196

ALSO BY DALE MAHARIDGE

(With photographer Michael Williamson)
The Last Great American Hobo (1993)
And Their Children After Them (1989)
Journey to Nowhere:
The Saga of the New Underclass (1985)

(With photographer Jay Mather)
Yosemite, A Landscape of Life (1990)

THE COMING WHITE MINORITY

THE COMING
WHITE
MINORITY

California's Eruptions
and America's Future

DALE MAHARIDGE

TIMES 𝕿 BOOKS
RANDOM HOUSE

Portions of this work were originally published in
The California Journal and *Mother Jones Magazine.*

Grateful acknowledgment is made to the following for
permission to reprint previously published material:

Donald Northcross: "Son of a Blackman" by Donald
Northcross. Reprinted by permission of the author.

Simon and Schuster: Excerpt from *Satisfied with Nothin'* by
Ernest Hill. Copyright © 1990, 1992, 1996 by Ernest Hill.
Reprinted by permission of Simon & Schuster.

ISBN 0-8129-2289-1

Library of Congress Cataloging-in-Publication information
is available.

Random House Web address:
http://www.randomhouse.com/

Printed in the United States of America on acid-free paper

2   4   6   8   9   7   5   3

FIRST EDITION
BOOK DESIGN BY MINA GREENSTEIN

"Remember, it's all an occupied country."

—Anonymous, scrawled on the bathroom wall
at Cody's Books in Berkeley, California.

Acknowledgments

Many thanks to Jeffrey Klein, Katharine Fong, Patti Wolter, and others at *Mother Jones* magazine, which serialized parts of this book beginning in 1993; all were a source of guidance.

Financial support came from the Pope Foundation in New York: a generous grant helped underwrite many drives and flights spanning the 1,000 round-trip miles between northern and southern California. Many thanks to Catherine Pope. Additional funding came from the professors' publishing program of the Freedom Forum. Assistance also came from Bob Love, a senior editor at *Rolling Stone,* from an ill-fated but ultimately valuable assignment on the decline of the University of California. I thank Bob for the excellent editing; to Jann Wenner, thanks for the money.

When I was living in New York in 1991 and 1992, ideas were shaped over Tex-Mex and many beers in Greenwich Village with Peter Ediden, then editor of *New Republic Books.* Going back even further, I continually heard the voice of social justice from Sister Ruthmary Powers, a nun from grade school whose influence has been felt ever since.

In California, many people provided invaluable assistance. Suzanne Wierbinski, chief of staff for Assemblywoman Martha Escutia, was helpful in ways that can never be repaid. Others include

Gretchen Kell at the public affairs office at the University of California at Berkeley; Lee Steelman, head of the South Orange County Community Services Council; Dana Point Mayor Judy Curreri, Councilwoman Eileen Krause, Juana Ortiz, an interpreter in the local school district, and many other city officials too numerous to name; Nancy Austin and Mary Heim at the population research unit of the California Department of Finance; Deborah Ortiz, a Sacramento city councilwoman and expert on the history of modern California Latino politics; Los Angeles writer Elizabeth Kadetsky for sharing ideas over bad coffee all those nights at the Astro; journalists Andrea Adelman, Yvette Doss, and Katherine Corcoran; and Stanford student Cate Cavanagh, who did some fact checking.

Of course, I thank Bill, Don, Maria, Martha, and others for allowing me into their lives and for sharing their experiences.

Once again, Gloria Loomis proved to be not only an excellent agent but an insightful editorial voice. And above all, I want to thank Ruth Fecych at *Times Books* for the uncountable hours she spent shaping this book.

Contents

PART THREE

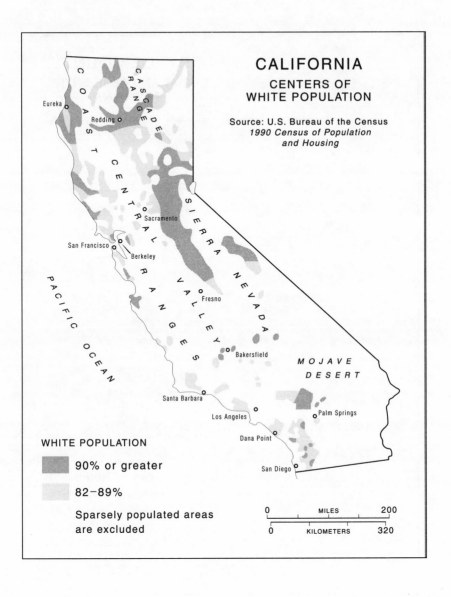

CALIFORNIA

CENTERS OF
WHITE POPULATION

Source: U.S. Bureau of the Census
*1990 Census of Population
and Housing*

Eureka

Redding

Sacramento

San Francisco

Berkeley

Fresno

Bakersfield

Santa Barbara

Los Angeles

Dana Point

Palm Springs

San Diego

PACIFIC OCEAN

COAST

CASCADE RANGE

CENTRAL

RANGES

VALLEY

SIERRA NEVADA

*MOJAVE
DESERT*

WHITE POPULATION

90% or greater

82–89%

Sparsely populated areas
are excluded

0	MILES	200
0	KILOMETERS	320

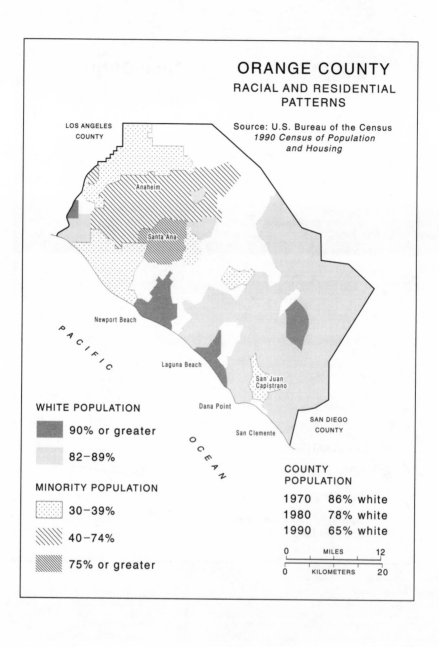

ORANGE COUNTY
RACIAL AND RESIDENTIAL
PATTERNS

LOS ANGELES
COUNTY

Source: U.S. Bureau of the Census
*1990 Census of Population
and Housing*

Anaheim

Santa Ana

Newport Beach

PACIFIC

Laguna Beach

San Juan
Capistrano

Dana Point

SAN DIEGO
COUNTY

San Clemente

OCEAN

WHITE POPULATION

90% or greater

82–89%

MINORITY POPULATION

30–39%

40–74%

75% or greater

COUNTY
POPULATION

1970   86% white
1980   78% white
1990   65% white

| 0 | MILES | 12 |
| 0 | KILOMETERS | 20 |

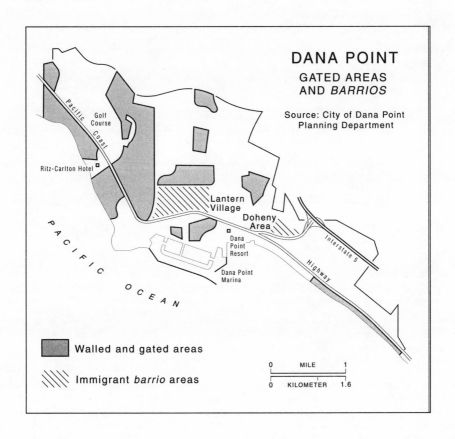

DANA POINT

GATED AREAS
AND *BARRIOS*

Source: City of Dana Point
Planning Department

Pacific Coast

Golf
Course

Ritz-Carlton Hotel

PACIFIC

OCEAN

Lantern
Village

Doheny
Area

Dana
Point
Resort

Dana Point
Marina

Interstate 5

Highway

Walled and gated areas

Immigrant *barrio* areas

0   MILE   1

0   KILOMETER   1.6

PART ONE

1

The Brink

In 1998 and 2000 California will observe sesquicentennials for, respectively, the discovery of gold and its admission as a state. Sometime between these dates, probably close to the first, California will make new history when whites officially fall to less than half its total population, which today stands at 31.6 million.[1] "Minorities" will be in the majority.

In the 150 years since California lured gold seekers to its lands, well-known political and social trends have started there and rolled east (in some cases around the world), and so it goes with the racial transition. California will become polyracial, joining Hawaii and New Mexico. Other states will follow, Texas sometime around 2015, and in later years Arizona, New York, Nevada, New Jersey, and Maryland. By 2050 the nation will be almost half nonwhite.[2] Other white societies, from France to Australia, are also growing increasingly mixed.

What will happen in California after 1998 or so will eclipse any of the real or imagined hype about California's sway in matters beyond its borders. No white society of the industrial world has ever evolved into a mixed culture. Multiethnic places exist—Brazil comes to mind—but they have never been dominated by whites.

As is well known, California's racial evolution is not happening quietly. Campus protesters have waged hunger strikes to win funding for ethnic studies departments, and the 1992 Los Angeles riots were America's first experience with major polyethnic urban unrest. Other seemingly unconnected events, such as the revolutionary tax-cutting Proposition 13, are also linked to the widening diversity, but in more complex ways. California is one of several states that allow citizen-generated initiatives, and when this measure was passed by California voters in 1978, it set off a nationwide antitax wave. The story of Proposition 13 is a good place to begin understanding the impact of the changing demographics. It demonstrates the complexity of what is happening in California.

Most people dislike paying taxes. But why did the revolt against taxes begin in California and not Ohio or New Jersey? As is now widely known, California seemed the logical place for the antitax movement to flex its muscle because this was the nation's most populous state, and the message would resonate. Also, property values in the state's vast suburbs had undergone enormous inflation and the resulting property tax bite was more serious than in other regions. These were major concerns, but as with so many other issues in California, the "other" factor—the rapidly changing demographics—acted as the catalyst.

Between 1900 and 1970 California's white population dropped from 90 percent to 78 percent of the total. But by 1980 the percentage of whites dropped as much as it had in the century's first seven decades. Between 1980 and 1990 it plummeted another 10 percent—and has continued declining about 1 percent a year since then. In 1996 California was officially estimated to be about 52 percent white. (Critics of the 1990 census charge minorities were undercounted, and if this is true, whites are already slightly below the majority.) Demographers say the state will be some 40 percent white by 2010.

Many people on the front line of government and social services now view the passage of Proposition 13 as a turning point in the disassociation of white society from the growing number of "strangers" among them. By 1978 more than one in three of the state's residents was nonwhite. Whites felt an underlying antipathy to what they viewed as a third-world society in their midst. They simply did not want to pay taxes for services that would benefit people different from them. Under Proposition 13, schools, parks, and police services were severely defunded. This did not affect many whites because more and more of them were living in communities apart from Latins, blacks, and Asians. They could send their children to private schools, pay for private police.

Even now as the number of whites hovers around the 50 percent level, they are able to maintain political control because electoral power among the various ethnic groups has not reached parity. When California votes, it is largely a white vote, between 80 and 85 percent of the votes cast in any given election.[3] These 6.5 million or so whites, many of them older property owners, have a stake in the system and thus trek faithfully to the polls. Politicians cater to this electorate, not so much leading it as mirroring it. The other 25 million or more residents simply do not take part in elections: they are too young, have entered the country illegally, are apathetic, or, in the case of many nonwhites, live in a society isolated from the one in which they would vote and often struggle to survive in third-world conditions.

With each drop in the white population, fear among white voters rose commensurately. There are various milestones. This concern led California voters to pass a ballot measure in 1986 declaring English the official language. The backlash continued on a small scale over the next few years. Then everything changed on April 29, 1992, with the start of the Los Angeles riots—which resulted in 58 deaths, 2,500 injuries, 16,000 arrests, and $1 billion in damages.

If Proposition 13 was a veiled reaction to cultural change, and the English-only law a somewhat more overt response, the reactionary pitch that followed the riots erased any subtlety. Two movements stand out—one against immigrants and the other against affirmative action.

In 1994 voters approved Proposition 187, which denied public services such as hospitals and schools to illegal immigrants and mandated that teachers report nonresident children; the measure was a mark of white resentment toward the Latinization of California. If upheld by the courts, it will punish immigrants but will not stop anyone at the border, nor will it impose sanctions on the many businesses that hire undocumented workers for substandard wages. The anti-immigrant sentiments also came out in numerous small ways in the early 1990s, such as local laws forbidding Mexicans to hang laundry on apartment railings and whites picketing and harassing streetcorner Latino job seekers.

Another defining vote will occur in November 1996, when the California Civil Rights Initiative (CCRI) will be on the ballot, proposing to end affirmative action in all aspects of state government and contracting. Proponents gathered nearly 1.1 million signatures to place CCRI before the voters, and polls showed widespread support. If approved, it is expected to have an enormous impact on the fate of affirmative action nationwide.

The anti-immigration wave generated by California rapidly spread around the country. But the speed at which it moved was nothing compared with the strength of the response to California's attack on affirmative action. In the eight or so months after the California Civil Rights Initiative was proposed in 1995, 20 states moved on bills or resolutions to limit affirmative action: 15 of them copied the wording of the California initiative.[4] The CCRI was also the model for groups in other states that allow initiatives, including Colorado. They collected signatures to get a similar proposition before the voters. In Congress, Republican Senator Bob Dole and Republican Representative Charles Canady introduced a bill known as the Equal Opportunities Act of 1996 that would eviscerate federal policies giving women and nonwhites special consideration in the workplace and in government contracting.

In most of the United States, affirmative action is commonly associated with programs for blacks. In California it also applies to some, but not all, Latinos and some, but not all, Asians. Thus while affirmative action and immigration often seem to be separate issues, they are very much interconnected.

Immigration and affirmative action are emotional issues, whose mere mention can set off a feverish debate. But it is important to keep certain facts in mind, especially with respect to affirmative action. At the University of California, where conservative forces succeeded in rolling back affirmative action in 1995, only 1,000 blacks who graduated from high school in the entire state qualified for admission to the university's nine campuses. For all the talk of competent people (meaning whites) being displaced by lesser-qualified minorities (usually meaning blacks), there really has not been much so-called reverse discrimination.

Whites themselves are sometimes on the receiving end of affirmative action in California schools because Asians excel academically. At the University of California at Berkeley, whites have shrunk to one-third of the undergraduate student body, down from half in the 1980s, to make room not for "unqualified" blacks and Latinos but for Asians who outperformed whites. Rather than lowering standards, the school has raised them five times over 15 years.[5]

Most California whites do not know this. Given a level playing field, there likely would be more Asians and fewer whites in many of the state's schools. One official predicted that without affirmative action, the student body at the University of California at Los Angeles would be 60 percent Asian and 40 percent white. This could create an entirely different kind of anti-immigrant sentiment. The point is that many whites dislike cultural change because it is seen as working against their interests. A white revolt is at the root of what is happening in California.

California is leading the nation in this revolt, and the affirmative action initiative is the latest in a series of actions fueling it. This is not to say that affirmative action does not need fine tuning—there are flaws that could be corrected—or that the nation should welcome unlimited immigration, which would be foolish. But rational discussion is not in vogue. Instead, California is creating a racist climate as it heads toward the 1998 racial turning point. The growing hostility toward nonwhites that is being spawned in California presents a grave threat as the nation becomes increasingly nonwhite.

The immigration issue is closely identified with California. According to a 1995 U.S. census report, 25 percent, or 7.7 million, of the state's residents were born outside the United States, most in nonwhite nations; this group makes up one-third of the foreign-born in the country. Some demographers predict the United States will develop a white core with brown edges, since nonwhites are expected to settle and remain in Texas, Florida, and New York, with the majority in California. But demographer Hans Johnson says many nonwhites are migrating inland and that California now plays a role long held by New York City—it is a receiving point from which future generations will fan out.[6]

By the early 1990s California had become the epicenter of an anti-immigrant mood sweeping the country. The tempo of hate increased in California as defense contractors and other industries began downsizing. On a national scale, Americans seeking an outlet for their anger over the state of the economy have scapegoated immigrants.

The popular complaint of the day, epitomized by Proposition 187, is that America has an "immigration problem," coded language for the arrival of too many brown-skinned people. There are actually far fewer immigrants coming today than arrived at the turn of the century, when another anti-immigrant wave swept the country. The foundation of North American culture is immigration. In the eyes of native Americans, who now make up just some 1 percent of the nation's population, there has always been an immigration problem.

Are there too many immigrants? Maybe. Or maybe not. That is not the real issue. The Mexican maid making beds in San Diego or the *campesino* picking peaches in Marysville are not the ones causing, for instance, the layoff in 1996 of 40,000 AT & T workers. Many of these workers were laid off to boost Wall Street stock prices in companies that are quite profitable. Nor are immigrants responsible for the fact that 1 percent of American households own 42 percent of the wealth, a proportion almost double that in 1978. This concentration of riches at the expense of the middle and lower classes places America more on par with Brazil, rather than its industrial rivals in Europe or Asia.

There is a boot kicking Americans in the head, and instead of looking down for the source—at the workers—Americans should look up. Conservative politicians who decry immigration ignore one of the real villains: unbridled multinational capitalism that has no allegiance to the nation's citizens, regardless of their race. Middle-class workers—white, black, Latino, Asian—are all losers in the Brazilianization of the United States. Class differences have sharpened across the nation, and in California they are extremely pronounced. In 1995, when many middle-class Americans feared being laid off and saw their incomes fall, chief executives at the largest companies in one survey saw their compensation rise 31 percent over the previous year, when all benefits are added to their salaries, to a median of $5 million each.[7] Racism may always be with us, but in times of economic despair it heightens and expands.

The multicultural transformation of America is happening precisely at a time when the so-called world economy is wreaking havoc on the nation's middle class.

California is at the forefront of a banana republic society, rife with race baiting and hatred. The rich have become isolated from everyone else and the masses economically deprived.

In examining California's influence on race and immigration matters at the national level, it is important to steer clear of some erroneous assumptions. It is a mistake to think that events in California are singular. It is also wrong to assume that California is exactly like everywhere else and that what occurs here is just like what happens in Ohio or New Jersey, only on a more massive scale.

As former Governor Edmund "Pat" Brown once wrote, "California is part and apart from the larger American society. It is both representative and unique."[8] Carey McWilliams, the state's noted biographer, called the state the "great exception." According to McWilliams, "The nation needs to understand this tawny tiger by the western sea, and to understand this tiger all the rules must be laid to one side."[9]

Although McWilliams was referring to various social trends, the same advice applies when it comes to understanding California's impact on the multicultural future of the country: one must lay aside rules. What is happening in California politically and culturally has implications for race relations throughout the country, even though at first glance it might be difficult to see how it applies to other regions. In the end, as it usually does, the part of California that is different will pull the rest of America along with it.

An example of the state's representativeness and uniqueness is found in its residential separation of races and social classes. In the East and Great Lakes region, whites do not like living near blacks. Detroit is the epitome of this detachment: it has a central urban black community living in wretched poverty surrounded by suburbs filled with whites who have fled. It has a chocolate core surrounded by vanilla, as one study described it.[10] The same thing is seen outside New York City on Long Island or in Connecticut.

Similarly, whites in California do not like living amid large numbers of nonwhites. But the pattern of the ruling class's separation is different. In plotting 1,551 major California census survey tracts by race, I found two contrasting patterns above and below a line extending on a northeast axis from San Francisco to just above Sacramento. North of the line, for a distance of 300 miles to the Oregon border, the state resembles the rest of America: it is largely white, with a few Latino and American Indian pockets. Below that line, for the 500 miles reaching to Mexico, the pattern is different. This is what the rest of America might become.

Instead of ringing the minority areas, the white communities form "islands" that are surrounded by vast ethnic or transitional communities, as well as deserts, mountain wilderness, and the ocean.[11] These white islands are usually found high above mixed neighborhoods—in the hills near San Diego, Santa Barbara, and San Jose, and in the canyons of West Los Angeles. These islands contain walled and gated neighborhoods, the numbers of which exploded in the 1980s as developers met the growing demand for private enclaves. In Los Angeles between 1990 and 1995, one-third of all new developments had locked gates.[12] There are no expansive wealthy communities that are more than 80 percent minority. Many nonwhites are disproportionately poor and live in sprawling lowland ghettolike suburbs abandoned by the walled whites.

Yet even in the whitest of the wealthy islands, on average 8 to 10 percent of the population consists of minority groups, largely Asian, with a smaller number Latino. Very few are black. The reason is that the segregation is class-based. It is not hard to find up-scale nonwhites who aspire to move into rich white areas. If they can afford the price of admission, these different ethnicities are welcome. What is happening in California is not traditional white flight. It is class flight, mostly white, because whites have more money and can afford to live in the hills.

California has become a checkerboard of "reservations": of walled, dominant white communities; middle-class and lower-middle-class mixed suburbs in transition; blacks and Latinos in ghettos and barrios; and clusters of ethnic students, some living in racially specialized theme houses on college campuses. Sprinkled throughout all these areas are Asians. Some of these reservations are quite small—just a few blocks of despair in an otherwise wealthy zone, the place for the working poor to call home, with two and three families sharing a small apartment. Other reservations have been specifically created through the electoral process to house blacks, along with some Latinos and whites; their population tripled between 1980 and the early 1990s and is guaranteed to increase sixfold or more from their 1980 number just after the turn of the century. These are called prisons.

The Golden State is not really any more or any less racist than the rest of the nation. But because of its sheer size and its global address where both East meets West and North meets South, California is setting the trend, as it has with other less substantial fads. In this case, the cultural change is creating a great deal of friction. One must keep the following points in mind when looking at the events leading up to the racial brink that will be crossed sometime after 1998.

First, whites are scared. The depth of white fear is underestimated and misunderstood by progressive thinkers and the media. Whites dread the unknown and not-so-distant tomorrow when a statistical turning point will be reached that could have very bad consequences for them. They fear the change that seems to be transforming their state into something different from the rest of the United States. They fear losing not only their jobs but also their culture. Some feel that California will become a version of South Africa, in which whites will lose power when minorities are the majority. It is an ill-founded fear because most nonwhites have the same economic and social interests as whites, but in interviews across the state I found this fear permeating the thinking of many whites. These anxieties will blow east like a bad Pacific storm as whites are outnumbered in other parts of the country.

Second, whites are not a monolithic group, though they are often treated as such in discussions about race and ethnicity. There are conservative whites and liberal whites, rich whites and poor whites, whites who live in cultures as vastly different as the gay enclaves in San Francisco, hippies in the north coast redwood country, and new immigrants from Russia, Ireland, and Eastern Europe. Many whites are not part of the backlash. At the same time, because whites are still the dominant group and many of them are afraid (and because the conservative among them vote in disproportionately high numbers), they are the most powerful group in the state in what often seems like a de facto apartheid system. The term "whites" in this book usually refers to conservative white voters.

Third, one must abandon the simplistic and common notion that it is whites versus everyone else. In many parts of the country, race relations are mostly binary, black and white. On the Pacific shore, the split is between Asians, Latinos, blacks, and whites, with no end to the multiplicity of rancor. If race relations between blacks and whites are complex, those in a four-sided society are byzantine in nature. There are Japanese who dislike the Vietnamese, blacks who do not like Koreans, Mexicans who bristle at the presence of Central Americans, and so on, not to mention the whites who do not like blacks or other groups.

Fourth, class is as important as race. Many Asians are part of the "overclass" and are Republican, voting along with the whites in favor of building prisons, punishing immigrants, or ending affirmative action, as do a significant number of well-off Latinos and blacks. Anti-immigrant Proposition 187, for instance, was supported by one in five Latino voters and roughly half of California's Asians and blacks. In many situations, the conflict is between the overclass (whites and nonwhites) and the underclass (nonwhites).

Fifth, whites themselves are responsible for the racial transformation of the United States. It began when slaves were imported from Africa and when the Chinese were encouraged to emigrate to the California frontier. Later, military actions in the Philippines, Korea, Vietnam, and elsewhere brought refugees and war brides home. The Cold War helped bring Cubans. And finally, despite the current outcry over immigration, Mexican nationals continue to be encouraged by American business to work in the service industry and in the fields—labor that citizens refuse to do.

Sixth, the state has a long history of racial eruptions. The Chinese were hounded in the 1870s, burned out of their laundries, and lynched. The Japanese were assailed after the turn of the century and again during World War II, when 70,000 citizens of Japanese heritage (plus additional Japanese nationals) were imprisoned. There was also a reaction against Filipinos and Mexicans in the 1930s and 1950s, although on a smaller scale. The state was relatively quiet during the post–World War II boom, until the recession of the 1990s. During the early anti-Asian waves, Washington politicians bowed to pressure from the state and passed laws that it wanted, excluding Chinese immigrants in 1882 and later the Japanese. Because California was a meeting ground for Latin and Asian cultures, there was a natural inclination for the state to become multiethnic. If it had not been for a serious legislative effort on the part of the young United States to keep out nonwhites, California never would have been a white majority state.[13]

History has shown that when California erupts, America does, too.

The California "problem" is as old as the state's black and white racial differences, but it is also something new. What happens when you throw almost 9 million Latinos, some 3 million Asians, and over 2 million blacks together with an aggregate number of whites? One of the many results is that the meaning of race changes. The 1990 census showed a quadrupling of interracial couples from the previous two decades, to 1.4 million nationwide. Their offspring defy easy categorization: one in four California children are now of mixed race. And 9.8 million people checked "other race" on the 1990 census—a huge increase from 1980. The Census Bureau is now considering introducing a multiracial category.

All nonwhite groups are lumped together as "minorities," but the Latino family in Los Angeles that arrived from Mexico City last year has little in common with the black mother and child in Oakland whose ancestors came to this country as slaves three centuries ago. The Chinese Asian student at the University of California at Berkeley can despise affirmative action as much as the white student sitting at the next desk because more Chinese Asians at the university have been subjected to "reverse discrimination" than whites. When conservatives from these two groups get together, blacks are usually on the losing end of their shared sentiment. There is no rainbow of common interest.

Nationwide, blacks are the largest minority group: at present they account for 12 percent of the population, Hispanics for 9 percent. But after 2010, Hispanics are expected to surpass blacks, who will then be just a small portion of the total minority slice. By 2050 Hispanics will make up about 21 percent of the American population, blacks 15 percent, and Asians and Pacific Islanders 10 percent, according to midrange estimates by the U.S. Census Bureau.

While California leads with the mixing of cultures, there are pockets in other regions that give a hint of the future demographics. The 1990 census found that 51 out of 200 cities with populations over 100,000 were minority-majority communities. New York City is, of course, a prime example. Outer Queens or the lower Bronx are as diverse as anything found in Los Angeles. Growing numbers of Vietnamese are living in places like Kansas and more Mexicans are ending up in Chicago.

For many Americans, the terms "minority" and "black" are synonymous—yet the future lies with the Pacific Coast model, in which blacks are but one piece of the equation. The notion that the word "minority" would mean anything other than black or Native American is relatively new. It was not until the 1970s that there seemed to be any pressing reason for the U.S. census even to count Latinos as a separate category: before this, they were lumped in with "whites." In 1968 the commission impaneled by President Lyndon B. Johnson to study that year's urban riots presented a bifurcated racial view in the *Kerner Report,* with its now famous warning: "This is our basic conclusion: Our Nation is moving toward two societies, one black, one white—separate and unequal." [14]

The fate of Latinos and Asians never came up as the commissioners did their research, said panel member Katherine Graham Peden. In their view the only pressing race problem was the one between blacks and whites. The commission recommended a variety of solutions—in the areas of housing, education, and jobs, things that would bring blacks into the mainstream of economic and social success. The report was ignored. Three decades later, with four or more separate societies developing, Peden said of the new American racial dynamic, "Our melting pot would be a far stronger underpinning for our nation if we had faced these problems."

But the term "melting pot" was never more than a myth and was perhaps even a bald lie. It is common to think that by some arbitrarily chosen point after World War II, when European emigration slowed, the nation had become what it would always be, over 80 percent white, with most of the remaining percentage black, living in the South. This snapshot of culture was viewed as the American identity, bound by language and "Western" values (associated primarily with a consumer market culture).

With California leading the nation's polyracial evolution, the change has been cast as a war between cultures by the right wing. Their view is that American society is being invaded by ethnocentric Latin, African, and Asian separatists. This shrill message, when used by politicians, wins the votes of fearful whites. Some authors use the argument to gain attention in the same way that some celebrity hosts pump up their talk show ratings by pandering to base fears. Among those on the right, Peter Brimelow, in *Alien Nation,* says that foreigners cannot become Americans, even though Brimelow is himself a foreigner, albeit what he deems to be the good kind from the United Kingdom, not the unwashed kind from China or Mexico.[15] He is essentially recycling the anti-immigrant arguments made at the turn of the century. Among the neoliberals, Arthur Schlesinger Jr. argues against the "cult of ethnicity" found on college campuses, which he believes is tearing America apart.[16] On the left, a host of books from small presses are promoting ethnocentrism or radical separatism. In the current political climate, these books have not made the best-seller lists or headlines as have recent titles with right-wing extremist viewpoints, but they have great power in their small circles.

Seldom mentioned is the fact that most Americans, regardless of their cultural background, would not side with any of the extremists in this debate. The far Left sees a conspiracy of racist whites against minorities, which gives too much power to a small cadre of reactionaries. The Brimelow-Schlesinger view ignores human nature and fails to recognize that most people new to this country (especially their children) are actually being assimilated into the mainstream culture, just as generations of other immigrants have been. Conservatives place too much credence in the power of a small number of campus ethnic activists, whose politics of identity combines with their 18-year-old hormones to produce small and angry ethnocentric cliques. These young people are relatively impotent except in the eyes of those on the right, who use them as red flags to manipulate the distress of whites. The students have little off-campus influence in their own groups, much less in white society. When it comes to multiculturalism, a centrifugal force dominated by both the Left and Right flings the debate to the outermost edges, where it oscillates, never lining up in the center.

The conservative-driven political backlash in California can be described as old America rejecting the new America, according to Antonio Gonzalez, president of the Southwest Voter Research Institute. Old America is made up of European white stock that, despite the presence of blacks, used to dominate the culture. The new America is composed of dark-skinned people who have the same material and economic wants as whites. This America, Gonzalez says, must win, but he does not mean this in a militant sense. The reality is that its values are not very different from those of the old America. It just has a browner face.

Yet it does present a different dynamic. The impact of Latin and Asian cultures will influence America in the same way that black culture has: American blacks have lost their "Africanness" while whites have adopted many aspects of black culture, from its music to its dialects. Why should this be seen as bad? The infusion of new perspectives—not only into culture but into the solutions to society's economic and social problems—can only benefit the nation.

Why some people fear that multiculturalism will lead to cultural fragmentation is puzzling. In the nearly 15 years that I traveled the length of this giant state (over 10 of them as a newspaper reporter and the remainder working on this book), I never saw a splintering society but one that was striving to be whole. Many new Californians speak Spanish or Asian languages and are indeed quite different culturally, but their children are "assimilating" just as the offspring of other immigrants have done through the years. For good or ill, they have the same materialistic wants of fourth-generation Americans.

In many cases, their desire to achieve "success" is stronger. As one white Los Angeles man interviewed before the 1992 Los Angeles riots said, "For every complacent [white] 'C' student, there's some Korean, Central American, black who wants very, very badly to get into the middle class and is willing to work unbelievable hours and get straight 'A's and go to school at night to do anything to buy the dream. Nobody told white kids that all these Asians would want what they wanted more than they wanted it. They're the kind who take the complacent [white] San Fernando Valley kid and knocks him off the face of the map. But if you are a white semiliterate kid in the Valley, you don't like it. And if you are their parents, you don't like it. So we are rightfully being displaced by the new generation of immigrants, which has always been the dynamic of this country."

Not all whites are so progressive in their thinking, especially in the wake of the riots and economic shocks of the 1990s. California voters, which largely means suburban whites, have sought scapegoats. The brunt of their anger has been felt by immigrants, especially nonwhite immigrants.

The United States cannot and should not allow open borders, but strict immigration control alone will not stop the ethnic change, especially in the contemporary world, whose regions are connected by technology and markets that do not recognize borders. The United States can no longer close itself off as easily as it did during previous anti-immigration waves. Jetliners have rendered controls useless because anyone with a visa can easily come and overstay. And even if the borders were sealed shut today, the demographic trends show that nonwhites will double as a percentage of the population by the year 2050, to nearly 4 out of 10 Americans. There is no avoiding the fact that whites will no longer be the overwhelming majority in the United States.

The country is now entering the most fragile period in the history of its race relations. Despite the fact that so many nonwhites want to join the middle class, many will be unable to do so because of economic stagnation. Economics, more than racial differences, will determine how the new multicultural society will work, according to research by Dr. William Tafoya of the Federal Bureau of Investigation (FBI), who several years before the Los Angeles riots predicted riots by 1999 that would be more severe than the urban unrest of the 1960s.[17]

"My phone rang off the hook," Tafoya said of the calls from the press in the first days of the riots. "They said 'yeah, you were right, but you were early.' I said you don't understand, the riots exceeded what happened in Watts in 1965, but it didn't meet the 1999 criteria. What happened in L.A. will look like peanuts compared to what will occur."

Tafoya's prediction is based on a reality of the cultural change: whites still have most of the well-paying jobs. Even though some Latinos and Asians—especially Chinese Asians and some Japanese and Indian Asians—are among the overclass, many nonwhites are economically disenfranchised. This group of Latinos and Asians,

Tafoya says, will learn from what happened to many blacks. "They see the experience of blacks over the last 100 years. They aren't going to wait forever and ever."

The riots were not a rebellion, a term used by some on the left. There was nothing organized or political about the unrest. What happened in 1992 was an outpouring of frustration and rage. But in a counterriot, taking place at the ballot box, the overclass is rebelling against cultural change. In the face of these two oncoming trains, the Left ignores, even mocks white fear, and the Right maneuvers to put nonwhites in their place through ballot measures and other laws and in rarer cases, the specter of violence. Gun sales were brisk following the riots.[18] Some Californians seemed to be preparing for war, but that was not the real danger. Far more perilous was—and is—the politics of division that emerged after the riots. Guided by a handful of right-wingers, Californians voted for measures to punish nonwhites. As these extremists gained power, they were bolstered by the state's governor, Pete Wilson, a supposedly moderate Republican who latched on to their success and used the backlash for political gain.[19]

The conflict that has come with the cultural change has given rise to much spirited discussion; the statistics cited are imposing and impressive. While the numbers delight the researcher and are used and misused by partisans, they do not convey what is truly happening.

One could focus on the arguments of the Left and the Right and on the statistics and cobble together a polarized story. But it would be a gross misrepresentation. As California is poised to cross the threshold of a white-minority society, the last few years leading up to this change have carried a far different meaning for a majority of the state's residents. There is another California beyond the groups wallowing in caustic self-indulgence. It is a California that is bewildered and trying to adjust—people living everyday lives who are confronted by the extremes of the debate.

For four people rooted in the history and experiences of distinctly different California ethnic and racial groups—Asian, black, Latino, and white—the period that followed the 1992 riots was bruising. The latest wave of racial division that has arisen as the state heads toward a society in which no one race will be in the majority has deeply affected the lives of Martha Escutia, Maria Ha, Donald Northcross, and Bill Shepherd. For all four, the state in 1996 would become a different place from the one they knew in 1992.

In the Latino immigrant community of South East Los Angeles and in the state capital of Sacramento, freshman lawmaker Martha Escutia would be part of the frontline battle against immigrant bashing and Governor Wilson. Martha, the daughter of Mexican immigrants, sought public office not to fight immigration issues, but to push economic development.

In Berkeley, student Maria Ha, a young legal immigrant of Chinese heritage from Vietnam, would see her tuition skyrocket at the University of California at Berkeley as the state cut funding in favor of building prisons. She felt personally attacked in the backlash.

In Sacramento, black sheriff's deputy Donald Northcross worked to save a small group of black boys from the ravages of urban crime and despair with an innovative mentoring program. But he felt thwarted by the attacks on affirmative action.

In the Orange County city of Dana Point, a white-majority community, Bill Shepherd worked on the local level to stem a tide of change that brought an increase in crime, much of it among immigrants' children who joined gangs. Bill was like many whites—confused by the sudden cultural transformation in his neighborhood. Relatively liberal in the 1960s, he had grown steadily more conservative.

And there is a fifth character, the state itself. Its violent history in dealing with nonwhites dates back to the Gold Rush, and it has played a role in the nationwide rise of the politics of hate.

This book is the story of the lives of these people and the state between 1992 and 1996, a pivotal period of increasing discord. The actions of California in the 1990s will surpass previous bouts of xenophobia because the stakes are now higher. In times past, California's conservative forces were always able to keep out "foreigners" and thus maintain peace—at a high price. This is no longer possible. As the state takes the first steps into a multicultural society, the nation will finally have to face up to what it means to be a melting pot.

Up to the time of the Los Angeles riots, even with such electoral outbursts as Proposition 13, it did not take boosterism for most reasonable citizens to find themselves acknowledging that, for the most part, the state was racially hospitable. This attitude was found in the well-known 1988 report *LA 2000: A City for the Future,* authored by a blue ribbon panel commissioned by the city. This upbeat study came on the heels of the 1984 Olympics and extolled the mix of things that made Los Angeles the nation's model city, a host of economic and cultural advantages that were "drawing on the energy and ingenuity of one of the most diverse populations in the world." The report warned against "the fusion of individual cultures into a demotic polyglotism ominous with unresolved hostilities," but this was overshadowed by optimism.[20] Even though the report was later called "dreamlike" even by LA 2000 Commission President Jane G. Pisano, the authors cannot be faulted too heavily.[21] At the time the popular view was that California was a place where different people could get along. As one white woman said, "You can't live in California and be prejudiced." Many Californians are indeed not prejudiced. As for those who are, they can harbor prejudice as long as they do not openly show it. You have to do business, work with, or live next to a lot of different people. Amid this mix, there has been a great deal of natural acceptance of other groups. In the words of one sociologist, the untold story of California society is that so many people do get along.

The bad news is that all rules changed after the Los Angeles riots. Even though quiet everyday interactions are harmonious, recent events suggest that California is not on course to a smooth cultural changeover after 1998. Thus far, the example set in the final years of white numerical domination in California has not been a good one. The next few decades could continue to be filled with turmoil, riots, race baiting, and hate. California can be an archetype for how a new culture can work, or it can be the prototype of failure.

This book is an effort to uncover the underlying fears and desires of ordinary people, as well as to draw attention to the voices of reason and to help find a workable solution to the cultural problem. For all but the most extreme of those interviewed, people want this coming new society to succeed. Most are seeking a center ground. But what is the center? Does it mean a culture that is white, Western, and European? The best of all cultures? Something entirely new? Whatever the dynamic of the new center turns out to be, it can and should result in a stronger America.

The outcome will rest largely with those who hold overwhelming economic and electoral power: whites. Power has never been given up easily, but whites who are now resisting the change will eventually learn that it does not mean the end of civilization as they know it. They will come to understand that nonwhites want the same things they do. As for the small number of ethnocentric activists who shun "white society," they, too, will have to learn that going it alone is not only isolating but self-destructive in a polyethnic culture.

Even the most racist members of all ethnic and racial groups will have to realize that if for no other reason than economic self-interest the new cultural dynamic will have to work. After all, in a society such as California, where no one group will comprise more than 4 out of 10 residents, the economic future is tied to all cultures working toward a common goal. It is going to be people other than those of your race paying taxes, contributing to social security, helping to keep your neighborhood safe.

Given the nature of American culture, the best that can be hoped for is a multiracial capitalist society without a white majority—one that has some compassion for ethnic differences and one (unlike present society) that allows all of its citizens to partake in economic benefits, essentially a form of free-market integration. Another white-majority society, Australia, has been increasingly integrating itself with Asia rather than resisting nonwhite culture, as it did for most of its existence. California and the United States must adopt this same attitude of acceptance.

A multicultural society can work because on many levels it already is doing so in California. There is the risk of an explosion, unless the extremes, both left and right, are marginalized. The situation in California must be taken into account if one is to understand the future course that racial relations might take in the United States. California is America's multicultural tomorrow.

2

Californians and California

MARTHA ESCUTIA

It is curious that Latinos—California's largest "minority" group, which will soon make up one-third of the state's population—are considered foreigners by most of the whites there. The whites have forgotten that their state was once part of Mexico.

Propelled by Manifest Destiny, Americans stormed across the continent in the early 1800s, conquering as they went, until they ran up against Mexico, which then occupied most of the West. At the time of the Mexican-American War in 1846, Mexico was weak and in disarray, just two decades removed from Spanish rule. U.S. soldiers easily captured much of northern Mexico. The Americans decided to take Mexico City, and on March 9, 1847, 8,600 troops under the command of General Winfield Scott stormed ashore at Veracruz. Their battle plan was to trek inland to the capital to force the surrender of President Antonio López de Santa Anna.[1]

There was no easy route to Mexico City past heavily armed fortifications. Scott decided to launch an assault on the citadel of Chapultepec, atop a steep column of rock, 2 miles southwest of the city. The fort required 2,000 defenders, but Mexican Major General Nicolás Bravo had only 832 soldiers, including 100 military cadets aged 15 to 20. Nevertheless, the battle was fierce. After shelling Chapultepec all night, at the first light of September 13, 1847, Americans stormed the fort. The cadets fought "like demons," said one American officer, but most surrendered as the Americans overran it.

Six boys, however, held out. As American soldiers closed in, these youths, including Juan Escutia, 20, Martha Escutia's distant relative, wrapped themselves in a Mexican flag and leaped 20 stories to their deaths. They became known as *Los Niños Héroes,* the boy heroes, for their martyrdom.

The next day, Scott's troops occupied Mexico City. On February 2, 1848, the Mexican government signed the Treaty of Guadalupe Hidalgo. It ceded to the Americans the top two-fifths of Mexico, 529,017 square miles of land, which included much of what today is Arizona; parts of Colorado, New Mexico, and Wyoming; all of Utah, Nevada, and Alta (upper) California.

The fight against the Americans was a proud one, especially in the Mexico City home of young Raul Escutia, Martha's father. Raul's parents came from Juan Escutia's hometown of Tepic, and they revered their ancestor. There was, however, little hatred for the United States, and it was Raul's destiny to emigrate to the powerful country to the north. In 1945, when Raul was 10 years old, his mother died. The next year, he and an aunt and uncle waded the Rio Grande and traveled to Chicago. He became fluent in English within two years. Eventually, he settled in southern California, and he and his first wife gave birth to their only child, Martha.

Martha was not radicalized by the family's history. She worked hard, never getting involved in movements. Martha was a child of "firsts": the first generation to be born in the United States, the first to graduate high school, then the first to graduate from a university (the University of Southern California), with honors. She took a full course load while holding down a 45-hour-a-week job. Later, she was awarded a law degree from Georgetown University and studied trade at the World Court. In Washington, she went to work for the National Council of La Raza, a Latino interest group, where she pushed employment training, a tough sell in the Reagan years.

By 1986 Martha wondered how a progressive agenda could be sold in a conservative era. She knew the message of 1960s Chicano activism was passé. Terms like "societal justice" were not going to cut it.

"I figured people in the eighties are thinking about the pocketbook," she recalled. Martha decided to focus on Social Security, which everyone hopes someday to collect. The Census Bureau predicts that one in five Americans will be over the age of 65 early in the next century and that most of them will be white. At the same time, much of the younger workforce will be nonwhite.

Martha developed position papers based on the peril to the Social Security system. If most young nonwhite people are living in poverty or are underpaid, who will fund tomorrow's retirees? To ensure that nonwhites would be ready for skilled jobs, Martha wanted to help minorities become educated, and she took this message into the halls of the U.S. Capitol. "I told this congressman, I said don't you want to get your Social Security paycheck in 20 years? 'Yeah,' he said." Martha then told the congressman the country had better train nonwhites so there would be someone paying the taxes.

"You've got to realize that the only way whites will come into the picture is if they see an economic self-interest with blacks and Latinos and Chinese working together. The concept of economic justice, it's an argument they will not be able to tell me, 'you're wrong.' The security of the country is at risk if you do not train a viable segment of the labor pool who's going to be the bulk of the labor force in the future."

When Martha returned to California, she worked for the United Way, and later as an insurance lawyer. By 1992 she was ready to move from behind the scenes to a position where she could directly effect change, ready to try her brand of progressive politics. Through more hard work, at age 34, she was elected to the California State Assembly to represent a sprawling Latino-dominated district, at the center of which is the city of Huntington Park, in South East Los Angeles.

On a sunny day in December 1992 Martha was inaugurated in Sacramento with the other new legislators in the 80-member assembly, a body not unlike the House of Representatives: heavily partisan, immensely polarized, and unable to reach a consensus. But on this day, the mood was giddy. The mahogany chamber was crowded, the floor and balconies packed with spectators, some waving to Martha, who was easy to spot in a purple dress. It was a crowning achievement for the daughter of Mexican immigrants who had come north with nothing except a desire to work.

Martha went to the podium to tell the man who would read off the members' names how to pronounce "Escutia." "Ess-scoot-ee-ah," she said. Martha wanted it said perfectly for the sake of her non-English-speaking grandparents, Ricardo and Marina Ovilla; Martha kissed them on the cheeks as the gavel was lowered.

Assemblyman John Vasconcellos nominated long-time power-broker Willie Brown to become once again the speaker of the lower house. He said it was appropriate that a black man lead the increasingly multiethnic body. When Assemblyman Richard Polanco seconded the motion, he addressed the audience as *Estimada publico,* esteemed public. Polanco talked of an "era that reflects a more diverse California" and an "unprecedented" vitality in the body. As the members cast their votes on Brown's nomination, another newly elected Los Angeles assemblywoman, Hilda Solis, answered the roll call not with an "aye," but with a loud *"¡Sí!"*

In his acceptance speech, Brown noted the election of 21 assemblywomen, up from 1 when he was first elected in 1964, and the record 7 Latinos, as well as 7 blacks and 1 Asian, the first to be elected since 1978. "This House does not yet reflect the diversity of the state of California," Brown said of the 15 nonwhites making up some 19 percent of the members, "but it comes closer to what California is and will become."

Martha saw hope for political inclusion in 1992 because more minorities had been elected to the legislature that fall than at any time in the state's history. She came to office eager to bring economic development to her impoverished district, the poorest in the state. It is 90 percent Latino and filled with immigrants, legal and illegal, struggling to escape profound poverty. Near the end of the swearing-in ceremony, Martha leaned over to Vasconcellos, her seatmate, and good-naturedly whispered, "You ready to cause some trouble?"[2]

Trouble would come, but not the kind Martha wanted. She did not count on becoming engulfed in a cultural backlash. But as the Latino bashing began, Martha began fighting the underlying racism.

Martha would rather have focused her energy elsewhere. She

saw strength in the common interests of all groups, believing that economics was at the heart of many problems in California's multi-cultural society. If jobs are readily available, she reasoned, there will be less strife simply because there will be less cause to hate your neighbor. The lack of jobs makes the wave of Latino immigrants different from the eastern Europeans who came at the turn of the century: work in coal mines and steel mills is not there. If those Poles, Czechs, and others had found no jobs other than selling apples, the history of their adaptation would have been far different.

A large part of Martha's success as a politician would be measured by how she helped the new immigrants find access to jobs and the "American Dream" sought by her family and other immigrants. But it also entailed combating xenophobia. In the wake of the Los Angeles riots, she did not like the way different racial and ethnic groups were fighting it out in the courts and the media. "L.A. is on the verge of Balkanization," she said one afternoon eight weeks after the riots. "We're dividing into hostile groups. It's almost like piranhas."

Martha's postriot assessment was echoed by others. One does not have to travel very far to hear someone compare the situation in California to the strife and "ethnic cleansing" in parts of the former Yugoslavia—the result of centuries of friction between Muslims and Christians. In some respects the analogy is not entirely accurate: centuries-old religious differences do not exist in California, the soma of consumerism and television softens hatred, and the power of the "American Dream," no matter how illusory, is still strong. American myths, exported around the world via Hollywood, are difficult to destroy.

Nonetheless, Martha saw the right wing pushing tribalism and she took the attacks personally. The Right created an environment in which people looked at her as an outsider because of her skin color and ever so slight Spanish accent. She was becoming a stranger in the land of her birth.

BILL SHEPHERD

When the Mexican-American War came to a close, the United States needed to populate its newly acquired territory with citizens or risk losing it. The problem took care of itself days before Mexico signed the treaty surrendering its territory, on January 24, 1848, when gold was discovered in the American River east of Sacramento and miners flooded the state.

The flow of people into California was steady over the next century and a half. The motives changed, but the faces moving into the conquered territory were mostly white. First it was miners; in the 1880s, farmers and idealists; in the 1930s, Dust Bowl migrants; after 1945, men returning home from World War II; in the 1960s, more idealists and job seekers.

Each year following the Mexican-American War, California's population swelled almost without pause, doubling on average every 18.5 years, as the migration from the East continued.[3] The first period in memory when more people departed than came was between 1970 and 1974, when 71,000 people left, according to driver's license transfers within the United States. More typical was the pattern of 1979–80, when 42,000 people moved from other states to California.

As a result of the nearly ceaseless influx, in 1964 California surpassed New York as the nation's most populous state. The demographic milestone was marked at 4 p.m. on a Sunday afternoon when Governor Pat Brown asked citizens to ring church bells and blow car horns in celebration.[4] That was also the year Bill Shepherd moved from his native Pennsylvania to the coastal town of Huntington Beach in Orange County. A teenager, he had come with his parents. His father's job as a geotechnical consultant had brought the family to the West Coast.

California was on the minds of many Americans in 1964. The Beach Boy's hit "Surfin' USA" from the previous year was still on the radio, and the group's latest hit "Fun, Fun, Fun" was popularizing the California sound and the notion that the state was definitely a place to be. Though his parents moved on to another state, as an adult Bill remained in California. He was away for a significant amount of time only in 1969, when he joined the Air Force and was sent to Southeast Asia. He was stationed for one year at Nakhon Phanom, on the Laotian-Thailand border, as part of a unit that monitored troop flows through North Vietnam, Laos, and Cambodia.

When he came home, he went to the University of Southern

California, where he gained a master's degree in administration. Bill eventually started a consulting business called Team Performance, which shows companies how to improve their operations through cooperation, communication, and proper management.

Through the 1970s and early 1980s he bought, fixed, and sold homes all through Orange County, saving money along the way through the profit from each sale; it was not hard to miss in the real estate boom days. But Bill also invested a lot of sweat equity in night and weekend carpentry, plastering, and plumbing. Bill is a small and wiry turtle-faced man in his forties, whose mannerisms and dress are all yuppie. He bought his last house in 1985, in Dana Point in south Orange County, a rich coastal city 60 miles from both San Diego and Los Angeles. South Orange County is one of California's white "islands." Bill's house had a movie-set view of the ocean, which had long been his dream. It was even on a street named El Encanto, which in Spanish means enchantment. Everything was perfect. Bill even later learned how to surf, more than three decades after he had arrived in California.

But by 1990 there was a sudden surge of crime in his neighborhood. In a period of 10 days, there were two rapes and one shooting. "I heard *Bam! Bam! Bam!* one night," he said. "I thought it was gunfire. I got in my car and I went to where the sheriff's helicopter was shining a light down."

The wife of a physician was standing in the yard of their home adjacent to the crime scene, a shooting. "She said, 'That's it.' She wouldn't put up with it," Bill said. She told her husband they were moving.

Bill soon became active in his neighborhood, attending community association meetings and talking with people. He blamed a lot of the crime on immigrants from Mexico, specifically their children who joined gangs. He also saw problems stemming from environmental changes—when these immigrants hung laundry on railings or parked old cars on the street. He felt his neighborhood was looking more like Mexico. He also saw a leadership vacuum. On the promise that he would work to stem crime and other problems such as environmental blight, Bill was elected president of his community association, one month after Martha Escutia was sworn into office.

"The conflict here?" Bill said. "You have a community that is predominately white. I don't mind that we have Mexicans here. But the whites are being taken over by a culture that is not assimilating. The dominant culture does not want graffiti everywhere. It does not want a large group of guys congregating outside drinking beer. It does not want vendors going door to door. It does not want laundry hanging out windows. These were not part of our community five years ago."

Unlike some activists in California, Bill is opposed to illegal immigrants not because of deep philosophical reasons but because of gang activity and the visual deterioration of his neighborhood. If those problems had not arisen, he would never have become active. He felt immigrant children were joining gangs and not assimilating because cultural separatism was out of control—Mexicans were speaking Spanish and identifying heavily with their own culture while benefiting from living in the United States.

"I'm second generation," Bill said. "My parents were born here, but my parents' parents on both sides were born in Europe. People ask me what I am—I'm white and I'm American. I don't call myself a Euro-American. But I could appropriately, if someone is a Latin American, or an African American, or whatever, to really be correct and in sync. From my point of view, they created a culture," he said of the European immigrants who forged an American identity based on Western values.

"Now we have an established culture, established values, established guidelines. And we've got individuals coming here with very different lifestyles, culture, values. We aren't a melting pot any more. Who sees themselves as American? Does someone who's been here for four or five years, here from Mexico, or someone that's been here a year from China? How can people consider themselves American if they always use a hyphen [to indicate] where they are from?"

Bill believes this separation of cultures helped lead to the Los Angeles riots. "It was subculture against subculture. It wasn't like the sixties when it was blacks and whites. We have a clash of cultures."

Bill and Martha shared the same concern: that society was splitting. But Martha saw the division coming from right-wing whites, Asians, Latinos, and blacks. Bill was alarmed by the fragmentation coming from left-wing whites, Asians, Latinos, and blacks. At the start of the backlash, they were on either side of the middle of the debate, but several years into it, they would both grow more bitter and further apart.

Bill defied stereotypes. He is a strong supporter of equal rights for women and minorities. But he draws the line at the number of special preferences that should be given to these groups. Astute conservatives such as Governor Pete Wilson tapped into white concerns and reached out to the Bill Shepherds of California. It was the mistake of Martha Escutia and others not to find some way to reach the same people, or to realize how afraid whites were of the cultural change. Whites were shrinking in number, but they were still half the population and most of the voters, a significant "minority" that had to be dealt with.

A lot of whites throughout the state were worried. The whites who were not leaving were heading to the white islands. According to census data, one of these islands—in the foothill counties of the Sierra Nevada, the mountain range running up the state's eastern edge—experienced 100 percent growth from 1980 to 1990, largely from whites. One woman interviewed said, "We moved here, well, I don't want to sound like a racist, but to get away from the immigrants. We like it up here because we're surrounded by people just like us."

Many others were leaving the state. Driver's license transfers show a net departure of 426,000 people between 1990 and 1994, or 1.2 percent of the population.[5] Apparently this is the biggest reversal since the Mexican-American War. Many who departed were white, according to moving companies and anecdotal evidence. Some were fleeing the changing demographics. The first question asked by those thinking of moving to the Arizona town of Flagstaff was what was the racial breakdown of the city, a Flagstaff official told the *Los Angeles Times*.[6] Bill also had a time line—he wouldn't fight forever. "If the shooting continues, I go."

MARIA HA

As eastern whites were streaming into the Golden State in the 1950s and 1960s, Asians were all but forbidden entry because of a restrictive immigration policy known as the national origin quotas.

These quotas, which severely limited immigration from Asian countries, were first imposed after California's vicious backlash against the Chinese in the 1870s. In 1882 state officials succeeded in pressuring Congress to pass the first of the restrictive laws, the Chinese Exclusion Act. Over the decades, the laws were slightly amended, but the message was always the same: Asians were not wanted. The McCarran-Walter Act of 1952 eliminated race as a means of disqualifying entry, but the change was little more than a semantic one: the act allowed only 100 immigrants from each Asian country to be admitted each year.

In 1964 Attorney General Robert F. Kennedy testified before Congress, arguing against national origins quotas. Kennedy's testimony was hard to ignore given the climate of the civil rights movement. As segregation was eliminated, the same pressures came to bear against race-based immigration policies. How could the United States create equal rights for its black citizens but continue to say it was acceptable to discriminate against Asians? In 1965 Congress passed amendments to the Immigration and Nationality Act that by 1968 would allow into the United States as many as 20,000 immigrants from non-Western nations each year. President Lyndon Johnson signed the law at the base of the Statue of Liberty. There was a ripple effect in other white non-European nations. In 1966 Canada relaxed its nonwhite policy, and a few years later the White Australia Policy was abolished.

In 1965 there were 1.4 million Asians in the United States. Many were descendants of those who had come before the national origins quotas; others came through marriage to American soldiers after the wars in Korea and Vietnam, or as refugees. With the political obstructions out of the way, Asian immigration surged. From less than 1 percent of the U.S. population in 1965, Asians grew to more than 7 million, or 3 percent, by 1990. In California, Asians and Pacific Islanders now constitute almost 10 percent of the state's residents.

The Asian population more than doubled between 1980 and 1990; it was the fastest-growing group. One who arrived at the start of the decade was Maria Ha, then age six, who, like Bill Shepherd, came with her parents. The events leading to Maria's arrival were set in motion when the Japanese invaded China in 1939. Maria's grandmother fled Canton for the safety of Hanoi. Her son studied to become a mechanical engineer and married a woman who was half Chinese and Vietnamese. Near the end of the war with the Americans, the couple gave birth to Maria.

When China invaded Vietnam for four weeks in 1979, the ethnic Chinese were harassed. In 1980 Maria's family fled Hanoi and made the dangerous boat trip east to Hong Kong. They spent four months in Hong Kong before being relocated as legal immigrant refugees to the United States.

They moved to San Francisco's Tenderloin, a crowded district of cheap hotels and apartments, home to those either on their way up or down in the American system. Maria's father could not get work of the level he had in Vietnam because he did not speak English. He took a job as a mover, later a grocery clerk. Maria's parents did not want Maria in a gang-infested Tenderloin school, so she was enrolled in Presidio Middle School in the more stable western part of the city. The family then moved to San Francisco's Chinatown. They set ambitious goals for Maria, who was about to enter seventh grade. She had to work harder so she could get into Lowell High School, which, though a public school, has entrance requirements like those of a private academy and admits only the scholastically elite from the city's elementary schools. Among its alumni are the late Governor Pat Brown, the late *Gorillas in the Mist* anthropologist Dian Fossey, and Supreme Court Justice Stephen Breyer. Admission is an indication that students will make it to the Ivy League or the California Palm League equivalents, Stanford and the University of California at Berkeley, since Lowell sends as many as 150 students each year to Berkeley's freshman class.

"Sometimes I get a little bit frustrated," Maria said of her parents' pushing her to achieve, "because when I come home with my report card, and there's like all As and maybe one or two Bs, and they look at it and they say 'Hey, why are you getting a B in this class?'"

Maria's hard work paid off—she was accepted into the class of 1998 at Berkeley, which along with other colleges in the state, was engulfed in the so-called culture war. White undergraduates had become a minority at the time of protests, takeovers, and hunger strikes by nonwhite students who wanted more courses studying ethnic cultures. Asians were involved in ethnic activism, but far fewer than their black, Latino, and even white counterparts. Much to the chagrin of Asian activists, the image of Asians working hard and succeeding was typified by Maria. Though, as with most stereotypes, there were exceptions, this cliché of the "model minority" stuck.

While some whites saw all nonwhite young people imposing their culture on the United States, Maria did not want to go to Berkeley to promote her culture. She wanted to go to learn, like most students, and to succeed.

DONALD NORTHCROSS

With the great legal strides in civil rights in 1964, it seemed the United States would reverse its racism once and for all. By 1968 this dream was doomed to fade, but in the midst of the turmoil, life for blacks had improved in the Arkansas town of Ashdown, where 10-year-old Donald Northcross lived.

Prior to 1968, Ashdown schools had been segregated. That fall Don jumped at the chance to go to the white school. No longer would he have to use secondhand textbooks that white kids had worn out. And there was a pool, so he could finally learn to swim. When Don walked across the tracks separating blacks from the white part of town, he discovered the white school did have new books, but he also found that the pool had been cemented over.

The youngest of seven children, Don was embarrassed by his family's poverty. He wore socks with holes in the toes and heels and would tuck the socks lower on his foot so his skin would not rub, but then kids made fun of him for having low socks. Yet the family did not want for food, even if they did not always have meat on the table.

Don's ancestry was lost. His family only knew they came from slaves. According to family lore, their name came from a time when their forebears lived north of a giant cross. Don's parents did not finish school; his father left in third grade after both his parents died. Don's father had a job at an army depot across the Texas state line, an 80-mile commute. Despite the distance and fierce winter ice storms, he was often cited for perfect attendance. He also raised truck crops on Saturdays. While his father plowed behind a mule, Don followed and planted potatoes. In the fall the family picked cotton. On Sunday the elder Northcross was a deacon in the Pentecostal Church.

The young Don wanted to be a minister, the only profession open to a black man. Then for the first time he saw blacks rise to unheard-of positions in law, business, and government through affirmative action. In his freshman year at Northeast Louisiana University, he joined the football team. Study and football occupied Don's life. When he graduated, he turned pro. He first played for the Memphis Showboats, a U.S. Football League team; then he headed west hoping to be recruited by the San Francisco 49ers. But a hamstring injury forever ended his days in professional sports.

Don found California to his liking, and he decided to stay. It seemed so much more accepting than the South. Don sought a new career in law enforcement. In 1988 he was graduated from the Sacramento County Sheriff's Academy, voted the "most inspirational recruit" by his classmates. Don did not need any boost from affirmative action—he was extremely qualified for the job regardless of his skin color—but for many years, the Sacramento County Sheriff's Department was a very white place. He never would have been hired in the early 1960s. The color barrier was broken only because of affirmative action. Even by 1996, the department had not met its own affirmative action goals to match the force with the county's racial makeup; its employees were 8.3 percent black, while the county's population was nearly 12 percent black. Don's career experience was typical of that of many successful blacks— half of all blacks in professional and managerial positions work for government agencies on the local, state, and federal levels. In contrast, one-quarter of all whites work in these agencies. This is because the government has been more serious about affirmative action than other institutions. Only the largest corporations have provided equal opportunity. Many smaller businesses have not.

Don did not start at the top, however. Like all new employees, he was assigned to jail duty, which was depressing and difficult. A disproportionate number of black faces showed up behind the bars. "Everyday I would sit there and watch them come in. I'm talking about young guys, nice-looking big strong guys. I'd think, boy, what a shame."

Don said to himself, blacks are no different from any other

racial group: prison should not be the inevitable end for so many. Leaving the jail assignment in 1990, he went into a crime-prevention program and talked to fourth- through sixth-graders about drugs and gangs. He saw kids walking around mad at the world, probably headed for the jail he just left. When Don was elected president of the Sacramento County Black Deputy Sheriff's Association, he explored ways in which the group could work with young black men.

It was obvious to Don that environment was the key, just as it had been when he was growing up in rural Arkansas. Don decided he had to create a "community," an alternative to gangs. "That was the power of the black community when I was a kid. We *had* a community. People were proud." The kids who joined gangs formed replacement "families" in which negative acts were rewarded and peer pressure discouraged academic success.

For Don to create a community in a modern urban environment, he had to reach out to kids when they were still in junior high, before they had begun to get into trouble. Don came up with the "Our Kids" (OK) Program. The idea was relatively simple. Some 24 black officers on the force would each be assigned to several young black men. While this resembled a traditional one-on-one mentoring program, Don's program had one critical difference—almost all the black teenagers at one school—Mills Junior High in Rancho Cordova, a downwardly mobile suburb east of Sacramento—would participate. Each child would have *positive* peer pressure throughout the school day and an adult mentor on weekends. In a traditional program, a youth still has to deal with the larger society of school kids who are not being mentored. "If I'm going to have a lasting impact on these kids, I've got to not only change one kid; I've got to change his environment. Give all his peers the same rules, the same expectations, the same boundaries," Don said.

Rather than belong to a gang devoted to drugs and crime, the five dozen kids would belong to a structured group in which good deeds were supported and rewarded. In its first year the program had a budget of $10,000, not counting Don's salary. It would take a lot of hard work and even more luck to make the program a success.

Don believed that black people had to help themselves. Across

America, white society had given up caring about the black ghetto, but as the face of California changed, many blacks felt even more shunted aside. They were just another part of the mix. An Asian who arrived in California a decade ago and a recently arrived Mexican had the same minority status as blacks who had arrived three centuries earlier as slaves.

As Don struggled to help resolve age-old problems, he saw the attack on affirmative action as a move to blast blacks back to the pre-civil rights Arkansas of his youth. And it amazed him that California was being so reactionary. "I never thought I would live to see California leading the way in doing away with affirmative action, the most liberal-minded state in our union—supposedly. From Arkansas, I would expect that, Mississippi, Louisiana, Georgia."

Don found himself preferring old-style southern racism to the version he found on the Pacific Coast. He'd rather see a Confederate flag sticker on the locker of the white officer in his department than veiled racism. "I'd rather know who I'm dealing with," Don said.

CALIFORNIA

Racial friction in California is different from that in other regions of the country, for a unique mix of reasons: the state is at the end of the road for white European immigration, the people who have migrated to California fall into certain categories, and the four major racial and ethnic groups there interact in a complex way that is not evident in most other states.

Many events reflect this nation-state's racial disposition, but one of the most revealing occurred several years into the reactionary wave, on the morning of July 20, 1995, when the University of California regents met to vote on ending affirmative action at the nine-campus University of California, the nation's largest and most prestigious state university system.

The vote was pushed by Pete Wilson, who as governor is also head of the regents. Wilson was courting the so-called angry white male voter to boost his faltering campaign for the Republican presidential nomination. He decided to make a stand by abolishing race preferences at the university. It was a move guaranteed to attract media attention.

The university system is governed by 26 regents: 17 of the 18 core members were appointed by Wilson and his Republican predecessors, including 2 who date back to Governor Ronald Reagan's term; the others consist of a student, alumni, and politicians, mostly Democrats. Common Cause once estimated the average worth of the 18 core regents at $1.3 million. Wilson needed votes from these 18, some of whom contributed to his campaigns. Black developer Ward Connerly, a Wilson appointee, had first proposed killing affirmative action in the university system in January, two weeks after Wilson called for an end to the policy. Now it was time for the vote.

The 18 regents serve 12-year unpaid terms to insulate them from political pressure. Some Republicans bravely refused to go along with Wilson. He fiercely lobbied several swing votes and even considered stripping student regent Ed Gomez of his right to vote, Gomez later said in an interview.

Security was especially tight for the meeting in San Francisco: 155 cops had surrounded the grounds of the Laurel Heights campus, some marching lockstep, others standing guard, riot gear and paddy wagons at the ready. Even in quiet times, the board sometimes made reporters empty their briefcases and pockets at a checkpoint, but much of their paranoia was unfounded. This time, there was reason to expect turmoil. It was the opening salvo in a nationwide attack on the policy, and the point when the backers of the anti–affirmative action California Civil Rights Initiative were gathering forces.

Wilson was grim-faced and presidential before the television cameras. He looked reasonable in public, but off camera he raged. After UC Berkeley Chancellor Chang-Lin Tien publicly corrected Wilson's misuse of a stage-prop chart, Wilson cornered Tien and chewed him out.[7] When university officials refused to allow the CCRI backers in the press room—citing obvious partisan bias—Wilson's people brought in a representative, who fed releases and was not discovered until late in the day, when he was evicted.

Voices of reason among the dozens who testified at the meeting suggested that the matter should be studied and a vote taken after serious deliberation. There was no need to rush the issue. Eloquent speeches were made to a board that had already made up its mind. Assemblyman John Vasconcellos said in support of keeping affirmative action, "I come as a native Californian and a white male raised to believe we are one people." Acknowledging California's long history of bashing nonwhite people, he added: "We come from a history of shame."

Assemblyman Nao Takasugi, the only Asian in the assembly when Martha Escutia was elected in 1992, testified that affirmative action should be ended. He referred to his internment in an American prison camp for the Japanese during World War II, even though he was an American citizen. He charged that affirmative action "is state-mandated discrimination, the same kind that took my family away."

Tom Sayles, a recently appointed regent who is a black Republican, defied the man who seated him. He said he was voting to retain affirmative action because the week before, as he looked for a new house, he was reminded of why protections were needed.

"I was in my upscale car and my upscale clothes. There was a Caucasian couple looking at the house. I heard the realtor tell them that it was a good neighborhood, that only whites and a few Asians live here—so that I could hear it. That was extraordinarily hurtful." He said he could deal with this and other kinds of discrimination, but that "we cannot ask this of our young people entering our universities." That is why protections are needed for young people, he added.

Outside the meeting hall, many protestors were baffled to hear affirmative action being attacked in what they had considered a liberal state. The Reverend Jesse Jackson was among them. When he arrived, surrounded by television cameras and a throng, he flatly branded Wilson the "new George Wallace," a spin he would repeat throughout the long day and one the protesters embraced. Reinforcing the civil rights imagery, Jackson marched with the crowd of several hundred, singing "We Shall Overcome."

California's nonwhites were under siege, but Wilson is no more George Wallace than Jackson is Martin Luther King Jr. Most important, California is not the South. Even the South today is not the South of 30 years ago. Jackson was using the wrong imagery. Jackson did not seem to understand the dynamics of California's four-way society. He did not have a new message to cut through Wilson's rhetoric.

After the 12-hour meeting—amid a bomb threat and

protests—the regents voted 14–10 to end affirmative action in university admissions and 15–10 to end it in hiring. The new policy was supposed to be race-neutral while recognizing disadvantaged students regardless of their skin color. Jackson emerged and announced the vote as a historic moment in the "attempt to stop the second Reconstruction." Beneath the glare of a police helicopter's spotlight, Jackson led a march down California Street. But there were just 300 participants, an unusually low number for a city so liberal that protest is sometimes embraced for no other reason than to have a street party.

The affirmative action marchers continued to sing "We Shall Overcome" and chanted "out of the house and into the street!" to residents, whose faces filled the windows. Jackson stopped the march in the middle of the intersection at Geary and Divisadero and addressed the protesters for the last time.

"Tonight, the movement has been reborn," he said.

As Jackson spoke, a woman at the edge of the crowd worried about the dismal turnout. Eva Paterson, executive director of San Francisco's Lawyers Committee for Civil Rights, had participated in many local protests over the years and said when marchers call out to residents, people usually run into the street to join. "But no one came out," she said of the mostly white spectators. In fact, the crowd thinned, surprising even the police. If San Francisco liberals shunned participating with Jesse Jackson in behalf of affirmative action, how could moderates and conservatives in less progressive locales be persuaded it still had value?

Pete Wilson understood the feelings of those who peered from windows but did not join Jackson. Conservatives alone have not approved California's reactionary laws. That is why in 1994 two out of three voters approved Proposition 187 and three out of four voted for the draconian "three strikes and you're out" sentencing of even small-scale offenders to 25 years to life in prison. And that is why many will vote in 1996 to end affirmative action in state government. Right now, the fear among whites is tremendous, regardless of their politics. Wilson perfectly mirrors the collective anxieties of the Golden State's overclass, which includes some non-whites and even some liberals.

Wilson seemed to have answers for angry whites while Jackson did not. When I asked Jackson outside the regents' meeting hall that morning why California was out front in attacking brown-skinned people, he had no explanation. Either he did not know or would not say. When pushed on this point, he evaded the question. But some at the meeting had theories. Tanya Selig, who had made the trip from southern California by bus, said she saw a grand plot by forces of the Right to use the state as a staging ground because of its size. "This is the place to do it. They started 187 to see how that worked out. They're doing the same thing with affirmative action. It's all part of the same divide and conquer."

Businesswoman Elizabeth Peters, who moved to California in 1953, did not see a plot. She said racism is "the story of the United States. California is just as bad as the rest of the country." What makes it worse now, she said, is that California is engaged in one of its periodic eruptions. "It's hard to explain California to people outside the state. California always has the extremes. California has the best and worst of any given thing."

Peters is correct. How, after all, can one explain why the state would elect Ronald Reagan governor at one turn and then Jerry Brown at another? Or why the state is home to two counties of such ideological extremes as limousine-liberal Marin County and Libertarian-Bircher Orange County. Political schizophrenia is why the state has liberal cycles and then conservative ones, periods of acceptance followed by crackdown. It is why, when the economy sours, reactionary forces whip things wildly to the right.

Peters believes the "country was founded by misfits and ne'er-do-wells. They were misfits in Kansas and Iowa and then they came here. This makes them more cantankerous." The good part is that the state's restless residents are open to social experiments or new ideas and technologies. The bad part was happening inside the building where the regents were about to end affirmative action. She added, "I think California has always been the land of fruit and nuts. It's the last stop on people's dream train."

In writing about California's centennial, historian Carey McWilliams spent most of his book *California: The Great Exception* (perhaps the best history of the state) documenting why Californians are so different from their fellow Americans. According to McWilliams, the Gold Rush played a big role in making the state unique and fostered an intensity of feeling that was passed down to later generations. The Gold Rush was a "poor man's" bonanza, the most "democratic" mining rush in world history, and the news was telegraphed around the world. Anyone could come and take a chance, for unlike mining booms elsewhere in the West, the California Gold Rush was not controlled by big companies. Those who came were adventurous and independent. The state raced forward politically and economically. In four years, the state experienced 2,500 percent growth. California wielded great power from the start, gaining statehood in an unprecedented two short years, bypassing status as a territory. The state was separated from settled America by the empty prairies, deserts, and mountains, and its culture developed sequestered from the rest of the western frontier. McWilliams notes that prior to 1869 California was closer to China and South America than it was to Mississippi.[8]

Its residents were more inconstant than those in other parts of the frontier. The Indians, McWilliams notes, were killed more quickly and with more violence, in part because of the zealous invasion of so many miners. There were no "long drawn-out negotiations with Indians, Indian agents, and congressional committees, over land titles, water rights, and similar matters." Other western states have vast Indian reservations. There are only isolated "rancherias" in California. The Indians were simply exterminated or their rights trampled. The same attitude was reflected in the state's backlash against Asians and others.

The actual search for gold waned several decades after the rush, but it reemerged in a metaphorical guise. The state continued to attract seekers, not of gold but of dreams, and the fierce independence that the pioneers developed continued, mixed with the utopian ideals that brought many new settlers. California has long had more "edge" than other places. That is why so many trends emanate from there, from hot tubs to rollerblades, Hell's Angels to drive-in churches, "Valley talk," the Sierra Club, computers, and the cultural domination of the television and movie industry, to name but a few. That influence carries over to politics. Because of the pioneering and utopian roots of the state, individualism was nurtured. In 1911 the state allowed citizens to generate ballot initiatives to mold the law. Through one like Proposition 187, the state's reactionary mood erupts and carries over into policy.

In the 1990s a critical mass of history plus the mix of cultures exploded in the turmoil that so surprised Donald Northcross, Jesse

Jackson, and others. The complex multiethnicities created their own dynamic, especially among whites, who cross paths with a wide range of cultures. They might reside in self-segregated pockets but work and shop amid other races. Having long since learned that open racial comments would have negative results, even the ones uncomfortable with the change are relatively tolerant. Others have developed a certain degree of sophistication: they interact with all cultures, are virtual internationalists without ever leaving the country. But throw in a contracting economy and this generates fear even among reasonable people, along with confusion. The backlash against affirmative action, for instance, is not always directly racist inspired. At the forefront of the confusion among many whites is a question: why does special status exist if there are so many different minority groups deserving of special status: Central Americans, Chinese, Filipinos, Koreans, Mexicans, Middle Easterners, Pacific Islanders, and others, in addition to blacks? Plus, whites see some groups, such as Chinese Asians, outperforming them. Even some liberal whites quietly mutter.

With so many groups, some ask why whites are not considered a special group. This question is particularly important in a place like Lowell High School, where whites make up less than 20 percent of the student body, and at Berkeley, where they account for about a third of the students. Whites can object to the focus on group identity while sincerely believing they are not racist toward blacks and Latinos and Asians. Bill Shepherd in Orange County is somebody who would be horrified by a Bull Conner sicking dogs on blacks, and Bill is typical of many of the eight out of ten voters in the state who are white.

Against this background, many California whites are like whites elsewhere: they see themselves losing ground. They see the brown face taking the place of their white face or that of their son or daughter in jobs and college admissions, in a time of finite opportunities and resources. While some whites are scared and angry about this in the East and South—in places that are still between 80 and 95 percent white—this fear ratchets up exponentially in a state where whites form 52 percent of the population and their numbers are falling.

CALIFORNIA AND NATIONAL POLITICS

California's impact on modern race relations dates back to the latter years of the civil rights campaign and the growing urban unrest. After the urban riots, first in Watts in 1965, and Detroit, Newark, and elsewhere in 1966 and 1967, whites voted with their feet. Huntington Park in the center of Martha Escutia's district and not far from Watts, was a very white place before 1965. The town soon emptied of whites, and this, along with the flight from other areas, brought an economic boom to places such as southern Orange County. At that time, Bill Shepherd's neighborhood was a small village on an empty coast, not the gated suburban enclave it is today. The growth of California's white suburbs mirrors the flight of urban whites across America. For California, the political reaction and the anger that was waiting to be tapped proved unique.

To understand how this anger was consolidated politically, one must look at the California of 1964. Governor Pat Brown was an old-line politician who pushed investment in education, roads, and water projects. Brown was popular, and he had handily beaten Richard Nixon by 300,000 votes in the California governor's race of 1962. (In Nixon's campaign, Pete Wilson was a young advance man.) It was a relatively calm period for the state compared with the South. California had its share of racial conflicts, but they were minor. As Carey McWilliams noted in the 1940s, Californians were generally supportive of civil rights, especially voters in the major population centers. Many Midwestern whites who settled in Los Angeles favored equality, and San Franciscans were always very liberal. But in the 1950s, as was the case in northern cities, the number of blacks in Los Angeles County doubled as they migrated from the South. Also increasing in number were other nonwhites. The polyglot—and tension—was emerging.

In hindsight, there is plenty of evidence that trouble was coming. A few months after Congress passed the Civil Rights Act, California voters approved Proposition 14, an initiative that killed the state's fair housing law by a margin of two to one, in violation of the measure Congress had just passed.

This forgotten initiative would prove critical, both to Reagan's career—he was an early backer, supporting Proposition 14 on the

speech circuit and in the course of his ascendancy as state cochair-
man of Barry Goldwater's campaign—and to California's role in
racial politics. The positions that took shape in 1964 would control
the Republican Party for the next three decades. When Reagan
challenged Governor Pat Brown in 1966, he seized on the 1965
Watts riots, but unlike Wallace he was able to mask a conservative
message, interpreting events in a way that did not seem at all right-
wing to many voters. As one political commentator noted, Reagan
often sounded liberal when he was being very unliberal. He appealed to whites with a folksy demeanor and once said to black legislators that the fair housing law was wrong because "you wouldn't
want to sell your house to a red-headed Kiwanian if you didn't want
to, would you?" On another occasion, he argued, "There is no law
saying the Negro has to live in Harlem or Watts."[9]

Reagan made his message palatable by casting it in terms of
"law and order." Brown later wrote that he knew he was in trouble
when he went to a northern California cocktail party of "liberals"
and heard them calling for a crackdown. He also called for law and
order, but his mistake was to go beyond this and use words like
"justice, compassion, understanding." Brown appeared soft, Reagan tough.

Reagan's method fit a state that was steadily growing more
multicultural. Overt racism might work with the southerners who
had moved to California, but it would not work among the transplanted Midwesterners McWilliams wrote about who were now
filling the suburbs. They could not see themselves as racists. Reagan appealed to whites who would never cast a vote for a politician
as overtly racist as Wallace. He beat Brown by over 900,000 votes
in the 1966 election; in this same election, in a signal of a conservative trend nationwide, Republicans gained 47 seats in the House
of Representatives.

To Governor Brown, California's racial and cultural relations
became increasingly complex, what with white distress over the
Watts riots, and he resented Reagan's form of fear-based politics.
In his book, *Reagan and Reality: The Two Californias*, published
after his defeat, Brown wrote: "Reagan is a result, a symbol, and a
surface image of those currents. The tides of social tension, frustration, and fear probably run most clearly and swiftly in California,
but I know they are running elsewhere in America."

Alarmed California voters created Reagan, Brown says. (Or perhaps Reagan molded himself to their desires.) Brown cited the growing national racial polarization that California was fueling: the Watts riots that were followed by riots elsewhere, the formation in 1966 of the Black Panthers in Oakland, the John Birch Society "and [its] armed, violent offspring of the Right" with its strongest support in Orange County.

"Reagan remains both a force and a symbol of a new and negative type of politics, which *could* spread outside California and into the future . . . as the same social conflicts and complexities that have rocked California flair in the rest of the nation."

Brown's prediction proved utterly accurate. As Reagan was manipulating white fear for political gain in California's white suburbs, Richard Nixon, a native Californian, was also appealing to white anger about forced school busing without making whites feel like southern racists. Much like his protégé Pete Wilson, Nixon did not approach racial politics with Reagan's deep conservative convictions. He had learned what it took to win elections, and his use of race was a matter of convenience.

In *Chain Reaction,* Thomas Byrne Edsall and Mary D. Edsall document the rise of the politics of division in the Republican Party and the central role played by California politicians.[10] A rapid series of events after 1965 allowed Republicans to use race as a "wedge" issue to siphon off white voters from Democrats, with Nixon and Reagan building off each other and George Wallace.

In Nixon's case, the Edsalls note, "any direct attack on the principle of racial equality risked the loss of millions of traditional Republican voters." Nixon, the authors say, "developed strategies essential to capitalizing on the issue of race while avoiding the label of racism." Reagan, later in his run for the presidency, "consolidated, updated, and refined the right-populist, race-coded strategies of Wallace and Nixon."

There were myriad reasons for many working-class whites to suddenly feel fearful and for their support of black rights to erode. The dividing line, the Edsalls say, was the pre-1964 emphasis on the basic rights of citizenship, such as voting and equal opportunity, to the post-1964 "emphasizing equal outcomes or results for blacks, often achieved through racial preferences." Most whites could accept the former, but not the latter.

Success is naturally copied, and many politicians in the East and South adopted the same tactics of the Californians. George Bush is a prime example of the Reagan and Nixon mind-set. "The 1980s were marked less by Republican political innovation than by the drive to adjust, renovate, and strengthen messages established in the previous two decades," the Edsalls say.

Governor Wilson's approach is an extension of that of his California forebears. Take his position on immigration. As his campaign spokesman Dan Schnur pointed out, "Throughout Pete Wilson's discussion of the illegal immigration issue we have gone to extraordinary efforts to make sure the race or ethnic origin of an individual is not an issue."

Indeed, true. Wilson never said "Mexicans." But the television commercial Wilson used in New Hampshire in 1995 did not show hundreds of thousands of Europeans and Canadians who overstay their visas to remain in the United States illegally—it was of a "banzai run" on a border crossing by illegal Mexicans. And in 1995, when Wilson sued his own government to rescind all executive-mandated affirmative action, in the first minutes of his speech he invoked Hubert Humphrey, Thomas Jefferson, Martin Luther King Jr., and John F. Kennedy.[11]

Wilson used the softest language to say that affirmative action had outlived its time. It was now "reverse discrimination." In a twist, Wilson even alluded to the coming white minority and said affirmative action had to be overturned to protect nonwhites from unfairly competing with each other. It was more complicated than this, but like Nixon and Reagan, Wilson had simplified the message. There were many cases in which whites were granted admission to schools through affirmative action; at Maria Ha's high school, they were essentially given preferences. It was the same story at UC Berkeley: the proportion of Asians would be higher if some whites had not been admitted through what amounted to affirmative action.

Nixon set the national stage for Reagan, and in postriot California Wilson took the Nixon-Reagan message into new territory, expanding race fear to the fear of Latinos and campaigning for the end of affirmative action. Even Reagan did not try to scrap affirmative action directly. He relied on reshaping the judiciary. The fruits of this move were seen in 1993 and 1995, when Reagan-appointed

U.S. Supreme Court justices won narrow decisions that race cannot be a "predominant factor" in creating legislative districts to ensure minorities are elected, and other decisions in which race preferences were cast aside.

Wilson is far weaker than Nixon and Reagan. "Pete Wilson is Richard Nixon without the genitals," said Larry Remer, the editor of a weekly newspaper in San Diego when Wilson was mayor. At least in 1996, Wilson proved to be an insignificant presidential candidate. His bid failed for myriad reasons. Many Republicans were upset that he broke a promise not to run for president, and he was spurned by the usual financial backers. Plus he was handicapped by throat surgery earlier in 1995 that silenced him for weeks.

One Democratic Party leader crowed that Wilson's 1996 failure meant his policies were repudiated. This is a dangerous assumption, for Wilson is a metaphor for all the fears of California whites—he created himself in the image of those fears. Despite his presidential failure, Wilson helped propel the anti-immigration and anti–affirmative action movement into the national spotlight and sent California-based xenophobia on a march. Even in "defeat," a mailing sent out with Wilson's signature netted 145,000 of the 1.1 million names that placed the California Civil Rights Initiative on the 1996 ballot. He also raised $300,000 and put the force of his office behind the drive. Wilson has vowed to come back in 2000, and whether or not he succeeds, he has been a powerful player in shifting the debate on immigration and affirmative action.[12] The California backlash against immigration and affirmative action would have occurred without him, but as a catalyst, Wilson intensified these movements. He was in a position to be both a follower and a leader.

While one could blame Wilson for fueling negative politics, the Left has failed to articulate alternatives to reasonable people like Bill Shepherd. Wilson offered the only affirmative action option to many whites, and it was absolute: either throw it out, or keep it. The entire middle ground was not being talked about.

One state study shows that by 2003, when Wilson reaches the usual retirement age of 70, white males entering the workforce will only be 15 percent of the California labor pool. Census projections show that by 2010, white males will be just 36 percent of the national workforce.[13]

Progressives must educate whites of all political bents that their future is tied to nonwhites, that inclusion is not just a nice liberal idea. There will have to be de facto affirmative action regardless of the racial politics of California and the rest of the country. Hostility toward dark-skinned people is stupid and counterproductive. After all, as Martha Escutia said long before, who is going to do the work and pay the taxes?

In the next few decades, this question and others will be answered as the United States goes through the wrenching change associated with the shrinking white numbers now seen in California.

For Don Northcross, Martha Escutia, Maria Ha, Bill Shepherd, and Pete Wilson, California is a dream train of hopes and ideals at the end of the road. It drew Don from Arkansas to seek his chances outside the confines of the old South; Bill came with his family in California's heyday; the parents of Martha and Maria journeyed great distances to start new lives. Wilson settled here in 1959 after a stint in the Marines to take advantage of UC Berkeley, an institution that was then almost free, one that he would later choose to starve in favor of building prisons. In many ways, California and its residents exist on a frontier just as bold as the one present in 1849, only this time it is a cultural one.

3
White

Dusk. An Atchison, Topeka & Santa Fe freight barrels up the coast, entering Dana Point, a city of gently sloping hills above the Pacific. The train, as usual, is laden with Mexicans making profound but anonymous journeys. When it sides behind Price Club, men jump off and disappear in the jungle of bamboo growing along Capistrano Creek.

An early morning hike finds human woodchucks emerging from "spider holes," caves dug into the dry brush-covered mountainside south of the dusty creek bed. Those newer or less industrious, perhaps less confident of finding work, camp in an abandoned orange grove on top of the hill.

Mexicans have come north for work at least as long as there have been farms and hotels and sweat shops in California and legions of poor in Mexico. For many decades before whites made Orange County into a suburb of Los Angeles, Mexicans passed through Dana Point on their way to the groves to the north that gave the county its name. Martha Escutia's grandfather journeyed through here in the 1940s and 1950s; one of his jobs was picking oranges in an Anaheim grove and then cutting the trees down to make way for Disneyland.

It takes a creative mind today to picture the rural Orange

County that Martha's grandfather saw, the verdant orchards at the foot of dry hills. All that is gone and nowhere is the development more apparent than from Bill Shepherd's living room. When you stand at the long wall of windows near the indoor Jacuzzi, there is a view fit for a postcard, an endorsement of southern California suburban coastal living.The entire foreground is studded with red-tile-roof homes, some worth a million dollars. To the south, hidden just over a rise, is the hill pocked with "spider holes," the last undeveloped patch for miles around. Inland are the brown mountains above the Camp Pendleton Marine Corps base and the surf curves south to San Diego. On the clearest of days, Bill can see the faint outline of the Islas Los Coronados off the coast of Mexico, 80 miles distant.

For a long time, the cultures of the spider hole dwellers and white suburbanites like Bill were separate, but history and current events ensured their paths would cross.

THE ROOTS OF CONFLICT

For years, because Dana Point was never an agricultural center, Mexicans passed through on the road to hoped-for orchard jobs in the northern part of Orange County, or in Los Angeles, the Central Valley, and the apple country of Washington State. The town, which was not incorporated until 1989, came into existence in the 1920s when a developer designed it as a community of both apartments and homes. With an eye to promotion, he named the streets after different-colored lanterns: Street of the Golden Lantern, Street of the Blue Lantern, and so on. The Great Depression halted the ambitious project, and for a long time Dana Point was barely more than a gas stop on the Pacific Coast Highway, the main road before the San Diego Freeway was built.[1]

Many of the early homebuyers were working-class people— Dana Point was a place where they could live near the sea—and they were a bit more bohemian than most suburbanites. Those who had money did not flaunt it. The town never had the pretensions of Laguna Beach, an art colony immediately to the north. It was, as Bill's neighbor says, a place where you wore "scruffies," not caring how you looked.

Change came in the 1960s, when a huge harbor was blasted and dredged. A mile-long breakwall destroyed the best surfing, the spot known as "Killer Dana." The surfer community was subsequently overtaken by the culture that developed around the yachts and boats. Then as the southern California real estate market expanded in the 1980s, developers punched roads through the scrub and leveled mountaintops; Dana Point's hills sprouted houses like starthistles after spring rains.

The first of Dana Point's luxury hotels, the five-star Ritz-Carlton, opened in 1985, "positioned majestically atop a 150-foot bluff . . . the crown jewel of the California Riviera," where the best suite fetches $2,750 per night.[2] In 1988, between frequent business trips, Bill Shepherd watched from his window as the other big hotel, the four-star Dana Point Resort, went up.

With the explosive growth, the old part of town known as Lantern Village became surrounded by luxury homes. Bill, however, preferred the old part of town because it had charm. It was not a mass-produced tract. But many whites chose to live in developments with walls, gates, and sometimes guards. By the time the town was almost completely built out with 34,000 residents, save for the dying orange grove next to the noisy freeway where the spider hole people reside, roughly one-third of the 6.1-square-mile city was sealed off behind 17 walled—or, in local parlance, "gate-guarded"—neighborhoods, which means you can't go there unless invited.[3]

Dana Point's gated enclaves are typical of the communities in which as many as four million Americans now live, according to Edward J. Blakely, dean of urban planning at the University of Southern California.[4] He notes that walled estates began in the 1920s with East Coast oil and railroad magnates, but California made walled-in suburbs popular. Monarch Bay, a gate-guarded community at the northern edge of Dana Point, was among the first in a trend that accelerated in the 1970s. South Orange County probably has the most walled neighborhoods in California, 500 by one estimate.[5]

When whites fled the browning communities of Los Angeles, many ended up in places such as Dana Point, hoping they had left urban troubles behind. With their gates and high price tags, the new towns in south Orange County beckoned to homebuyers: this was a place where you would find people just like you, where you could control your environment.

Thus was born one of the major white "islands" in California in tune with the political message of Reagan and Nixon and later of Wilson. With the exception of San Juan Capistrano, home of the famous mission founded in 1776, whose Latino community has been in California for generations, the entire south county is between 82 and 90 percent white. The center of the county is a "de-militarized" zone of sorts, a mixed area that is some 70 percent white, and to the north of this, across an invisible border near Dis-neyland, is a dominant nonwhite community, with a 40 to 75 percent mix of Vietnamese, Mexican, Central American, and other cultures.

The census tract covering Lantern Village (and some adjoining white-dominated housing) shows that 64 percent of the residents were white in 1990; the remaining 2,200 residents were Latino, though this is likely an undercount, as many undocumented immigrants did not participate in the census. By contrast, the census tract with 1,500 residents in the northern part of town, which includes gate-guarded neighborhoods, is 91 percent white, as is the case in Dana Point outside Lantern Village. Of the nonwhite 9 percent in that neighborhood, there were 78 Latinos, 52 Asians, 19 blacks, and 1 American Indian.

The mixed population settled in the north partly because it is the oldest part of the county, and thus it has more apartments. It is no accident that many south county cities have virtually no low-cost housing. Dana Point has so many apartments because Lantern Village predates the flight of the whites in the 1960s and govern-ment planning boards that later forbade the construction of new apartments.

The Dana Point hotels became the city's largest employers, with a combined staff of 1,100. The multitude of newly arrived rich spawned a demand for workers to mow lawns, clean homes, baby-sit, and work in restaurants. Whites and blacks did not exactly scramble to fill these jobs, but word reached the little towns in the Mexican states of Oaxaca, Guerrero, Sinaloa, and Morelos, and in-stead of passing through Dana Point, Mexicans began staying.

A casual visitor might not suspect that Latinos are so important to the economy. In Orange County and much of California, many of the "front" positions—workers seen by the public—are fluent English speakers, which usually means whites and blacks and occasionally Asians. The host who seats you, the person who waits on you, the clerk who checks you in are usually citizens, but a peek through many restaurant doors finds the kitchen filled with undocumented Latinos. At one Orange County El Pollo Loco, a fast-food chicken franchise, workers put up a sign "United States/Mexico" at the point dividing the cash registers from the area where the food is prepared.[6]

This service industry fuels the economy of south Orange County. In 1994 alone, the Dana Point hotels had a combined gross income of $36.5 million—some 80 percent of which came from the Ritz-Carlton Hotel and the Dana Point Resort—which netted the city $3.65 million in bed taxes.[7] This was one-third of the city's budget, and officials estimated that if the attendant business was factored in, including what tourists spend in sales taxes at local restaurants, the hotels were generating about half of all city revenues.

Lantern Village and its apartments became home for many of the Mexicans whose labor supports this industry. There is one other barrio, in the Capistrano Beach area in the southern part of town. Because Lantern Village rents often exceed $1,000 a month—more than the income generated by two full-time minimum-wage jobs—two and three families often share one unit. Behind these apartment doors is Mexico, with handmade *maize* tortillas on the counter, eggs stacked unrefrigerated in cartons, families sleeping in shifts. A Dana Point code enforcement officer said he once found 16 people living in a two-bedroom apartment.[8]

Graffiti and old cars appeared. In the evening, Latino men gathered on corners, talking and drinking, a common way of socializing in Mexican neighborhoods. Such cultural change was upsetting to Bill's neighbors, who saw it as the beginning of decay. Their fear centered on Latino gangs comprised of the children of the immigrants who had come to take the low-wage jobs.

It is unclear how much crime is attributable to immigrant Latinos—the Orange County Sheriff's Department that patrols Dana Point will not give out ethnic arrest statistics. But the department says that 30 to 40 percent of all Dana Point crime happens in Lantern Village, roughly a 15-by-7-block quadrant north of U.S.

1, the Pacific Coast Highway. It has the highest rates of vehicle and commercial burglary, narcotics arrests, and residential burglary—twice that of any other part of the city.[9] Some crime is certainly being committed by whites, but poverty can cause crime, and a lot of Latinos are poor.

The sheriff does release information on gangs—and many young Latinos are involved. One report about the south county gangs stated: "Criminal street gangs have become one of our most serious problems and account for one of the largest, single, personal threats to public safety in the area."[10] No gangs operate in Dana Point, considered neutral territory by the two largest gangs —the San Juan Boys, with 130 members, and the San Clemente Varrio Chicos, with 146 members. But some members live in Dana Point.

Much of this change occurred over many months when Bill was busy traveling on business. He did not see it. He did notice that his street had fallen into disrepair, and he circulated a petition to have the road repaved. Visiting many of his neighbors for the first time, Bill was startled by what he heard. They described shootings and drug busts. They were afraid. Some said they were moving out. All this contrasted sharply with the town many of these white residents had moved to years before. Bill suddenly became aware of changes in the town's environment, and he saw that he had a choice: get out while the going was good, or work to change things.

Dana Point could be the story of a hundred California communities—people who exist in two worlds, who do not talk, do not understand each other, a third-world *campesino* culture thrust into the heart of a yuppie universe.

What do you do if you're a law-abiding illegal immigrant who just wants to make a buck and better your life—and a business is eager to hire you and even encouraged you to come to a new country—but a bunch of other people want you to quickly become just like them, or vanish?

What do you do if you are an American taxpayer who has worked all your life to buy a dream home, and suddenly the neighborhood becomes more dangerous because a small number of the children of the new immigrants join gangs?

THE WHITE RESPONSE

The first eruption of anti-immigrant sentiment in Dana Point occurred in the late 1980s. On some days as many as 150 men would stand on one streetcorner in Capistrano Beach hoping landscape contractors and others would hire them.[11] The sight of so many dark-skinned people hungry for work was unsettling to the social order, and it sparked a call for a crackdown. Dana Point Mayor Judy Curreri, a Republican who would be a Democrat anywhere else, brokered a compromise. The city outlawed streetcorner job solicitation, but set up a telephone hot line to connect employers with workers. "My theory is I can't control the people who come to Dana Point," Judy said. "That's a national issue. But we have to deal with the people once they are here. Let's make the best of it."

Things more or less quieted, until a second eruption that came after April of 1992. It did not seem a coincidence: the anxiety level of whites throughout the country went way up after the Los Angeles riots. Then Bill became a major player in Dana Point's sharpening reaction toward immigrants. He joined the Lantern Village Association and was elected president in January 1993.

This was no plum. When he began his term, the group and the town were heavily factionalized. The issues, mundane to an outsider, provoked deep passions. To understand this, one only has to attend a Dana Point City Council session. The biweekly meeting is a local sport for a few dozen souls, eager to watch their elected leaders in action, and their active participation includes hoots, catcalls, and hisses that have occasionally caused a council member to burst into tears.

Some members were amazed when Bill pulled off the impossible: after six months, he got the Lantern Village people talking to each other. Realizing that they had to identify problems before they could move forward, he asked the association to come up with a list of concerns to present to the city council.

On May 8, 1993, the Lantern Village Neighborhood Steering Committee consisting of Bill Shepherd and some dozen and a half other members met in a daylong session. One prominent issue was a "lack of recreation and open space in the Village." A second was "poor community image of the Village." Third was the "residents' lack of feeling safe in the Village." As the morning wore on, the members brainstormed potential goals; they came up with 35 ideas.[12]

Committee members then were asked to vote for the five most important goals. The top four vote-getters were

1. Improve absentee Owners/Management (18–0).
2. City to hire a local immigration agent; send letters to government officials asking that they enforce existing immigration laws (15–0).
3. Have a proactive code enforcement (12–0).
4. Tenant education (how to be a good tenant and neighbor) (11–0).

Stronger housing code enforcement in the Mexican neighborhoods, they felt, would help. The overcrowded apartments with laundry hanging from railings drove down property values. Dana Point had three full-time code enforcement officers, unheard of for a city its size. Two of them patrolled Lantern Village to ensure there were no violations. The most reactionary proposal was to hire an agent of the Immigration and Naturalization Service; it was dropped.

A member of Bill's group put the situation in relation to the Mexicans simply: "They have nothing to lose. We have everything to lose." But Bill's idea was to work within the framework of existing laws and not to engage in activities such as picketing Latino job seekers, which was seen in other communities. He had faith in his neighborhood. "I don't give up," Bill said. "I love the area. One of the best hotels in the world is just blocks from my house. I travel all over the United States and if I found a better place, I'd move there."

He was so confident that not long after he became involved in the Lantern Village Association, he decided to remodel. Consulting work was slow, so he used the downtime to do all the labor himself. His home was suddenly transformed into a construction project. The garage was stacked with rolled carpeting, walls were ripped open, dust was everywhere. Early one summer afternoon, he came down from the roof where he had been hammering nails.

As Bill removed his work overalls, he said his group wanted to send out the message that anyone was welcome in Dana Point—as long as they conformed to community standards. "We can work together," he said of the immigrants. "But they need to be assimilated and educated."

This, of course, was the argument made at the turn of the century against immigrants from southern and eastern Europe. With the great surge of immigrants, the number of foreign-born residents in the United States reached almost 15 percent of the population in 1910, half of what it would be eight decades later. About the time of World War I, there were calls for the eastern and southern European immigrants to adapt and learn the language, to act like "Americans."

Is the current anti-immigrant wave any different? Perhaps it is that the newcomers this time have brown skin, but if anything or anyone is to prove wrong Jesse Jackson's assertion that Pete Wilson is the new George Wallace, thus inferring that Wilson's supporters are Wallace-like racists, it is Bill. It is difficult to categorize Bill, for whites like him reflect many sides of California's racial question.

At one time, Bill would have been called a liberal. He was compelled to do social work when he came home from military service in Southeast Asia, and in the early 1970s, he conducted research into the needs of veterans from the last three major wars. His work helped lead to the establishment of an outreach program that would refer veterans for counseling, educational, and vocational training programs.

Bill was next the director of a center in Garden Grove, where he matched one community's poor residents with jobs and health care. He also empowered them to help themselves, organizing a group of eight women to pool child care while the others went into job training. Bill created a point system that made the shared baby-sitting duties equitable; the women learned typing or other skills. When most women in the group got jobs and left for a better neighborhood, Bill started over with new residents. Eventually he felt burned out. "I was so naive," he said. "It was never-ending."

He left the job having learned two things: when people were able to do something for themselves, they were more likely to succeed, and when the city improved the neighborhood by planting trees, tearing down some buildings to reduce crowding, the resi-

dents' lives were enhanced and they felt safer. That convinced Bill
that the environment was a key to a community's stability.

To illustrate his theory about the negative impact of "small"
problems, he placed his hands together in a pyramid. At the bottom is the vast majority of problems the police do not consider
crimes: junk cars on the street, guys hanging out and drinking,
graffiti. In the middle are things like spousal abuse, vandalism, and
various misdemeanors. At the top in the narrow space where his
fingers touched, perhaps 2 percent of all crime, were the murders
and rapes. The police understandably want to focus on those
things, he said.

But by tolerating the behavior at the bottom, the community
suggests that it does not care. Unsightliness, he feels, encourages
crime to escalate.

"Before I felt really compelled to provide programs that would
work toward self-enabling and training and systems. My approach
here is to ignore that part of it. I'm now concentrating on the
physical state of the community. Let's determine how the community looks. I was trying to have an impact on what was going on inside. Now I'm working on the outside."

Bill knew, however, that the rich could not hide and let the rest
of society crumble. He'd visited some residents behind the walls
and told them they should be worried. "I tell them, 'Your walls will
not protect you. They will be climbed over and overtaken with
graffiti.' That's not a threat. Just what's going to happen."

One of the outreach programs the city started after the Lantern
Village Association began presenting its concerns was a "fotonovela," *Good Home/Good Neighbor,* illustrated with pictures of a
couple and how they should lead their lives in Dana Point. It was
written in both Spanish and English, distributed to Latino families.
The pamphlet's introduction states: "This fotonovela was produced and is being distributed as a bilingual campaign to provide
residents of Dana Point with some of the resources necessary to
mainstream into the community."

In part, it said:

> You live in Dana Point. People from all over the world have come
> to live in Dana Point. We must respect one another and live in
> harmony.

The city of Dana Point provides many services for its residents. You should feel free to call on them at any time.

In this book you will learn about being a good neighbor in Dana Point.

This is Aurelio and Rosalba. They just moved to Dana Point from another country. Did you just move to Dana Point?

When someone has moved to a new home in a new country, they must learn many new things. Let's see what they are learning.

If you want to socialize with your friends, your own yard or patio gives you more privacy. It also helps you to be a good neighbor by keeping you from disturbing those around you.

Rosalba is learning a lot about her new apartment. One thing she is learning about is the washing machines. . . . After the clothes are washed, she sometimes does not want to use the electric dryer. Instead she hangs the clothes on hangers inside her apartment to dry. She always hangs the clothes inside the apartment, not on the balcony.

Aurelio and Rosalba are glad they live in Dana Point. They will try very hard to keep Dana Point clean and safe.[13]

HISTORY: UTOPIA AT THE END
OF THE ROAD

Looking out Bill Shepherd's window, you know you are at the edge of the continent. Before you is Mexico blocked by an arbitrary border built across the desert, steel walls, a moat, and guards and sensors. To the right, beyond the arcing blue line of the Pacific covering half the planet, which the poet Robinson Jeffers called the "eye of the earth," lies the vastness of Asia.[14] To your left is the American continent, and behind it, Europe.

When conquistador Hernando Cortés set sail for the New World and landed in Mexico in 1519, this land was unknown to the Europeans. Cortés was no doubt influenced by *Las Sergas de Esplandián,* a work of fiction printed in 1510 by Garcia Ordóñez de Montalvo. Ordóñez, perhaps influenced by mythology dating to ancient Persia, wrote of the New World, "Know that, on the right hand of the Indies, there is an island called California, very near to the Terrestrial Paradise, which was peopled with black women. . . . Their arms were all of gold."[15]

Cortés's soldiers landed on Mexico's Atlantic coast and conquered the country. Years later his men pushed west to the Pacific and built and sailed new ships up the coast to a seemingly huge island where Cortés landed on May 5, 1535, convinced he had found a place deserving of the mythological name of California, though he learned months later that the island he called California was really a peninsula, later called Baja, or lower, California.

Another island influenced the Europeans and would have an impact on the settling of California's Orange County: the imaginary one in Sir Thomas More's *Utopia*, published in 1516. On Utopia, with a nonsecular communist government, perfection ruled, in stark contrast to the greed and religious strife then found in Europe. The island supported religious pluralism, state-run schools, women's rights, and legalized divorce. Utopian aspirations would launch many Europeans on a quest for a better life in the New World.

In the years leading up to the Mexican-American War, the region of Alta California that is now Orange County was no Utopia, but a dusty land of huge ranchos. These ranchos, some as large as 40,000 acres, were fiefdoms of dons descended from the Spaniards. Their primary commodity was cattle, whose hides and tallow were exported. The hides were tanned by Indians coerced into serfdom at the Mission San Juan Capistrano. A Boston firm was engaged in the transport of these hides, and a new sailor for the company, Richard Henry Dana Jr., arrived in May, 1835, when his ship anchored off the bluffs near the outpost. Dana (who wrote about his adventures in *Two Years before the Mast*) later inspired the naming of a rocky outcrop and the town, but he returned only once again.

The Gold Rush had sent most settlers to northern California. In 1850 there were just 3,530 people in Los Angeles County, which then included what is now Orange County. After the 1860s a severe drought killed thousands of cattle, and the owners of the ranchos decided to subdivide their holdings into small farms.

Left to a free world market, many Asians would have liked to have bought them. Just as Europeans with dreams were headed west, Asians with dreams were headed east. As Carey McWilliams noted, it was easier to reach California from Asia than it was from New York. But there were plans afoot to make sure that Asians did not dominate. It is no accident that California became overwhelmingly white. Careful planning funneled white immigrants into the state, as did restrictive federal laws. Without this orchestration, California would have long ago have had a minority white population—and the racial makeup of the United States would now be vastly different.

The plans for white migration were boosted by the completion of the transcontinental railroad on May 10, 1869. To ensure that the newcomers were white, the California Immigrant Union was created in late 1869 "to encourage immigration from Europe and the eastern parts of the United States to the State of California."

Word reached James W. Towner in central New York State. He was a member of the Oneida Community, a utopian colony founded in 1848 by John Humphrey Noyes. These "Bible Communists," shared a belief that everything in life should be communal, including sexual relations. Noyes felt marriage made women the property of men, but that Mormon polygamy made them slaves. "Complex marriage," in which all men and women belonged to each other, would free them of jealousy; sharing wealth would end greed. They also practiced mutual criticism, similar to modern group therapy. The group prospered for three decades, making silver goods. But by 1881 factionalism had divided the colony. Towner led a dissident group that pooled $26,200 to buy a 458-acre tract in what had been the Rancho Santiago de Santa Ana, from James Irvine, one of the first subdividers of Orange County.[16]

In California, Towner and 35 or so followers played down their Oneida practices, but the intensity of their beliefs seems to have metamorphosed into something more mean-spirited. Towner became chairman of a commission to carve a new entity out of the bottom of Los Angeles County. Voters overwhelmingly approved the creation of Orange County on June 4, 1889.

Towner became a Superior Court judge and epitomized the schizophrenic swings to the left and right that would come to typify the state's electorate. Towner once sentenced a woman to three years in San Quentin after she spread her laundry in protest over the Santa Fe Railroad tracks; the woman died two years into her sentence.

The conservative nature of the county soon became entrenched, in part because of its proximity to the Mexican border. In 1892 Francisco Torres was accused of killing a white foreman who withheld a $2 poll tax from his wages. While Towner was away on business, vigilantes seized Torres from the jail and lynched him.

One newspaper editorial praised the act, saying "Torres was a low type of the Mexican race, and was evidently more Indian than white. True to his savage nature, he had no more regard for human life than for the merest trifle. The sooner such savages are exterminated the better for decent civilization."

In the summer of 1924, the Ku Klux Klan held a rally that drew between 10,000 and 20,000 members to the city of Anaheim. That fall, a majority of Klan candidates won seats in the city government. The police chief and most officers were Klansmen.

Orange County's reputation attracted Midwest Republicans as well as Dixiecrats. It became a stronghold of conservatism in the same way Berkeley and Greenwich Village are liberal bastions. It grew rapidly, especially in the post-Watts riot years of white flight, increasing from almost 704,000 in 1960 to 2.4 million in 1990, which made it the fifth most populous county in the nation.

A prime mover was the Irvine Company, the successor to the firm started by James Irvine. In *Postsuburban California, The Transformation of Orange County since World War II* (1991), edited by University of California professors Rob Kling, Spencer Olin, and Mark Poster, the authors say: "The Irvine Company has explicitly marketed Irvine as a carefully planned, middle-class, suburban Utopia. Its advertisements project images of neatly landscaped communities, convivial village life, freedom from crime and congestion, upscale consumer conveniences, and other pleasant amenities." [17]

If suburbs are the result of white America's search for Utopia, the gated and walled neighborhoods of Dana Point represents its pinnacle. Monarch Bay, one of these neighborhoods on the ocean bluffs north of Lantern Village, has everything: a semitropical climate, a beach, an adjacent golf course, views, sunsets, privacy, a sentry on duty, walls reminiscent of circled wagons.

Ethnic activists often derisively call the sterile world of malls and tract housing found in suburbia the "dominant culture." Some Latinos, blacks, and Asians resent having to conform to it, or study their heritage in relation to it. But while the influence appears to be white, it is really *automobile* culture, built around merchandising. One suspects that if all Orange County whites suddenly vaporized and were replaced with wealthy blacks and Latinos and Asians, they would act just like the middle-class whites, living as any people would in an environment built for cars and consumerism. A small but significant number of minorities amid the gated enclaves of south Orange County do live just like the whites.

To cater to this community, the Orange County *Register* created a "mall beat," and by the early 1990s it was running front-page news stories and maps showing residents the best ways to reach the megamalls to avoid Christmas traffic jams.[18]

A visit to the South Coast Plaza megamall reveals who has the money in the county. A decidedly unscientific count of the shoppers who passed Amato's Espresso Cafe in a 10-minute period showed that of 94 shoppers who strolled past, 68 were white, 21 Asian, 4 Latino, and 1 of unknown ethnicity—not one was black. In Orange County, city halls are located in strip shopping centers and schools in trailers, but the equivalent of town squares that define the community are located in big malls such as South Coast Plaza.

A kid growing up in the Orange County suburbs can be just as alienated and angry and lost as a kid in the ghetto. In South Orange County, the bad press goes to Latinos who dominate gang membership. Many whites know of the two big Latino gangs, the San Juan Boys and the San Clemente Varrio Chicos, but few realize that suburban gangs come in all colors. The Orange County Sheriff's Department has identified three white gangs besides the Latinos: the Ball Sac Suburban Death Squad in San Clemente, the Laguna Hills Homicidal Punks, and the San Clemente Aryan Resistance.[19]

In Dana Point, the residents of a gate-guarded community saw Bill Shepherd's prophecy come true: graffiti would come their way, with the appearance of spray-painted tags "TSC," for "The Smart Criminals." But the culprits did not have to climb over the walls; a city investigation found that three white kids who lived inside were responsible. The average annual income of their parents was half a million dollars.

WHITE SOCIETY AND DANA POINT

The fourplex rental unit at 24621 La Cresta Drive in Dana Point is on the corner of the Street of the Violet Lantern, or "Violent Lantern," as it was called by Dennis Vlach, paintbrush in hand, as he emerged from the open garage door of the unit, an unremarkable dwelling in a town with houses that have closets the size of master bedrooms. But to Dennis, a Los Angeles paramedic and a member of Bill's group, it represented his nest egg for the future: he paid $440,000 for the building in 1989 as an investment toward retirement. Five years later, a similar fourplex nearby sold for $290,000.

Dennis's asset was vaporizing before his very eyes; and he was having trouble keeping tenants because of an increase in petty crimes. Not long before, one tenant had been burglarized. Dennis found a pile of feces and cigarette butts at the base of a forced window. The only items stolen were housewares, mostly pots and pans. Dennis believed the culprit was a Mexican immigrant who needed cooking utensils.

He pointed to an apartment across the street: the owner rented to a Latino couple who brought in friends, until 20 people were living there. The owner evicted them when the carpet became so encrusted it resembled earth. To Dennis, the third world was moving into first-world Dana Point. He does not want to live by the standards of the third world. "We have a lower culture coming into a higher culture," but he added, "we're doomed if the new cultures don't assimilate. To me, we're already going around in the bowl of the toilet—somebody's flushed it." Dennis feared other cultures living apart from the main society would drive wedges between all the major ethnic groups and lead to strife.

This conflict of cultures is not limited to Dana Point. Resentment and acts of violence against nonwhites have occurred in other white societies. In the late 1980s, London's Brixton area saw race riots; the French are openly antagonistic toward Arabs and North Africans, and the government has identified 400 communities that are "highly volatile"; on a number of occasions, skinheads in Germany have burned immigrant housing or have attacked nonwhites.[20]

The racial unrest in these European countries and California has its roots in five centuries of white global hegemony and can be tracked in demographic trends. Immigrants might be drawn to Dana Point by the same forces that brought white Europeans there.

Whites spread across the earth as Europe's population flared. (At the time of Christ, the world's population was some 200 million; by 1650 it had grown to 500 million; but by 1800 it had hit 1 billion.) Europe, in particular, was teeming with people. This increase led Thomas Robert Malthus to predict in 1798 that the population of the United Kingdom would outstrip its food and job resources. Malthus's theory has been endlessly debated. It was never tested because vast outmigration and the industrial and agricultural revolution altered his more dire predictions about labor and the food supply.

The eighteenth-century population explosion was due to an important development: the reduced infant mortality among Europeans. Today, it is the population of the third world that is out of control—or so it appears to the xenophobes in northern white societies who point with alarm to the fecundity of nonwhites. But these countries are merely following a course through which white societies have already passed, the "demographic transition model," which has three phases.[21]

In the first, found in preindustrial societies, deaths and births canceled each other: in primitive societies, half the children died before reaching age 10. A woman might have five or six children just to ensure that one or two survived. Europe was the first to move out of this phase, and Africa south of the Sahara in the 1950s was the last region to be in it.

The second phase, in the early industrial period, was marked by declining infant deaths owing to medical and sanitary advances. With the decrease in deaths and concomitant explosion in births (since women were pressed by their culture to continue having many children), the result was a massive increase in population. It takes several generations to orient people toward smaller families. Much of Africa and South America is now in this stage.

In the third, or modern phase, births and deaths are again equal. It has the first phase's static population—but the birth rate and death rate are low. Most white societies are in this phase. By the time whites solidly entered this phase at the beginning of the 1960s, undeveloped nations were in phase two.

When all cultures reach phase three, the world population will be overwhelmingly aged. The population will eventually decrease, though the numbers will still be far higher than current population levels, barring wars, famine, and epidemics.

These phases can occur simultaneously within a society. In the United States, many immigrants are still in phase two and continue having large families. The U.S. Census Bureau estimates that minorities, who now constitute 24 percent of the population, will increase to 38 percent by 2050, even if the borders are sealed to new immigration.

Many countries with high birth rates are showing signs of entering phase three, but their populations continue to climb, because even as third-world women have fewer children, large numbers of women are entering their childbearing years, and they will present staggering numbers of offspring.

Contrary to the observations of some, nonwhites are not taking over Dana Point or the earth from whites. Whites never were a global majority. Between 1750 and 1900, the developed—meaning white—countries increased from an estimated 21.6 to 31.4 percent of the world's population as they worked through the second phase of the demographic transition model. By 1950, according to estimates of the United Nations, the proportion had dipped to 29.9 percent; it is now about 25 percent; and by 2025 it is expected to be 17 percent. Whites are merely returning to roughly their original percentage of the earth's population.[22]

The world's population will jump to a UN median estimate of 8.5 billion by 2025; the high estimate is 10 billion. An additional 1 billion people will be added every 11 to 13 years into the next century. The United Nations estimates 94 percent of world population growth—the extra 3 to 5 billion people who will appear by 2025—will take place in southern, nonwhite societies.[23] For example, Mexico's 1990 population of 90 million is projected to reach 148 million by 2020.

This growth presumably will cause pressure for nonwhite immigration into white societies beyond anything imaginable today. But the situation is much more complex than this. Population growth is a factor, but not the only factor to consider. The United Nations estimates that even though international migration is at record levels in terms of absolute numbers, only 1 percent of the growth of the third world is heading to developed nations.[24]

In 1960, according to United Nations estimates, 3.2 million people from undeveloped regions lived in western Europe, the United States, and Australia. By 1974 the number had increased to 9.5 million. More recent UN data are unavailable, but in California alone the estimates of illegal immigrants range from 1.4 to 2.1 million; California has about half of the illegal immigrants in the nation. In the United States, the 1990 census found 19.7 million foreign-born people—nearly 16 million from non-European nations.[25]

For international migration, 1960 was a pivotal year. This is the point at which the equilibrium between the first and third worlds changed. That year, Europe stopped being a net exporter of people. Not only did whites solidly enter phase three of the population transition model about this time, but colonialism came to an end. By the 1970s there was migration *into* Europe, many from the former colonies, including one million repatriated citizens. Latin America went from being a destination for emigrants to being a net exporter. The reason in part is population growth: once an underpopulated region, Latin America is now overpopulated, suffering the same problem Europe faced in the time of Malthus.

Most white-majority countries are feeling the post-1960 demographic shift to increasing polyethnicism. The change is greatest in the United States, Canada, and Australia because these nations have encouraged immigration throughout their history.

The change is also happening in Europe, but at a slower rate. Countries such as Germany and Belgium have more restrictive immigration policies, according to Stephen Castles and Mark J. Miller in their 1993 book, *The Age of Migration,* because their nationalities are based on *ius sanguinis,* the law of the blood, whereas the United States, Canada, and Australia base citizenship on *ius soli,* the law of the soil, which views residency as a concept of place.[26]

Often, the authors argue, white countries are most responsible for the movement of nonwhite people into their nations. It is obvious that New World whites imported Africans. But there are other connections. During the period of colonization and imperialism, European and American powers forged ties with their subject countries. The native populations learned the language and grew economically linked to the mother countries. Thus when colonization ended about 1960, according to Castles and Miller, it was common to find Indians migrating to the United Kingdom and Algerians to France, because of language and cultural connections. In the United States, much immigration is due to the semicolonial relation of America to the countries it inherited after the Spanish-American War, which brought the later influx of Filipinos and Puerto Ricans.

In addition, during the labor shortage between World War II and the oil crisis of 1973, Germany, France, and other nations invited "guest" workers from Turkey, Greece, and Morocco, with the naive expectation that they would return home when their services were no longer needed. Now some of those "guests" have third-generation children who speak only German or French but are not citizens. Yet the demographic change in these countries has been small—Western Europe is still roughly 95 percent white. Only 5.5 percent of the United Kingdom's population is nonwhite, according to the 1991 census; exact data do not exist for France and Germany, but the estimates range from 4 to 6 percent.[27]

Most European countries have clamped down on immigration much more tightly than the United States, Canada, and Australia. European minority populations will continue to climb, however, just as in the United States, owing to higher birth rates among the nonwhites within their borders and continued illegal immigration. Italy, which by the 1990s was deep in the third phase of the demographic transition model, saw its birthrate fall to 1.3 babies per woman, far below replacement level. Since there was no way its natives could provide all the menial labor, a demand for Africans developed.

So what is happening below Bill's window behind the apartment walls of the Lantern Village is exactly what is happening in all white societies. In the case of Dana Point, its "guest" workers are the foundation of a multimillion dollar industry that supports the tax base, and the overclass of whites lives off it very well in a form of modern feudalism. The situation in Dana Point and in all white societies is a boomerang to the five centuries of white domination since Columbus.

4

Latino

The pictures on the wall across from the receptionist's desk inside Huntington Park City Hall—a mission-revival building of stone archways and long corridors in Martha Escutia's assembly district—give a vivid history of the town. Displayed are the portraits of 36 mayors, from Louis W. Weber, elected in 1906, to Herbert A. Kennes Jr., whose final term began in 1987. The stern faces of these white men are arranged in six equal rows. Set far off to the lower right, as if avoiding this crowd, is the 37th picture, the current mayor—Raul R. Peres—a very Latin-looking man.

Huntington Park was mostly white until the flight that followed the 1965 riots in nearby Watts and the exodus of steel and auto plants, which had been an economic mainstay. Today, most remaining white residents are retired and too old to want to move. Even as their numbers dwindled, they formed a strong bloc of voters and thus hung on to their political power long after they became a minority—that is, until the white percentage fell into the single digits. It was inevitable that Latinos would then start winning political office.

Huntington Park, known locally as "HP," is more or less at the center of California Assembly District 50. The local name for the district is South East. It is due east of South Central, now a pop icon in American culture because of rap songs and the riots. No songs about South East have entered the popular culture.

District 50 has 372,000 residents, half under the age of 18. Latinos make up 89 percent of the population, whites 8 percent, and blacks 2 percent. Most blacks live on the western fringe, near South Central. Most whites are in the south. District 50 is a *very* Mexican place. HP is the most "Mexican" city in the United States—almost 60 percent of its 56,000 residents were born in Mexico, according to the census. There are also Guatemalans, Salvadorans, and some Cubans and Puerto Ricans scattered throughout the area. But the Mexicans dominate.

South East's biggest distinguishing feature is that it has none. It is an endless march of crowded apartments, bungalows, faded strip shopping centers with barred windows, with any available wall, window, curb, and sign scrawled on with bursts of graffiti. The Los Angeles skyline just 6 miles distant looms like a Necropolis through an ever-present veil of smog.

District 50 encompasses eight small anonymous cities that are really just names on a map—Bell, Bell Gardens, City of Commerce, Cudahy, HP, Maywood, South Gate, Vernon—as well as some unincorporated areas of Los Angeles County. These cities are the most thickly populated in California. The city of Cudahy, slightly more than 1 square mile in size, has a population density of 21,304, while HP has 18,577 people per square mile. New York City has 11,480 people per square mile.[1]

Unlike New York, these cities are organized like huge decaying suburbs. They have palms and citrus trees and lawns, but for the most part two and three families live in each housing unit. Many in Martha's district work to find hope and hope to find work. The annual per capita income in Cudahy is $5,486; in HP it is $6,480; statewide, it is $20,952. Jobs are scarce, so many resort to entrepreneurialism. It is common to see corners dotted with Latino vendors selling everything from coconuts to oranges.

In numerous ways, HP and surrounding District 50 are the economic and cultural opposite of Dana Point, where the average per capita income is $30,176 and the population density is 5,163 people per square mile. It is hard to believe the two communities exist in the same state, much less in adjoining counties. Anyone driving from Orange County to downtown Los Angeles via Interstate 5 or Interstate 710 passes through District 50, but few Dana Point residents have any reason or desire to set foot here. One can travel great distances on its surface streets and never see a white person.

The residents of Dana Point, however, have an osmotic knowledge of District 50: it is rooted in the fear that the entire state will become just like Huntington Park. One man on the fringe of Bill Shepherd's group referred to the growth of huge Latino areas like District 50 as the *reconquista,* the taking back of the lands that were appropriated in the Mexican-American War.

But HP is not a place where a wild-eyed army of Mexicans is flirting with the notion of conquering California. That ideology exists among a handful of college students, not in District 50, where the sole desire of most residents from one day to the next is to scrabble together enough to eat. In the century and a half since the Treaty of Guadalupe Hidalgo, Latinos have come north because for much of that time they were invited and could find work there. In other cases, U.S. military adventuring in Central America forced refugees to flee to the very country that caused their exile.

THE ROLE OF CONSERVATIVES
AND LIBERALS

Just as Europeans imported foreign guest workers who now have second- and third-generation children, the United States has played a role in enticing many residents in District 50 to move north.

Most recently, the United States lured Mexicans in 1986, when Congress, after much debate, was about to approve the Immigration Reform Control Act (IRCA). Intended to drastically curtail illegal immigration, the act had just the opposite effect. IRCA was pushed by Republican U.S. Senator Alan Simpson of Wyoming. At the time, Martha Escutia was a lawyer working for the National Council of La Raza in Washington, and she lobbied strongly to soften the bill. Martha feared two things: that a huge Latino population that had been here for decades (which included her grandparents) would remain illegal; and that the employer sanctions Simpson wanted would lead firms to stop hiring Latinos, even if they were citizens, to avoid running into problems with the law, and this would fuel discrimination.

Martha knew Simpson's bill was going to pass, so she pragmatically pushed the National Council of La Raza to seek a compromise. Agreeing not to fight employer sanctions so long as safeguards were written into the law to ensure that Latino citizens would not be discriminated against, she told Simpson her group would not fight IRCA if it legalized all those who had come before 1982.

Martha later said she felt the bill was a victory because it helped those "living in the shadows" to partake in American society. But, she added, groups further to the left, such as the Mexican-American Legal Defense Fund, assailed the National Council of La Raza for selling out: "God, we took the heat for it. I was not willing to make the immigration bill our Waterloo."

Actually, the immigration bill that seemed so draconian turned out to be soft by the standards of California's immigration backlash a decade later. That Congress legalized some 1.7 million noncitizens in exchange for invoking what turned out to be virtually nonenforced employer sanctions was an incredible victory, one that makes Senator Simpson appear liberal.

Softness, however, was not Simpson's goal. The employer sanctions of his proposal failed after Pete Wilson did some lobbying of his own among senators. Along with other congressional leaders, Wilson (four years before he returned to California as governor), refused to endorse IRCA unless it allowed Mexican immigrants into the country temporarily to harvest crops.

Wilson, whose campaign was supported by agricultural interests, had pushed an amendment to allow 350,000 "aliens"—meaning Mexicans—into the country as "guest workers." Democrats offered a compromise. If farmworkers could prove they had previously worked in the United States as agricultural laborers, they would agree. This "special agricultural worker" exemption changed Wilson's mind and allowed him to vote for the plan. It passed with these amendments, as well as with Martha's amnesty provisions.[2]

Wilson later got into a fight with Alan Nelson, commissioner of the Immigration and Naturalization Service (later a coauthor of Proposition 187). Nelson wanted hard proof—written documentation—that the immigrants had previously been farmworkers in the United States. Wilson strongly protested; he sent a letter to President Reagan calling the requirements "burdensome." He said crops were wasting in the fields. Wilson won the battle, and a compromise on documentation was reached.

An industry in forged documents grew, and as many as 1.1 million Mexican nationals entered the country, most into California. While some entries were legitimate, those arriving brought spouses and children who were illegal and could not gain legal status. To this day, one can drive through almost any Latino neighborhood and find guys standing on corners selling *micas,* forged identification that will "prove" you are legal. *Micas* cost as little as $100. Many of those buying forged documents never set foot in the fields.

Wilson's actions actually set in motion events that brought in immigrants and thus aroused fear and anger among whites. But Wilson alone is not to blame if one views the opening of the immigration door as an adverse development: liberals had a hand in it as well, and not only in softening the IRCA act. Significantly, they helped bring in immigrants when at least one dozen American cities—from Seattle to San Francisco to Cambridge, Massachusetts—passed ordinances declaring themselves sanctuaries for Central Americans because of their opposition to Washington's support of right-wing governments in El Salvador and Guatemala. These cities forbade their police to cooperate with federal immigration officials, which had the effect of sending a message that it was okay to come north. They came by the thousands—Los Angeles has over 100,000 Salvadorans, more than the capital city of San Salvador.

In the 1980s, both sides of the political fence were sensitive about appearing racist against Latinos. Environmentalists were concerned that so much immigration would add to California's explosive growth, but it was politically incorrect to discuss the issue openly. And some on the left felt they could not object since they were also supporters of political sanctuary.

But the IRCA, Wilson's actions, and the sanctuary movement had a huge influential precedent, the "Bracero [strong-arm] Program," a federal labor contract system that was enacted during the labor shortage of World War II. The orange growers of San Diego and Orange counties were especially hard hit by this shortage, and on February 11, 1943, they and other agricultural interests petitioned the government to import Mexicans. The program that resulted lasted through 1964, bringing north between 2 and 4 million people.

Martha Escutia's grandfather was among those enticed by advertisements to come to America. Ricardo Ovilla, a Chamula Indian from the Mexican state of Chiapas on the Guatemalan border, was making a scant living with his family by growing mangos and vegetables on a small patch of ground and selling tortillas to ranches. On June 1, 1945, he was given a number, 153728, by the U.S. Department of Agriculture's Production and Marketing Administration with instructions to head north immediately, to the border entry in El Paso. On June 5, 1945, one month after Germany surrendered and two months before the atom bombs were dropped on Japan, Ricardo entered the United States. He picked sugar beets, fixed track for the Great Northern Railroad, tended sheep, and worked next to German prisoners of war.

After his Bracero papers expired, he was arrested by immigration authorities, but like so many Mexicans, his employer, a subsidiary of Sunkist Oranges, came to the rescue and pleaded his case. The letter written to support him said, "This to certify that Ricardo Ovilla . . . is a reliable and earnest worker. He earns approximately $45 per week. Upon his return we would be willing to employ him again."

The blessing of a corporation was enough to set things straight. Not only could he remain, but he was allowed to bring his family north in 1949. The passport photo of the family shows Martha's mother at the age of 12, a beautiful wide-eyed Indian girl. But after tearing out the orange trees for Disneyland, Ricardo never again did farm work. Until he retired, he was a factory hand.

EAST LOS ANGELES:
THE LATINO POWER BASE

In 1956 Ricardo and his wife Marina bought a house on 4th Street in East Los Angeles. A modest two-bedroom bungalow measuring 900 square feet, it was grand by the standards of Mexico. At the time Ricardo and Marina became homeowners, Los Angeles was segregated. Many neighborhoods had covenants that kept out blacks, and when covenants did not work, bombings did. Mexicans were not viewed any more favorably.

East Los Angeles was not coveted by whites. In 1900 some 90 percent of the entire state was white, from the great influx of easterners and Europeans that followed the Mexican-American War. But all whites were not equal, and some settled in enclaves. In the early decades of the century, the Jews and Serbo-Croatians who fled the sweatshops of the East Coast and Chicago had settled in East Los Angeles. By World War II, the area was thriving, with delicatessens and synagogues: many residents were New Yorkers enticed by a late nineteenth-century developer who had named one of the main streets Brooklyn Avenue.[3]

As the Jewish population moved up and on to West Los Angeles, Mexicans replaced them. Ricardo and Marina were the first Mexicans to buy a home on their block. By the 1960s, East Los Angeles was a very Latin place. It is hard to believe now, given the size of California's Latino population, but in those days, the term "Latino community" meant East Los Angeles. District 50 to the south was still a white place. Martha grew up within this emerging Latino middle class. Even if the elders did not speak English, they were content to settle into an American lifestyle.

In 1968 Martha was 10 years old and being raised very conservatively by her grandparents. Martha's mother had run off to Mexico, where she worked as an international telephone operator. Trying to organize a union, she was blacklisted by the government. She got caught up in the 1968 student uprising, and her new husband became a political prisoner. After that, her family north of the border never heard from her again.

Latino culture is inherently conservative, and unlike Martha's mother, Ricardo and Marina typified many Mexicans. The couple believed that in order to succeed Martha had to embrace the culture and language of the United States. The couple felt that either you were a Mexican or an American, that you should not hyphenate your identity. But some other older children of East Los Angeles immigrants were anything but conservative. They were being sent to Vietnam, returning dead or maimed. The youth saw no avenues to power. Police and politicians were virtually all white. The token Latinos at the top in business and politics at best were considered *vendidos,* sellouts; at worst, *tio tacos,* the Mexican equivalent of Uncle Tom. The dissatisfaction of the youth spread among Latinos and to the same kind of whites who marched in the South against segregation; they joined Latinos and embraced César Chávez's farmworker movement. This new Latino empowerment contrasted sharply with the conservative nature of Mexican culture.

The first rumble of Latino power occurred on March 3, 1968, when 1,000 students walked out of Abraham Lincoln High School in East Los Angeles. The students demanded Latino teachers and Mexican history classes. It was the first racially based mass protest by Latinos in the United States, according to Carlos Muñoz, a student in those marches who later became an ethnic studies professor at the University of California at Berkeley.[4]

These young people did not call themselves "Mexican" or "Mexican American," and certainly not "Hispanic" or "Latino," terms that came along later. They preferred *Chicano,* increasingly heard after the Lincoln High walkout. Chicano, a pejorative for trashy Mexicans, was embraced by the youth.

By 1970 *La Raza* Magazine appeared in East Los Angeles, and the first issue's cover carried the cry "Chicano Power!" It contained stories about racism and racist images. One story chastised the April 6, 1970, *Tonight Show* with Johnny Carson. Carson in his monologue called his producer Rudy Vellez a "wetback." Other stories blasted advertising: Philco-Ford, a maker of televisions, showed a sleeping Mexican. Frito Lay had the "Frito Bandito." Arrid underarm deodorant used a Mexican bandit in one commercial, with a voiceover saying, "If it works for him, it will work for you." It was the first time anyone had ever complained about the depiction of Mexicans as lazy, shiftless, or stinky.[5]

Frito Lay said the commercial was effective and was reluctant to give it up. It must be recalled that the California of 1970 was still almost 80 percent white—California blacks and a small but significant percentage of Asians took up a large portion of the minority population—and nationwide, those of Mexican heritage were statistically insignificant.

Unlike their parents who shrugged off these things—keep quiet, work hard, assimilate—Chicanos rejected silence or joining European society, that of the *gabachos,* a negative term more common than *gringo*. These youths ignored the Spanish influence, both genetic and cultural, preferring instead to stress their Aztec roots. The Chicanos had a name for California and the rest of the lands taken by the gabachos during the Mexican-American war: *Aztlán*. Aztlán was the Aztec name for the place of their birth, a mythical land somewhere north of Mexico City. A tenet of the Chicano movement was that Aztlán should be returned to Mexico.

The rage of the *Aztlánistas* grew to encompass other issues, such as *why* so many Latinos were coming back maimed or dead from Vietnam. On the afternoon of August 29, 1970, Martha, then aged 12, was mowing her grandparents's lawn while eight blocks due south an army of Los Angeles County sheriff's deputies were swarming over 5,000 Latinos who had gathered in Laguna Park—where Martha in quieter times took swimming and art lessons. The anti–Vietnam War rally turned into a riot that left 3 dead and 60 wounded and caused $1 million in damage. About the time Martha was putting away the mower, the cops had finished tear-gassing and pummeling.

As things quieted, journalist Rubén Salazar, who had been covering the event, headed to The Silver Dollar, a bar on Whittier Avenue 1 mile east of the riot. He went through the arched entry with its painting of two women, naked except for stars over their nipples, to have a badly needed beer.

He never took a sip. Sheriff's deputies materialized and surrounded the bar. The reason was vague—there was an anonymous report of a gun inside. When Deputy Thomas Wilson arrived, he ordered several patrons standing in the street to go back inside. Moments later, to empty the bar, Wilson leveled a tear gas launcher and without warning fired through the thin drape that served as a door. The projectile took off half of Salazar's head.[6]

Salazar was the voice for Latinos at a time when few were employed in the media: he was a *Los Angeles Times* columnist and KMEX-TV news director. Salazar was no Latino version of Malcolm X, but he pushed hard on stories about police abuse and the mysterious deaths of Latinos while in sheriff's custody. Salazar's death smacked of an execution. It was ruled accidental.

The killing was talked about everywhere, even in Martha's house—and Martha's house was not political. The official report was doubted even by the most conservative Latinos. The journalist would forever remain on the minds of East Los Angeles residents—and with him the knowledge that the American system of justice was not equally stacked. At the time of Salazar's death, Latinos had almost no political voice: there was just one in the 120-member California Legislature.

The Aztlánistas had a martyr in Salazar. The movement seemed ready to spread into a real political force on the basis of his death alone. But like so many things from the 1960s, as the nation spilled into the 1970s a lot of momentum died along with those who did not make it. The Chicano movement suffered the same fate of the Students for a Democratic Society and other white left groups: the war ended, younger people did not relate to the original cause, some leaders grew bitter and fell out.

These days, "Chicano" is used only on college campuses—over the years in conversations with Latinos around California, I never heard the word uttered by anyone other than a student or professor. Then, as now, a majority of Latinos disdain the term. As for Rubén Salazar, to many newcomers, his name signals nothing more than the name of a park—Laguna Park was renamed in his honor.

Martha would never refer to herself as a Chicana. She vowed she would be active in a different way, by first being successful.

THE POLITICS OF INVISIBLE PEOPLE

Martha did not inherit District 50 when she won the election in 1992. In fact, she is responsible for its creation. Prior to 1992 there was no District 50 in its present form. In 1974 it was dismembered by Sacramento politicians.

When California legislative districts were redrawn as they are each decade, the area was considered marginal; during the 1974 makeover, it was cherry-picked into adjoining districts, in part because the legislature wanted to create a few districts in which minorities could win elected office. This political real estate was parceled out to nearby black seats, as well as to East Los Angeles, which as the oldest Latino urban area became their first political power base. In 1974 East Los Angeles was a maturing community. The port of entry had shifted to South East, where new Latino immigrants were pouring in. They did not vote and lacked political power. As the years wore on, community leaders felt like stepchildren with no one looking out for their interests. The district was in terrible economic shape. Factories closed. There were few hospitals, no county facilities.

After the 1990 census, the Southeast Coalition was formed, composed of area politicians and community activists. The goal was to re-create the assembly district that existed before 1974. This group recruited Martha, then an attorney at United Way, to research their chances. Martha dug in, excited about the prospect of empowering the huge new Latino population base. Her bedroom walls were plastered with maps with plastic overlays of different alternatives for a perfect assembly district.

Martha repeatedly heard the plan would never succeed because it meant black and Latino politicians in neighboring districts would have to give up some turf. While there is much talk of rainbow coalitions, in the real world, minority politicians are no different from their white counterparts—they do not want to give up power.

"It made no political sense," Martha said, "because it assumes [they] would willingly give up these cities in order to form a new district for the greater good. I ain't no dummy. I just pushed these people to the north, a little south, and everyone is one big happy family. And I thought it would happen. But it didn't."

A fight ensued. Martha prepared legal briefs as testimony before an assembly committee, but the plan died. All looked lost until Democrats and Republicans became gridlocked over the entire redistricting effort and the matter went to the California Supreme Court. To everyone's surprise, the court's decision included District 50 as Martha envisioned. The new Latino political stronghold was born.[7]

One question remained: who would run for the office? None of the likely leaders stepped forward. Martha presented herself to the coalition. After getting the nod, a small group of friends held a long-delayed birthday party for Martha—she was so involved in the district battle that she had never celebrated. At the party, Martha asked her friends for support. She dubbed them her "chorizo cabinet," after the popular Mexican sausage.

Martha recruited campaign workers at Huntington Park High School. Of the 20 students, many were undocumented Mexicans and Central Americans. Martha and the students walked door-to-door, each hitting the homes of 60 registered voters each day.

Martha won the Democratic primary with 6,299 votes, or 47 percent, the next highest candidate getting just 35 percent. Turnout was low—just 13,462 votes were cast out of 58,835 registered voters (almost half of them white). That meant that just over 3 percent of the 372,000 residents participated.

When sprawling District 50 is compared with 6-square-mile Dana Point and its 34,000 residents, the impotency of the Latino vote is clear. In Dana Point, virtually the same number of people vote as in Martha's much larger district—13,500 citizens go to the polls in most elections. A comparable turnout in District 50 would mean over 130,000 voters.

Latinos have not exactly turned out in droves at the polls. In the 1988 presidential election, just 7.5 percent of the California votes cast came from Latinos. But the 1992 election in which Martha handily beat her Republican opponent, it rose to 10 percent, or 1.1 million California Latinos. The minor surge was credited in part to support for Bill Clinton.

With nearly 28 percent of the state's population, Latinos could swing elections if they voted proportionally like blacks, who comprise about 6 percent of the voters and 7 percent of the population. Latinos have been called the "sleeping giant" of California politics. If it ever awakens, the giant could control the state.

One reason Latinos do not vote is that many are undocumented. Another is the repressive political history south of the border. "I don't know if it's a built-in apathy because of our history of bloody revolutions and dictator governments, but a lot of the immigrants bring with them that apathy," Martha said. "They think they're still in Mexico where it's a one-party system." And Latinos do not have the church as an organizing force. The conservative hierarchy coming out of Rome tends to shun politics. For blacks, the civil rights struggle in America began in churches.

With such apathy, Martha felt pressured to deliver. Her worries were obvious one summer day in 1992 as she clutched a soda at Avila's El Ranchito restaurant in HP. Her big priority would be to help get approval for the Alameda Corridor, a $1.8 billion project to build a sunken railroad line through District 50 from Los Angeles to the Long Beach Harbor. The center of the district is difficult to reach. The freeways are on its edges, and busy train tracks criss-cross the surface roads; the trains often pull tanker cars of toxic chemicals. The Alameda Corridor project would free 159 intersections where trains block roads and make the district's cheap land and willing labor accessible to companies interested in Pacific Rim trade. The payoff was distant, but it was the best economic shot.[8]

"By creating jobs, all other issues will be taken care of," Martha said. "It doesn't take a rocket scientist to figure that out. I've got economic development problems up the kazoo. Poverty, unemployment, whatever. This [district] is a microcosm, frankly, of California."

Leaving the restaurant, she walked past a mural on the outside north wall. The mural depicts Spanish conquistadors holding a native's feet to the flames. The Mayan resembles Jesus, strangely peaceful in the knowledge that someday he would be resurrected victorious.

Martha drove around her district, pointing to stores looted in the riots, the latest in a long series of blows to this place of dead factories, immigrants, gangs, poverty, and crowded schools. She felt the burden of "doing something." Politics as usual would not cut it. "I don't know how I'm going to do it. My ass is on the line," she said as she gripped the wheel.

One worry was a term limit initiative recently passed by California's voters. Martha could only serve three terms, or six years. "Realistically, what am I going to do in six years?"

As the car crossed the Los Angeles River and the 710 Freeway into Bell Gardens, she said, "Look at that, three homes on one lot. Real poor people rent here. Look at that one," she added, gesturing to a weathered shack-like building. "I got people to vote out of that one. I literally dragged them out."

Fresh from the riots, Martha worried about the cultural integration of Latinos with other groups. She was in her campaign office on Florence Boulevard in Huntington Park the day of the Rodney King verdict. She watched carloads of unfamiliar—meaning black—youths passing by. Few blacks ever ventured through the Latino neighborhood. She called the police chief and warned that trouble might be coming; that night, several nearby stores sustained some $5 million in damage.

"But then all the looting was not done by just the black community," Martha said. "It was our own residents who looted. It was a disgrace. It was an embarrassment for all of us as humans. We really turned out to be barbarians."

The second embarrassment, she said, was the riot's aftermath. Ethnic leaders preferred to combat each other, rather than unite to work for common economic goals. The ethnocentrists who were gathering headlines in postriot Los Angeles troubled Martha. She disdained black activist Danny Bakewell and his group Brotherhood Crusade, which picketed job sites that employed Latinos and insisted that they be fired and blacks hired in their place.[9]

"Another crazy xenophobe, a Hispanic counterpart, is a guy by the name of Xavier Hermosillo, who is out there saying if you take a Latino off the job, we're going to get after you. My poor city of Los Angeles is going through the most terrible kind of tribalism now after the riot. It's not 'Let's help the victims,' it's little groups who just want to help blacks, or just help Hispanics. It's crazy. We're all in it together."

The conflicts are not just panethnic. It is a grave mistake to look at any ethnic group as a monolithic entity, and Latinos are no exception. There is a stratification not only in terms of class, but among the different kinds of Latinos. Beneath the political apathy in Martha's district is internal strife. Mexicans have no love for Central Americans, who in some quarters are referred to as *cerrotes,* a local slang for cowchips. In turn, the Cubans and South Americans look down upon Mexicans.

While conservatives were pandering to white fear, and ethnocentric activists were appealing to group fears in their own circles, Latinos were further split among themselves.

THE "OTHER" LATINOS

Of the 20 high school students who helped Martha's campaign, most were undocumented or were in the process of becoming documented. One of them was Ivan Muñoz, a Guatemalan who recruited several members of his family to work for Martha's election. (He and his family later became legally documented.) Ivan's parents, Lucía and Carlos Muñoz, would have been content to remain in Guatemala. When they married in 1971, they took over running the family *finca* near a volcano in the Guatemalan jungle, growing coffee and other export crops. Their first children were born on the *finca*: Karla, then Ivan. When Ivan was a toddler, local Indians were fighting the military junta; one of the family's workers was killed. Lucía does not know which side was responsible.

"They hacked off his head and limbs," Lucía said. "He was then reassembled in bed, the covers put over him, and that is how he was found in the morning."

Then one night the army descended, ordering the family to leave the *finca* so it could be used for staging operations against the Indians. They fled to Guatemala City, where Lucía opened a bookstore. The military grew more repressive. Threats were made against Carlos. A banker friend of his was slain. When they went into exile in 1983, they took nothing. The trouble dates to U.S. intervention. Colonel Jacobo Arbenz, the first democratically elected Guatemalan leader, had instituted land reform. In 1953 his government confiscated 400,000 acres of uncultivated United Fruit Company land to redistribute to Indians. In 1954, a CIA-planned coup overthrew Arbenz. Land reform ended, thousands of Indians were killed, and decades of repression and war followed.[10]

They wanted to go to Spain but landed instead in HP, where they bunked with relatives. Tension grew. The Muñozes then lived out of a bashed-up green 1967 Javelin. They slept on the seats sitting up, washing in the rest rooms of public parks.

"I was too young to know how bad it was," Ivan recalled. "I thought it was great that we went to the park each day and ate, did our homework."

Carlos, who besides running the *finca* was a psychiatrist back home, stood on streetcorners begging for day labor, and the family collected aluminum cans to sell for scrap. Slowly they gained a toehold and were able to rent a house. Carlos studied and got a real estate broker's license. Lucía worked in a casino, then got a position with the county library doing outreach among immigrants. At night, she had dreams of the hundreds of books she left on the *finca*. The couple wants to reclaim the life they once had by buying a small farm in Santa Barbara or San Diego counties where they can grow oranges and avocados.

The Muñoz children were making their way in the new country. Ivan was president of the student body and was active in the

Sierra Club. One afternoon, Ivan stood to face the "leadership class" at Huntington Park High School, the most academically involved among the 3,900 students. A thin young man with dark skin, he was *muy Guatemalteco*. A Guatemalan is easy to spot in a crowd. Most have Indian features such as diminutive noses and they carry themselves quietly. Ivan also had a silver nose ring. Behind Ivan on the fireplace mantle stood a class photo from 1923. All 1,300 students in it are white.

Ivan cleared his throat and reprimanded the 19 students for doing little to help prepare for a dance to benefit the student fund. "It's pretty disturbing to see people blowing things off—that's how low morale is," Ivan told the class, which was affected by a looming teacher's strike.

It had not always been so. From this class, Martha recruited many of her volunteers. Ivan and a few other students had studied all the candidates, choosing to put their effort into Martha's race. Yet even this activism masks strong indifference, Ivan said after class as he sat in a Slauson Avenue donut shop with Zoila Escobar, a Salvadoran who was student vice president. Most students do not care about anything. Many are involved in the local gangs—the Bratz and Florencia—or are drifting. Many see little evidence that a reward exists for rushing to greet the school day. Zoila was saddened by the apathy. When she walked precincts for Martha, doors were slammed in her face.

This environment of poverty, depression, and malaise has an obvious outcome: unfocused anger. In this way, Latinos are just like inner city impoverished blacks. According to a *Los Angeles Times* survey of 694 people convicted of riot-related felonies, 50 percent of the looters were black, 43 percent Latino, 4 percent white, 3 percent other.[11] Latinos were likely undercounted because some were turned over to immigration authorities and not prosecuted; some 80 percent of the Latinos convicted were here illegally. The important fact in this survey is that none of the 694 convicted were college graduates and two-thirds were unemployed. Those with jobs were in low-skilled fields—many were security guards. Of the Latinos, 40 percent had jobs, compared with 29 percent of the blacks, and 21 percent of the whites.

PUSH-PULL

The well-known "push-pull" argument dominates the debate over why people leave their native land. The "push" argument says they emigrate to escape miserable conditions. The "pull" argument says they are lured by opportunity. Thousands of Latinos like Martha's grandfather Ricardo have been directly lured to the United States. Others like the Muñoz family were forced into exile. And others came of their own accord.

Those who subscribe to the "push" theory point to the burgeoning population of Mexico and Central America and say the overcrowding and poverty drive people to emigrate. Many demographers now dispute this notion. One needs only to look at historic European migration to see that it was not just the poorest huddled masses that fled. Some historians have held that much emigration from the United Kingdom to the United States in the early to mid-1800s was due to the "push" of agriculturalists and craft workers displaced by industrialization. But sociologist Charlotte J. Erickson, who studied logs from U.S.-bound British passenger ships in 1841, found that the majority of emigrants were not the poor but farmers and workers from trades then in demand.[12] And in terms of modern third world migration, if push-pull were as strong a force as it appears, the northern countries would already be overwhelmed with hundreds of millions of third world people: half of Africa or Mexico, or Central and South America would have already packed their bags and come north. Regardless of the factors, only a small percentage of people migrate. On the other hand, many poor did migrate, from Ireland, eastern Europe, and Italy. The truth is probably in the middle. Some people are pushed, but these are the more adventurous and the more energetic types. The pull argument is tempting, but equally fraught with questions. The kind of people who emigrate are the ones who could make a living in their native lands. Like the trade workers in England, they did not have to make the journey across the ocean—they could have carved out an existence at home.

Although each argument has both its merits and weak points, today's global economy has made the push-pull debate even more complex. "Pulled" by cheap labor, companies are moving whole factories abroad.

Governor Pete Wilson threw his voice behind the pull crowd not long after he was elected in 1991. Faced with an incredible budget deficit in a state that, unlike the federal government, is not allowed to run in the red from year to year, he blamed immigrants for "taking" more government services than they gave back in taxes. Wilson cited the "magnetic effect" of the state's services to draw immigrants.[13]

A numbing numbers debate ensued. Those against Wilson argued that undocumented workers pay federal and state taxes on their wages as well as a sales tax when they purchase goods. In addition, through their phony Social Security numbers they contribute to a system from which they are forbidden to collect. They also contribute to the economy, picking fruit and making hotel beds, jobs that Americans do not want to do. On the other hand, although illegal immigrants cannot receive welfare (but legal immigrants are eligible), their children born on U.S. soil qualify for assistance. At the time Wilson was making his pull argument, there were 97,000 citizen children with illegal immigrant mothers enrolled in Aid to Families with Dependent Children, the leading welfare program, out of a total California caseload of almost 776,000.[14] And all children are entitled to a public education, with each child receiving on average $4,500 spent on schooling each year.

But before 1992 Wilson did not become personal or racist in his speeches. He may have remembered that in 1986 he had done some pulling of his own to lure immigrants to the state. Or he may have been testing the waters to see how his message would be received. Wilson blamed mostly the federal government for not helping pay its share for immigrants. The state took 35 percent of all legal foreign immigrants in the 1980s and half of all illegal immigrants, but federal funding did not increase to help it cope with this burden.

Back then, Martha Escutia was not overly concerned about Wilson's rhetoric: immigration was one of a number of issues Wilson was voicing concern about, including crime and prisons, and it did not seem to stand out.

HISTORY

Wilson never mentioned Mexicans, but that is what he meant when he talked about illegal immigrants. It was not the first time politicians attacked Mexicans in California, but oddly enough, they were not the subject of much controversy until decades after the Mexican-American War. One reason was that Mexicans did not come north in great numbers in the years after statehood, and those who did usually went back to Mexico after working. Prior to 1900, no more than 1,000 Mexicans came north during any given year, according to S. J. Holmes, a University of California professor.[15]

The unrest in Mexico prior to and during its revolution and the labor shortage following World War I changed everything. In 1924 the U.S. Congress passed an immigration bill drastically curbing immigration (mostly from eastern and southern Europe) from 1 million a year prior to the war to 150,000. When American business's pipeline to cheap European labor was cut off, Mexicans were substituted. As Holmes notes, "In 1908 the recorded number suddenly shot up from 915 to 5,682. In the following year it became 15,591, and then increased . . . reaching its climax in 1924 with a figure of 87,648. The numbers for 1925, 1926 and 1927 were 32,378, 42,638 and 66,766 respectively."

In addition, between 1920 and 1929 California agriculture imported 31,000 men from the Philippines. Few women were allowed, and race laws forbade the men to marry. The Filipinos were not seen as much of a threat, though there was agitation against them. The Mexicans were more worrisome.

Holmes cited a 1926 report made to the governor by the California Commission on Immigration and Housing. It foreshadowed similar complaints about immigrants six and a half decades later:

1. They drain our charities.
2. They or their children become a large portion of our jail population.
3. They affect the health of our communities.
4. They create a problem in labor camps.
5. They require special attention in our schools and are of low mentality.

6. They diminish the percentage of our white population.
7. They remain foreign.

Holmes said:

The Mexican peon has proved a great boon to employers in the Southwest. There has gradually come to be a dependence upon Mexican labor to such an extent that many important industries would be handicapped, at least temporarily, if the supply of this labor were suddenly shut off . . . it must be admitted that white labor is practically unobtainable for this work at the prices paid.

Holmes's article appeared on the eve of the Great Depression and the Dust Bowl emigration. White migrants fled Oklahoma and other affected states for California, doing the work that had been dominated by Mexicans. The backlash Holmes documented was California's first major outburst against Mexicans. But the antagonism may not yet have reached its full force because many Mexicans retreated across the border when faced with the influx of an army of poor whites competing with them for work. There were reports of the "return of entire trainloads" of Mexicans.[16] Many, however, remained.

There were great similarities between the Okies and Mexicans. They picked the same crops, lived in the same meager conditions, were equally ill-treated. At the height of the Dust Bowl period, California set up border checkpoints to stop a tide of its own nation's citizens from entering. This was a class-based act of hatred, the only time the state acted against both white and nonwhite strangers.

Modern Americans know the story of the migrant workers through *The Grapes of Wrath,* which reported the conditions surrounding them so accurately that it seemed like a work of nonfiction. Traces of that era can still be found. The peach country of Marysville, north of Sacramento, still has some remnants of a camp started by Tom Collins, who was instrumental in helping John Steinbeck research a series of articles on Dust Bowl migrants published in the *San Francisco News* in 1936.

Collins had opened this first New Deal migrant labor camp as a demonstration project for what he hoped would be a number of permanent government camps, a dream never fulfilled. There was not much left a half century later. I was about a month too late. The rotting administration building had just been torn down by a farmer planting a new orchard. All that remained were concrete pads and a shack nearby that the farmer rented for $54 a month to an old white woman, who remembered the camp but had never lived in it.

When one heads south down Highway 99 through the Central Valley, there are other Steinbeck landmarks. Below Fresno, there is a Tagus Ranch exit. Tagus is the "Hooper Ranch" in *Grapes,* where the Joads picked peaches and were robbed of their labor. Years ago, I met a Fresno man who knew old woman Tagus before she died. She was bitter to the end, he said, cursing Steinbeck with such a rage that her arms would fly. At the bottom of the valley, just beyond Bakersfield in the crossroads of Weedpatch, is what Steinbeck named the "Wheatpatch Camp." It is now called the Sunset Labor Camp, the second and last of Collins's experimental camps, used these days by Mexicans. At the front of the complex surrounded by a melon and a tomato field and acres of cotton are three wooden buildings that are scabbed with peeling paint and that have settled off their foundations.

The buildings are unmarked but instantly recognizable to anyone who has seen the *Grapes of Wrath* movie: the camp scenes were filmed here in 1939, when it was still filled with Dust Bowl migrants. The camp office that the Joads's car lurched to a stop in front of is there, as well as the water tower. Today, few worry about what happens to the Mexicans living there. California newspapers periodically publish articles on the farm labor situation, decrying conditions, but nothing ever changes.

In the 1930s, however, Steinbeck caused the masses to care about the have-nots—if those have-nots were white. Any student of California labor history knows that Steinbeck ignored Mexicans who were subjected to even worse treatment. And he left out the uncomfortable fact that many Okies hated Mexicans. Martha Escutia's grandfather, Ricardo Ovilla, had run-ins with "Okies" twice during his migrant farmworker days. In 1946, a restaurant in Sidney, Montana, refused service to Ricardo and 25 other Mexicans. When they began an impromptu sit-in, they were attacked by a group Ricardo described as Okies.

Then in 1953 Ricardo traveled to Visalia, a town not far from the Tagus Ranch, to pick grapes. When he was refused service at a restaurant, a brawl ensued. He apparently got in his licks and was jailed; he paid a $25 fine.

"Los Okies nos trataban mal," the Okies treated us badly, Ricardo said years later, shaking his head.

Without alluding to these tensions, Steinbeck predicted in his *San Francisco News* series that Mexicans were on their way out of California agriculture. He saw Dust Bowl whites as the new lower class. "Foreign labor is on the wane in California," Steinbeck wrote, "and the future farm workers are to be white and American. This fact must be recognized and a rearrangement of the attitude toward and treatment of migrant labor must be achieved." [17]

But farmers were not keen on Dust Bowl refugees. They were "Americans" and entitled to better—they would not be pushed around—and farmers had to pay them more. The *Grapes of Wrath* did create a reform movement, though the farmers were saved from a unionized workforce by World War II, when many whites went off to the war or factories. The farmers quickly embraced the Bracero program, which whether by plan or accident ensured that whites would not be in the fields.

Talk of farm labor reform ended with the return of Mexicans. Oppression surfaced occasionally, as in "Operation Wetback," launched by the Immigration and Naturalization Service on June 10, 1954.[18] Over a period of two months, some one-half million Mexicans and even some citizens were driven out. This program received a warm reception among California citizens; there was resistance in Texas. (Texas was more hospitable to Mexicans possibly because it has a longer border and exports three times as much to Mexico than does California.)

Then things quieted. During the four-decade postwar boom, Mexicans could be more or less ignored at the same time they were being used by industry and agribusiness. It was only in the 1990s, when California felt its biggest economic downturn since the Great Depression, that they were eyed again as targets.

The dependence on Latino labor that Professor Holmes wrote about in 1929 had grown even more important. By the 1990s Latinos were vital not only to peach farmers in the Central Valley but to the $36.5 million hotel industry in Dana Point. Californians struck out at Latinos while directly profiting from their labor, either as stockholders or residents in cities enjoying the benefits from bed taxes.

Latino labor is coveted, yet hundreds of thousands of Latinos live in the hardscrabble world of District 50 just as they would in the poorest parts of Mexico. One woman interviewed said her cousin was excited about coming to America, but when he arrived in HP he quickly became depressed—it was just like Mexico, endlessly poor and troubled. For him, the idea that the United States was a land of opportunity proved to be a lie, and he soon returned to Mexico. Because of the proximity of the Mexican border, many Mexicans have an out that Asians and other immigrants do not. If all goes wrong, they can easily return to their homeland. To union organizer Robert Wilberg, who lives in Dana Point, the surplus labor of HP is exactly what American business wants: "There's always a pool of ready and willing workers." With a porous border, he says, it is almost impossible to organize workers in order to raise their wages and benefits, as did the Europeans early this century.

When traveling around District 50, with its orange sky, endless graffiti, rumbling trains with container boxes of toxic chemicals emblazoned with skulls and crossbones, lack of job opportunities beyond selling oranges and coconuts on the streetcorner, one is struck by a horrifying thought: What will happen to this place in a century if present economic trends continue? Martha Escutia, despite her political savvy, is not a miracle worker at creating jobs. Martha's dream of the Alameda Corridor rail project that would connect the district to the Long Beach Harbor and jobs there was becoming mired in a host of conflicting interest groups and political squabbles. It seemed a faint hope.

The ghettos and barrios of Los Angeles are vast, dwarfing those of even the South Bronx and East St. Louis. And these lowland third world zones are expanding at the same time the rich hill dwellers grow more nervous. As the percentage of nonwhites increases, Los Angeles and other cities are beginning to resemble San Salvador, where in the 1970s the hill-dwelling rich raised their walls as the political situation worsened. Some walls had three and four layers and were 20 feet high by the time the civil war was in full swing.

For many immigrants, the number-one goal is not to loathe the walled hill dwellers, but to travel far enough in the American system to move next door to them. HP is the place you come to and then get away from, if luck is with you. Many immigrants hope to head south to Downey, where many whites still live. The Muñozes, meanwhile, aspire to move up even further.

At the same time, HP residents want to make it a better place. Human nature does not abandon hope, even in this environment. The summer after Ivan Muñoz graduated from high school, a councilman organized an antigraffiti day, the "HP Wipe Out," with donated paint and rollers. The cleanup was an attention-getting maneuver for the councilman, who later lost an election, but he tapped into a desire for improvement: 170 people signed up to spend the day rolling over the graffiti that plagues HP.

For the most part high school kids, they gathered at 7 o'clock on a Saturday morning beneath the ever-present smog blotting the sun. Supplies were handed out—paint rollers on poles were carried like rifles by volunteers. Ivan was armed with maps that he handed to leaders—he had scouted the sites with the worst graffiti and had worked on the maps until 1:30 a.m.

The language flipped back and forth between Spanish and English.

"*¿El nombre, otra vez?*" asked the man signing in volunteers.

"Louis."

"I'm going to get you 13 people," the sign-in man then said.

"Great," said Louis, nodding.

Ivan and six kids piled into a van. At Slauson Avenue and Alameda streets they faced a 500-foot long corrugated metal wall smothered by uncountable *vandalismos* and rolled tan paint for several hours. As lunch hour approached, some cholos unhappy with the cleanup cursed the work as they drove past.

"*¡Chingadas!*" yelled a kid in Ivan's group. It was the first Spanish spoken by the seven youths. At noon, they were finished.

"Time to go," Ivan said.

The van showed up. All heads turned as it drove off, surveying their effort—the clean wall looked absolutely unnatural.

"Looks pretty good," Ivan said.

The next day, the wall was covered by more than a dozen patches of graffiti. Two weeks later, it was impossible to tell if the work had ever been done.

North of HP in the city of Vernon, a Farmer John's meat processing plant takes up a city block. The walls of the building for its entire circumference are covered by a mural depicting farm scenes: green fields, rivers, blue sky. Pigs eat and run, farmers do chores. Martha loved the mural as a child—her favorite scene is of a pig taking a mudbath.

She said that people always respected the mural. Three decades later, it was still untouched, a fragment of faux nature in stark contrast to its surroundings, about the only place off limits to graffiti.

5

Black

In January 1993, a little over a year after Donald Northcross signed up 60 of the 71 black boys at Mills Junior High School in the OK Program, he drove a blue van through Rancho Cordova one overcast winter morning, picking up sleepy-eyed young men for the Saturday morning study hall.

The van headed south into the Central Valley plains. A misting rain fell. The land is barely above sea level and the cow pastures had become temporary lakes. The van zipped into the parking lot of the Rancho Arroyo Sports Complex, a warehouse-sized private club with tennis courts and a giant swimming pool. Don hurried the youths, who trooped through the building heading for a room behind the pool. Two of the boys wore the "X" hats made popular by Spike Lee's movie about Malcolm X.

The air was heavy—steam rose from the pool—and the back room's mirror-covered walls dripped moisture. Before sitting at one of a dozen tables, one youth scrawled an "X" in the condensation, complete with the horizontal lines at the ends of each point.

Except for the pistol tucked in the back of Don's pants, nothing about him resembled a cop. He wore a tight red T-shirt, his muscles well-defined from years of weight lifting. On the front of the shirt was the image of Martin Luther King and the words, "Keep the Dream Alive."

What Don, 34, was trying to accomplish, all these years later in this cold room, was less sure than the aim of the civil rights movement, the goals more elusive, the outcome unpredictable. The program, though in its infancy and in need of tuning, was having an effect: gang influence was down at the school. In a survey of teachers Don found that 86 percent said students in the OK Program improved in their homework, and 90 percent reported improved attendance. They also reported that less than 2 percent of the kids were involved in gang activity, and 98 percent avoided negative contact with the law.

The study period lasted just about an hour. As it progressed, the restlessness grew; the decibel level of chatter increased with each minute.

Officer Charles Turner announced that in the future the kids would have to come to study halls with a short essay on something good they had done in the previous week. "What do you guys think of that idea?" Charles asked.

No one spoke—shy faces looked everywhere but at Charles.

"We hear a lot of negative stuff. We want to start hearing about positives," Don added. He told of one recent negative, the shooting death of a local 19-year-old black man a few days earlier.

A youth named Wayne was talking at his table. Don called on him to share his comments. Wayne acted as though he was being scolded. Don said he was not reprimanding him—he just wanted to hear what he thought.

After stammering, Wayne said of the shooting, "Well, we was saying it's just like the movies."

Don then asked for someone to step forward with a positive. "If you can speak in here in front of your righteous brothers, you can talk in front of anyone," Don said as encouragement.

Don called on Devan. Devan (not his real name) had moved from Oakland, where he sold drugs, living alone on the street for one year. The 13-year-old was now in a group home and on the brink of becoming a serious gangbanger. Don wanted to make sure he was awarded with approval.

"What good thing have you done in the past week?" Don asked.

"I went back home for a visit and didn't smoke no weed and didn't get in trouble," Devan said of a trip back to Oakland.

Don quieted the laughter and praised Devan, who stood uncomfortably.

"That's a big accomplishment for Devan," Don said. He added that Devan's grade point average had risen to 3.3 since he joined the program and that he was now a good role model.

Another officer said that they should keep on this track.

"I don't want to go to your-all funerals," said the officer. "Last week I was called out to a shooting in Lincoln Village. I never made it because I came on a car that matched the description of the suspects'. Four black men. At any point in that vehicle stop I could have shot any of them. How do you think that makes me feel? I think about that at night."

Don added, "If one of you guys dies, chances are it will be a homicide. When's the last time you heard of a Klansman killing a black man?"

Heads shook.

"When's the last time you heard of a black man killing a black man? Yesterday. We're killing ourselves. If you go to school and stay out of trouble, you have a good chance."

Don said the guys with the dope money usually get it taken from them. They might have fancy cars and cash to flash, but they make mistakes and get caught. He spoke with the passion of a man in a pulpit, the career he once considered.

"That blue van we came in—no one can take that from me. The dope dealer—it can be taken from him, his car, his house, his money, with the forfeiture laws. I just bought a brand new $225,000 house," Don said of the home he owned with his wife Gladys. "I'm proud. I worked for it. I moved in just a couple weeks ago. You can do that legitimately. You don't have to rob nobody to make it."

MAKING IT AS A BLACK MAN

Son of Black man,
Can't you see
How you affect
The economy.

When you sell drugs,
Steal and rob,
You provide
The Man a job.

More policemen
To make the arrest,
A public defender
at your request.

They hire more judges
To hear the cases
All those new jobs
But few black faces.

This system is a chess game
In which you are a pawn
And you're the one being sacrificed
Yes, you, the black man's son.

This poem, framed amid a number of others in a hall near the entry of Donald Northcross's new suburban Sacramento home, was written in 1989 when he worked as a jailer, at the peak of his search for answers to how he could help the black community. There were 1.1 million inmates in America's prisons, triple the number that existed in 1970, according to the Sentencing Project. Almost 50 percent—about half a million of those prisoners—were black men. (In 1920, just 21 percent of those imprisoned were black.) The incarceration rate for black males was five times higher than for black males in South Africa—3,370 per 100,000 in the United States compared with 681 per 100,000 in South Africa, then still under apartheid. The Sentencing Project also reported that on any given day in the United States, one in four black men between the ages 20 and 29 were in prison, on parole, or on probation.

Many American whites associate blacks with prison or the ghetto. In reality, a majority of blacks are like Don and have moved up into the middle and upper classes. But because the ghetto is visible and concentrated, it seems that most blacks are in poverty. The people who could easily leave the ghetto moved up and out, even in Don's hometown of Ashdown, Arkansas.

"There was a paper mill that came in and it provided jobs for a lot of people," Don said. "They started to make more money. They didn't have to borrow sugar from the neighbor anymore. In a way it created a different class. People weren't as close as they used to be. The cream of the crop, the thinkers, the people who had some abilities, got out."

Don was able to get out because he came of age at a time when overt discrimination was no longer tolerated. In a color-blind world, Don would not need the help of affirmative action or the federal government's watchful eye to ensure that he was not discriminated against. If the government had not forced the integration of his school in 1968, he would have studied with 50-year-old textbooks. Without affirmative action, it is also unlikely that he would have been hired as a sheriff's deputy.

The paths of Don Northcross and Pete Wilson parallel those of American racial groups in recent years: the awakening of society to the injustice of segregation, the elevation of many blacks like Don into the middle class, and the growing white animosity toward "preferences" for blacks and others, a cause which Wilson would come to champion.

When Don was born in 1959 and his father was picking cotton and plowing with a mule on weekends between commuting to his distant day job, Wilson was in his first year in law school at Berkeley. Then the school was filled with white males—there was only a handful of women present. There was no affirmative action to ensure access for blacks and other minorities.

In 1962, when Wilson graduated from Berkeley with a law degree, he headed to San Diego and began working in Republican circles. His hero, Richard Nixon, had settled there after his defeat in 1960. A self-described "eager young advance man," Wilson worked on Nixon's ill-fated run for the California governorship in 1962. The young Republican confided to his mentor that he was thinking of running for the California state assembly. Wilson later recalled that Nixon gave him a "cool look" and asked, "Pete, do you think you can win?" As a final word of encouragement, Nixon told Wilson "You've got to try, or you'll never forgive yourself." [1]

Wilson won on his first try and was in the assembly from 1966 through 1971.

In 1966 Don was already old enough to know the rules of Ashdown, Arkansas: where he was forbidden to walk, which stores made him go through the side door to be served, which water fountains were off limits.

California was ahead of the South in those days—the state did not have Jim Crow—but California was no different from much of the North in that it was not a hotbed of racial inclusion. When Wilson became mayor of San Diego, the city, like others in California, had little in the way of equal opportunity. In 1971 the most prominent city job for blacks was to be a garbage collector.

When Wilson became mayor, he aggressively hired minorities. In 1972 he announced he wanted to increase minority employment to 23.7 percent. A different increase was set for women. There was little resistance from the city hierarchy, where most people agreed that creating equal opportunity was the right thing to do. Any grumbling from whites was not widely aired.[2]

Wilson did more than set goals, however. He went into the community and sought out those who could help, such as LaQuita Robbins, a black community leader then working for a federal antipoverty program. Robbins attended one event in which Wilson drove himself in a "beat-up old Chevrolet" and helped her wash glasses in the kitchen when they ran out in the middle of the meeting. She added that "when Pete got up and said something, people didn't know he was the mayor. He was just another white man there talking."

At another event, Cleo Kearse, another community activist, recalled that Wilson "ate all my barbecued pigs' feet and he wanted some more. He got real black that time."

Wilson's desire for inclusion seemed genuine. In 1977 Carey McWilliams, who by then had become the editor of the *Nation* magazine, glowed that he was a "Republican . . . worth watching."[3] Robbins and Kearse were among the first hires made by the city in Wilson's new program to include blacks and women.

When Don was trying to get his fledgling program off the ground, he could not imagine that Wilson would lead a virulent attack against affirmative action. To get a small number of at-risk black youths to channel their energies into succeeding was daunting enough. It seemed inconceivable that there would be talk of a rollback of the basic rights of inclusion he understood to be part of modern society.

California, like the rest of the United States, presents mixed signals to blacks. In Don's case, his new home was evidence enough that society had advanced. His 2,400-square-foot house was so new that the lawn was still utterly weedless, the trees tiny sticks supported by stakes and wires. Don was talking to one of his two children; the girl ran to the arms of his mother, Lucy, visiting from Arkansas.

"We were poor," Lucy said as she did the dishes, looking out the window at the backyard pool. "Different now, things sure are."

While driving to a store to buy a patio table for an upcoming OK Program event, he ticked off the race of the owners of all 17 houses on his street: six white; four black, including his; three Latino; one a mixed white-Latino couple; one Asian Indian. In California, people will live next to different races—some of the white families on his street bought their home long after Don had moved in. The kind of trouble seen in eastern overclass suburbs is not as common in California. In the Great Lakes and East, realtors have created robust sales and profits by moving a single black family onto a street, driving the whites to sell, a practice known as "blockbusting." In Boston, Cleveland, and Chicago, blacks occupy de facto gulags. In California, despite the presence of traditional black areas of Compton and Watts (which are both now almost half Latino), it is much more common to find acceptance of blacks in rich areas—as long as those blacks are well-to-do. The last houses in Don's development sold for $240,000, which makes them elite by Sacramento standards. Whites on Don's street do not seem to mind living next to blacks who can afford houses just like theirs.

At the store Don's cellular phone rang. He stood talking near the entrance. Whites stared with alarm, as though they thought Don, a very dark-skinned black man, was a drug dealer. I was not sure if he noticed these stares.

Inside, Don found the table he wanted. He paid with a credit card and signed the receipt. The clerk, a white woman, compared the signature with the one on the card for an uncomfortably long time.

"Did you notice that?" he said outside the store. "Sometimes you think it's because you're black. Some people would have made a stink, would have hung around to see if they checked the next person who paid. I don't let it upset me." But it is clear that on some level it did bother him. The clerk's suspicion makes one wonder how thin the veneer of legal protection is. Even though he is accepted by his upscale neighbors and he earns more than three times the salary of the white clerk who studied his signature, outside of his quarter-million-dollar home and good job, Don was just another black man not to be trusted.

HISTORY: NO UTOPIA

The first non-European immigrants to arrive in North America landed in late August, 1619. The 20 Africans who were taken off a ship at Old Point Comfort on Chesapeake Bay were imported just a dozen years after the British made their first successful settlement at nearby Jamestown.

The traffic in slaves escalated. By 1770 there were 2.5 million Africans in the colonies, numbers that would continue to grow. But most blacks remained in the cotton South. For many years the black presence in California was small. There were only 962 blacks in the state in 1850. By 1870 blacks were just 1 percent of the population.

Whether California would be admitted to the union as a free or slave state was a hotly debated issue, but it came in free. A decade later, Abraham Lincoln carried the state by less than 1,000 votes. Slavery may have been rejected because the moguls who needed cheap labor looked elsewhere—China was closer than Africa. When the Central Pacific Railroad was built, the Chinese were the muscle, although in 1867, blacks were used as leverage when several thousand Chinese workers went on strike to protest the brutal conditions. The railroad threatened to send for 10,000 black replacements and the strike ended after a week.

Yet Gold Rush–era blacks met with the same mixed acceptance Donald Northcross would find a century and a half later. From the beginning, one's past was irrelevant in California. Many pioneers could start anew, their history forgotten. To a degree, this included blacks in the Gold Rush mining fields. In Marysville, a saloon advertised that it welcomed customers "with no regard to distinction or color." And "a negro cook is one of the most independent men alive," wrote Leonard Kip in *California Sketches with Recollections of the Gold Mines.* "He is allowed to enter into certain familiarities, which would ensure him a cowhiding in almost any other part of the globe."[4]

In the 1850s the famous case of a fugitive slave by the name of Archy Lee wound its way through the courts and created a stir: sympathetic whites intervened in his behalf, and after a seesaw court battle, during which there was a foiled kidnapping of Lee by his ex-master and a small-scale riot by blacks in Sacramento, the state refused to extradite Lee back to the South.

Racism, however, was plentiful. From the start, California had a schizophrenic attitude toward blacks. Not long after the Archy Lee case, there was a move in the legislature to exclude blacks from the state. The debate was essentially between gold miners who had come from the South and those who had come from the North. The state addressed the issue in a circular pattern, passing repressive laws, overturning them, then quickly winding back the clock. One reason for this uneven record was that the fate of blacks became tied to that of the Chinese. Even a century and a half ago the polyethnic nature of the state was complicating race matters. For most of the nineteenth century, it was against California law for blacks to testify for or against whites in court, and some whites were opposed to changing the law for fear that the state might then have to grant the same right to the Chinese. This prohibition was changed near the end of the century, and sunny observations were made about the acceptance of blacks. In 1904 the *San Francisco Chronicle* noted that it was the Chinese who occupied low-level jobs, thus leaving to "select" blacks a large number of "responsible positions." That same year the *Los Angeles Herald* ran an article saying that blacks "will find no race problem in Los Angeles, only prosperity."

Along with the Townerites in Orange County there were black Utopian experiments. In 1908 Lieutenant Colonel Allen Allensworth, a former slave who had fought for the Union, founded a black town in the San Joaquin Valley as a haven from the repression he met in the South. Allensworth grew to 300 families and at first prospered. Its strength was its sense of community—the town had a history of cooperative effort—something Don Northcross was trying to recreate eight decades later. The founding of Allensworth met with some resistance. The Pacific Farming Co., which controlled the area surrounding the small town, stopped selling additional land to blacks. The company then tried to take over the water rights of those already there. Later, surrounding towns built new water systems and froze out Allensworth. The community banded together to dig new water lines. It survived as a black town into the 1960s, when arsenic in its natural state was found in the water system; many residents then drifted away. Today, half of it is empty, protected in a state park, and the other half is occupied by a small number of Latino families. In 1990 I met a black woman there who had just moved from Los Angeles with her children to escape drug and gang influence.[5]

Early in the century, California's growing dislike for blacks seemed to coincide with a surge of hatred toward the Japanese, who were under attack for most of the first two decades. In 1910 only three of 200 bars would reportedly serve blacks in Los Angeles. By 1930, restrictive covenants kept the estimated 40,000 blacks in the Los Angeles area out of white neighborhoods. The Depression made things worse. In 1920 blacks had some 11,000 domestic and service jobs in the state. By 1934, with more than twice the population, blacks had less than 3,000 of these jobs. Whites took the work.[6]

A political bright spot came in 1919, when the first black was elected to the California Assembly. Frederick Madison Roberts represented a district that was two-thirds white. He served for 16 years, pushing through several key bills, including one in 1921 that forbade schools to use textbooks that stereotyped minorities; in 1927 he authored an antidiscrimination housing measure; in 1933 he got an antilynching bill passed.

During the Second World War, jobs in defense lured blacks in large numbers when $35 billion, or 10 percent of all money spent for the war effort, went to California. In 1944 one out of 10 shipbuilding workers was black. But at the end of the war blacks were the first to be laid off. They kept coming west, however, as the cotton culture in the South came to an end. By 1950 blacks had risen from roughly 1 percent to 4.4 percent of California's population, and they reached 7 percent in the 1990s.

With the state's growing polyethnicity, conflict was inevitable. For years, blacks were the mainstay of the service industry, especially union jobs in hotels. Then as civil rights laws took effect, many blacks started moving into government positions. Latinos shifted into the service jobs behind blacks. When blacks started joining the middle class and left places like Watts in growing numbers, Latinos also moved into their neighborhoods. Some economically deprived blacks increasingly saw Latinos as competition.

Examples of friction abound. In the city of Compton, south of Watts, blacks once sued white leaders for not enforcing their civil rights and eventually came to dominate the city's politics. Meanwhile, as more Latino residents moved in, the Latinos in turn asked the U.S. Justice Department to file a lawsuit against the black-run city government to enforce *their* civil rights. Other Latinos began attacking policies that favor blacks for government agency affirmative action—in Los Angeles, blacks account for 28 percent of the county government workforce and for 10.5 percent of the population. Latinos, on the other hand, hold 21 percent of those jobs but make up more than 40 percent of the population.[7]

When Martha Escutia fought to create Assembly District 50, several black lawmakers resisted giving up pieces of their districts. Assemblywoman Marguerite Archie-Hudson, who like Don is a black southerner, argued that the Latino area could be better served if it remained fragmented into adjoining black and Latino districts because it would have more representatives in Sacramento.[8] For Watts and Compton, long black strongholds but now half Latino, the day may come when blacks lose these seats.

This black–Latino discord (along with the strain between Koreans and blacks) is occurring even as black and white tension continues.

The contemporary battle over job resources was avoidable and has its roots in the Civil War, said Lawrence Bobo, a black sociology professor and director of the Center for Research on Race, Politics and Society at the University of California at Los Angeles. Bobo notes that blacks should have been economically empowered immediately after the Civil War. The breaking of the promise of 40 acres and a mule was a grave injustice to former slaves, but Bobo sees a much larger issue.

"American history could have unfolded in a radically different path than it did if rather than importing millions of people from southern and central and eastern Europe to man the industrial expansion in this country, we had taken a bunch of newly freed slaves and done that." The years between 1870 and 1910 "were critical . . . in terms of the upward trajectory of the American economy," Bobo added. "They provided a remarkable economic footing for those otherwise desperately poor folks coming over from Europe."

During these years, blacks remained locked in southern agriculture. After they finally migrated north and west to partake in the industrial economy, it had already peaked. "At the point that blacks get a serious foothold and begin to establish a middle class, a whole series of other economic transformations take place that begin to undermine that," said Bobo. This shift toward deindustrialization started in the 1960s and accelerated rapidly: the number of high-wage jobs in steel mills and factories shrank greatly as jobs were shipped overseas or lost because of automation. For the jobs that remained, blacks were often the last hired and thus the first to be released.

Blacks today, especially in multiracial California, are being passed over for a second time, Bobo argues. After the 1960s, many blacks were let down once again when America began letting a new wave of immigrants take the jobs that blacks had long held. Illegal migrants from Latin America have offered American business an easy out—rather than paying decent wages, companies have a never-ending supply of willing low-cost labor. As an example, Bobo pointed to hotel workers in Los Angeles. Between the 1940s and 1970s, it was a largely black and unionized workforce. Now it is Latino and largely nonunion. "I don't think one can argue that it's simply a stepladder kind of thing, where blacks moved up to the next job. I think there was a fair amount of displacement."

In view of what has happened in California, blacks could be even more displaced in other regions of the country as Latinos and Asians migrate inland in search of work.

BEYOND UTOPIA: THE REALITY OF
COMMUNITY BUILDING

Donald Northcross was trying to re-create the Utopian experiment of Allensworth in an urban environment. He wanted blacks to take control of their own fortunes, especially in the complexities of California's economy, in which they would be competing to succeed not only in a white world but also in one dominated by Latinos and Asians.

In the three decades since civil rights began to be respected, a majority of blacks have joined the middle class. For those who did not make it, the 1980s and 1990s saw the war on poverty abandoned. In its place came a move by white voters to spend money almost gleefully in the opposite direction: in California, voters approved any prison-building measure that appeared on the ballot, the not-so-hidden motive being to incarcerate black criminals. Given this attitude, it is not surprising that Don gave up relying on societal solutions. But he is not naive enough to believe there was absolutely no role for society. Equal opportunity and affirmative action were necessary to ensure that resentful whites did not shut blacks out. All Don wanted was a level playing field. The black community's responsibility was to ensure that kids came to school prepared to compete.

One can look at this approach as self-help. Or one can take a more conservative view, as do many whites, and see programs such as Don's as "tribalism." It does not take much to evoke this fear. When in public, the sight of several dozen young black men always turned heads. "They think we're a gang," said one of the kids. Among conservative commentators, the de facto presence of a black group like Don's kids is automatically considered antiwhite and part of the Balkanization of America.

Blacks could not win, it seemed. Conservative whites do not like it when ghetto blacks are on welfare. They do not like it when blacks help themselves. And they do not want blacks to have affirmative action, either. There is no easy solution, yet conservatives are providing none beyond building more prisons or ending affirmative action.

For years, Don searched for answers. Long before he started

the OK Program, he and a former college football teammate listened to disciples of Louis Farrakhan, the black radical leader of the Nation of Islam. But Don found no solution in Farrakhan's bitterness and anger. Ethnocentrism probably would not work even in a society that was just white and black, and in polyethnic California it was simply out of the question: many blacks were already economically and politically on the edge and could hardly be further isolated. Blacks had to get along with others if they were going to succeed. Don decided on self-help, not ethnocentric chauvinism. He would try to teach the kids how to get along in a society that was filled with racism without using it as an excuse or becoming racist themselves.

"I understand racism, I know it exists," Don said of the problems the kids faced. "I want to let [them] know where we come from in this society, and I'll be durned if I'm going to watch us go back." He taught the kids how to make it in spite of racism. "Every time somebody says something you don't like, it ain't racism," Don said of what he tells the youths. Don shows them the difference between a teacher who is not being fair and one who disciplines them when they need it.

"When they tell me, 'Officer Northcross, I can't learn in Miss What's-her-call-its room,' I say 'Why not?' 'Man, she doesn't like the black guys.' I say 'Okay, what's that got to do with you learning? I've had boss men that don't like me, but I went to work everyday. She can be a racist. Now I have a problem if she's going to the white kids and whispering answers in their ears and not telling you. I don't care if it's David Duke, if he stands up in front of that classroom and he's teaching you the same thing he's teaching everybody else, then you're learning something. You can be his worst nightmare.'"

Don prefers to think of the program and its goals as if it were a football team. Don explained, you train the components separately: running backs, defense, the fullback. "If you train them all the same, you get chaos." In the end, "We're still a team. We can have different positions and train for these positions individually. Once every ethnic group does that, we can start to move the ball. When we get involved, get collective, then we'll build a strong America. America is diversity. When we deny the diversity, we don't have a strong America."

Don said each group should help its own "players." He pointed out that young skinheads need to be helped by white men. "I don't think I'm going to be too effective as a black man going to that kid showing him I care, talk to him about treating me as an equal. If somebody is going to get through [to] that kid, it's going to have to be a white male." But young black men need the most help. Don said of all the demographic groups in California, black males in junior high are by far the most likely to end up in jail or jobless. Black girls, while facing many problems, are not at such risk. Many of the children in his program came from single-parent homes, or the mothers were dead, drugged, homeless, and the children lived with relatives. There was no place for "family values" to start. If society waited for responsibility to start at home, it would not happen for these children.

The program is somewhat conservative in its approach. Kids follow certain strict rules—good attendance and behavior is mandatory, they have to come to class prepared. Every two weeks, teachers fill out progress reports. If these steps are met, there are rewards. Each quarter, they go to a sporting event. At the end of the year, kids with good performance get a free trip to Disneyland.

Mills Junior High was an ideal place to test community building. One in three blacks in America now lives in the suburbs, but often in marginalized ones like Rancho Cordova, so typical of the expanding medium-core ghettos. It once had been home to whites who worked at the nearby Aerojet-General Corporation, a rocket manufacturer, but in the early 1970s a round of government cuts forced the company to lay off thousands of workers. The whites fled and were replaced by blacks, Vietnamese boat people, Laotians, and most recently Russians fleeing the former Soviet Union. Even though Rancho Cordova wears a suburban mask—fast-food joints, discount marts, ranch-style homes—behind it is a world of drugs, drive-by shootings, and despair. Some kids had never seen an adult going to work as Don had seen his father do, with its cycle often going back three generations.

In this environment, the OK Program kids would form a community of sorts, reaching for the same goals, supporting each other as much as being helped by the adults. "Then when one kid is taking his books and stuff to class, he doesn't stick out like a sore thumb because all the kids know that's what's expected in this community," Don said. The program was not made for "bad" kids. "You may be a straight-A student, but if you're in the wrong neighborhood and you're a black male, you're at risk.

"I use a vehicle analogy when I talk about kids. You can't fix a vehicle one time and expect it to run forever. You've got to put a wrench on it every now and then. Otherwise, you're going to have a car going down the road rattling, parts falling off. Kids are the same way. You can't tell them to do the right thing one time. You got to keep that wrench on them. They may need a little more maintenance than other kids. You got to be willing to put that maintenance on them. I'm crazy enough to believe that after a while that it's going to have an impact. If they hear it over again, whatever the message is, sooner or later it's going to play into their decision making process somewhere along the way."

It was not all that long before results were seen. Susan Socal, a white woman who teaches special education classes at Mills Junior High, said the program's impact was rapid. "The majority of these kids weren't making it. They weren't involved in school." After Don, grades went up and problems went down. "A lot of them just want attention. When they act up, the bad ones, it's often just them saying 'Look at me, I came to school today.'" She said the toughest kids hug Don. "They hang on him and want to be close. [They] know he really cares about them." Even students of other races run up to hug Don when he is on the campus. They want a similar program for their groups.

"We need to get different ethnic females. I've worked with groups of black girls. There is a big cultural difference. They discovered things about me and I discovered things I didn't know, but they still need role models from their own culture.

"We need to understand other cultures, given how things are changing. As a white middle-class person, you have to learn to be tolerant. You have to learn to listen. For so long we've felt we are the only culture that exists, that we should have things our way. It's not going to work that way anymore."

BLACKS ON BLACKS

As the OK Program entered its second year, the federal trial of the officers accused of beating Rodney King was under way. The media were poised for a repeat of the riots that followed the first Simi Valley jury verdict. But anyone connected to the street did not expect problems for a host of reasons, the biggest being that the tension was like the pressure of an earthquake: once some of it was released, it would be a while before another burst of rage erupted.

The papers and airwaves were filled with stories about blacks, about poverty, gangs, the usual—but most missed the point. Absent was any discussion of black middle-class anger, and white fear. The press did not want to touch this issue. The affirmative action backlash had not yet matured into the force it would become in two short years—and pressure was building among whites for an eruption of their own.

Bill Shepherd seemed to typify the feelings of many whites. One day while eating lunch in a small Dana Point cafe, Bill sat beneath the poster of a white model who had appeared on the Arsenio Hall show a few nights before. Bill said that when the model walked on stage, the black host told her, "The only way you could be more beautiful is if you were black." Bill asked what would happen if Hall were white and had told a black model that the only way she could have been more beautiful would be if she were white? He imagined a major scandal. The dual standard bothered Bill, and it then prompted a discussion about affirmative action. Bill knew some blacks were successful and did not need any government help. He questioned the value of keeping programs that seemed to have outlived their time. Bill, of course, did not have contact with kids like Don's, but his anger was as typical as it was unaddressed by the media.

While this white anger was building, some blacks were asking themselves hard questions. Don had decided it was a good time to explore the issue of blacks in society in a community forum. He organized a panel discussion at California State University in Sacramento. The featured speaker was Ernest Hill, who had played college football with Don. He was completing his doctorate in history at UCLA and had recently published his first novel, *Satisfied with Nothin'*.[9] Its title perfectly describes the plot. It tells the story of Jamie Ray Griffin, a young black man who comes of age in the South of the 1970s, an unsophisticated rural youth trying to succeed in a world of racism and black apathy. As Jamie Ray heads to a tragic end, the novel looks at racism as well as how blacks have allowed themselves to become complacent in the post–civil rights era. Early chapters are based on Don's childhood and include one of his poems.

It was a rainy evening—unusual weather for May—and that may have explained why only 24 people, all black, came to the meeting to explore why blacks do not seem to care about their community. The audience, spanning all ages but heavily in the 45-plus range, was scattered amid the many empty chairs. On stage were Don, Ernest, the head of the Sacramento Urban League, a professor from the school, and a local black television personality who moderated the discussion. The first question was: why are so many blacks not succeeding—is it racism or is the problem within the black community itself?

Ernest told a story about the integration of his Deep South school. The first term after he went to the white school, he came home with a report card that had a C in one class—he knew he was in trouble because his father was strict and would not accept anything less than a B. Ernest's solution was to tell his father the teacher was a racist. It was a poor excuse and his father gave him a hard time.

"This is one of the most common things I hear when a kid has trouble," Don said. "I point out that they aren't experiencing as much racism as I had growing up in the South—and I've made it."

There were no scowls, only nods. Don said blacks have to use caution when claiming racism. He told about an incident at a local mall where some black kids were thrown out because they resembled gang members, with their pants hanging down off their rumps. "I have a problem with that and I'm as black as they are."

"We have to have community," Don said, alluding to his program, which was working to help young black boys.

Ernest said that many blacks talk about black pride, yet they live with bars on their windows, not knowing each other. "Our ancestors deserve more than this."

Worse, Ernest said, many blacks view success with contempt, as something that is part of the "white" world. He said he would bet money that if he could read the thoughts of some in the audience, he would hear a few saying that some of the people on stage were "Uncle Toms." He and Don agreed that being successful does not mean you are any less black. But this did not seem to be a universal notion. It was easier to blame racism, Don said, and he was interrupted by applause when he added, "There's not a white man in this country who stands outside my house and says I can't spend time with black kids."

BLACKS AND ASIANS

Months later, Ernest Hill sat at a coffeehouse on the UCLA campus and said black students came to him asking for help in fighting the low black graduation rates. He was bothered that they blamed racism.

"Let's identify where the racism exists [so] we can eradicate it," Ernest said. "But we also have to talk about apathy. When I grade their papers, they're half done. If I walk through the library . . . I won't see these black kids studying. If you fail, you should have utilized every source, have gone to every tutoring session, you should have been in the library every night. You should understand this is your job. This is a problem that permeates society, this sense of entitlement. The only thing that anybody is entitled to, be they black, white, whatever, is an opportunity." He said the kids often do not understand what they need to do in order to achieve.

"I went to this high school once. These kids said, 'I ain't flipping no burgers.' I said okay, 'I've got a job over here that pays a couple of hundred thousand a year. Now what can you do to earn it? Can you do what I need for you to do?'"

Without planning it, the Sacramento conference really had been about the role of blacks in a multicultural society. As the smallest major minority group in the state, blacks not only have to fit in a white world, they have to adjust to other cultures.

Ernest's novel *Satisfied with Nothin'* explored this relationship. The protagonist, Jamie Ray Griffin, succeeds by playing football. Whites begin to accept him for his feats on the field but he is viewed with suspicion by blacks. At one point, he is upset that he is not doing well in school and blames racism. The mentor tells Jamie Ray he felt the same way when he first went to Yale and got poor grades. Then he met a Taiwanese student who not only faced worse cultural barriers but hardly spoke English. Yet in no time, the man was earning top grades. The mentor said he realized the Taiwanese man was outworking him—he studied morning and night, seven days a week.

> I thought he was crazy until I took the time to talk to him. In the course of our conversation he used words like 'discipline,' 'motivation,' 'self-determination' and 'obligation.' But Jamie, it wasn't so much the words he used that impressed me as the ones he didn't—'racism,' 'discrimination,' and 'equality.'
>
> . . . I realized that he was self-directed while I was other-directed. And as I began to pay more attention to the other minorities on campus—Koreans, West Indians, Chinese, Japanese, Africans—I realized that all of them emphasized what they had to do and did it. Few of them found time to sit around looking at the white man . . . it was at that time that I realized that black folks were getting outworked. Son, if we're going to make it as a people we must not only learn words like discipline, motivation, self-determination, and obligation; we must incorporate them into our lifestyles, we must act on them.[10]

Ernest wrote this situation as a lesson on what can be learned from other cultures. "People tell me how cruel they are," Ernest said of Asian parents. "But I'm going to tell you one thing. Nobody reaches the upper echelons without that kind of work."

Others are seeing the same lesson. Edward N. Luttwak, in a study for the Center for Strategic and International Studies, said the Confucian ethos brought to America by Chinese, Japanese, and Korean immigrants might be a fitting replacement for the "spent power of Calvinism"; it could be a salvation for American business.[11]

The declaration of Calvinism's death may be premature, for there is still plenty of enterprise in American society. But races and ethnicities do differ in their attitudes toward the nature of work, according to a report released by the UCLA Center for the Study of Urban Poverty.

The principal author, Lawrence Bobo, and three other professors conducted focus groups with the four major races. About the only common denominator, the authors say, is that "regardless of race, native-born American status appears to bring with it a strong presumption of having options other than menial labor." More specifically,

> Latinos, both English and Spanish-speaking, saw almost any form of paid employment as honorable. Among Blacks, however, there were mixed feelings. Several Black participants, especially Black men, voiced strong objection to jobs in fast-food restaurants, as janitors, and other jobs that were stereotypical 'dead-end.' They were adamantly opposed to seeing their children take jobs they regarded as beneath them.[12]

Whites were found to assume overwhelmingly that they will have good jobs. While Asians were even more successful than the whites interviewed—they had higher earnings—they were "considerably more anxious about their economic futures." But whites said that creative expression in their work was more important than wages or benefits—Asians were the exact opposite.

A shared belief of Chinese and Koreans and whites was that their children would go to college and pursue professional careers. This was not true of Latinos and blacks, whose concern was that the "current younger generation was in serious trouble."

Don's OK Program addressed these concerns, but by late 1993 it was faltering because of a lack of volunteer officers. Don turned to the community to recruit citizens. The early success of the program was proof that young black boys could work hard and improve, but also proof that it was very difficult to create a community in modern society. Dr. Alvin Poussaint, a Harvard psychiatrist who has studied the black community, noted that there are many programs like Don's scattered across the nation and all face the same dilemma—trying to get time from busy role models. "Mentoring is a big commitment," he said. It is difficult, he added, to expect people to sacrifice time from their own families. "The need is so enormous, if you had 1,000 men out there it would only help a small number of those who need help." But if the 1,000 Northcrosses each had 20 committed men, that would make a difference. The question is how to get them involved.

The grim outlook did not dissuade Don. Yet in a rare moment of doubt, he worried about the white fear and anger he saw building in the days before the affirmative action backlash took off. Despite supposed advances in private industry, there really has not been a big influx of minorities into top positions. "But a large number of whites are very concerned about the little change that has taken place," Don said. "It's unnerving to some of them. I can see that as more progress is made by minorities, the greater the resistance is going to be. Inclusion in many cases means a loss of power to the people who are in power, particularly white males. And correct me if I'm wrong, but I can't remember any time in history when power has been given away or shared without a war or without battle. It's going to take a lot of rearranging in this society for it to work."

6

Asian

If Maria Ha had landed in California in 1848, about the time the treaty ending the war with Mexico was signed, she would have been welcome. The first Asians who trickled into the state were greeted with acceptance. Those who followed met a backlash, further acceptance, and then the most severe ethnic hatred ever seen in California except during the war against the Indians. The reaction against the Chinese set the tone for California's attitude toward nonwhite outsiders.

In the anti-immigration wave after 1993, however, animosity toward Asians barely registered. The backlash that generated new laws or calls for the repeal of old protections was aimed primarily at Latinos and blacks, though it is true that some whites mutter about the "overachieving" Asians, and a furor arose nationally when a ship filled with illegal Chinese immigrants tried to dock in New York and other ships were headed for the West Coast. But these are mild sentiments compared with California's vitriolic attacks against Asians in the latter half of the nineteenth century and the early years of the twentieth. China presented California with its first "immigration problem." Mexico was sparsely populated at that time, and it did not have the pool of readily exploitable labor the young state needed.

THE FIRST WHITE RIOT

In 1848 just 54 Asians were counted in California. That changed after San Francisco merchant Chum Ming wrote to a friend in China about the discovery of gold. By 1850 there were 4,000 Chinese; in 1852 some 20,000 landed in San Francisco. Many had come as laborers under contract—in debt to the masters who brought them. The Chinese were motivated by the gold, and the masters wanted their labor.[1]

The demand for labor was overshadowed in other white quarters by resentment against the hard-working strangers. In the tough election battle of 1852, Governor John Bigler blamed the "Asiatics" for California's economic troubles—the very charge Pete Wilson would level against Mexican immigrants 14 decades later. White miners, worried that the Chinese would outdo them in the gold fields, succeeded in getting the state legislature to pass a $3-a-month tax on foreign miners. This tax was raised in subsequent years. But the economic value of the Chinese forestalled more severe measures. Aaron H. Palmer, a federal policy maker, advocated using Chinese labor to build a transcontinental railroad immediately after the war with Mexico. Talk of such a railroad had been circulating since 1836, but the division over slavery in Congress held up approval. Palmer argued for Chinese laborers because they had already proved their ability to do hard work in Hawaii's sugar fields. Immediately after the Central Pacific Railroad was formed in 1862, Anson Burlingame, the American ambassador to China, was instructed to tell the Ta-Tsing government that immigrants would be "welcome in unlimited numbers." The Burlingame treaty went on to state, "The United States of America and the Emperor of China cordially recognize the inherent and inalienable right of man to change his home and allegiance . . . for purposes of curiosity, of trade, or as permanent residents."

The Central Pacific hired the first 50 Chinese laborers in early 1865. Leland Stanford, one of the "Big Four" backers of the railroad, liked them because they worked harder and were one-third cheaper than white labor. By 1867 there were 12,000 Chinese—90 percent of the construction workforce—blasting and chipping tunnels through the Sierra Nevada granite. After the railroad was completed, the unemployed Chinese came down from the mountains, setting off a "yellow peril" alarm. A few years after Stanford drove the final golden spike at Promontory, Utah, the Chinese accounted for half of all factory workers in San Francisco. The 1870 census found 63,000 Chinese in the nation, most in California.

Hatred against the Chinese was fueled by the very railroad they helped build, said the June 1900 *Forum*. The magazine noted that whites flooded the state over the new train route, "each with the belief that jobs were to be had in plenty, and that wages were high."[2] The whites who paid stiff ticket prices were not pleased that "strange" people were doing the work they felt was rightfully theirs—work on farms, in factories, independent businesses.

In 1871 Los Angeles's Chinatown was looted, and 19 Chinese were lynched. For two days starting July 23, 1877, several thousand white rioters torched Chinese laundries in San Francisco and burned the docks of ships bringing Chinese immigrants.

In a speech on May 18, 1876, to his fellow members of the U.S. House of Representatives, William A. Piper of California summed up the feelings of many in the state when he said:

> Now, toward the close of the nineteenth century, the globe is portioned out among four distinct races, destined hereafter to keep separate and apart. The four great races of mankind—the white, the yellow, the black, and the red—in their migrations have divided the earth among themselves in unequal proportions. The white race, excelling in strength, activity, and intelligence, and possessing a high degree of civilization . . . has conquered three-fifths of the habitable globe, leaving the remaining two-fifths for the semi-civilized yellow race, the savage African, and the perishing red man.[3]

Piper said there were 150,000 Chinese among California's population of 800,000, a twofold exaggeration. Underlying Piper's comments was his fear that many more of China's 450 million people were poised to come.

> The alarm excited by this invasion is wide-spread, and the aid of Congress is invoked to put a stop to this influx of semi-barbarians now threatening to outnumber the white population of the Pacific coast. . . . They have monopolized menial labor and the

lighter mechanical arts, thus depriving American boys and girls of opportunities of employment, closing the avenues of labor, and driving many to enforced idleness and want, resulting in confirmed poverty and crime. The people of the Pacific coast regard these hordes with fear and alarm, believing that superiority of race and intelligence will probably not be able to resist such overwhelming superiority of numbers.

When a constitutional convention was called in 1879, Californians revised their voting laws, forbidding idiots, lunatics, convicted criminals, and any "native of China" to cast a ballot. That same year, at the instigation of California representatives, the U.S. Congress passed a Chinese exclusion bill, but it was vetoed by President Rutherford B. Hayes. In 1882 exclusion proponents succeeded when Congress barred Chinese immigration. As in the following decades, the fears of California caused Washington to pass laws or otherwise react against nonwhites. The 1882 act marked the first time the United States had ever placed controls on immigration from a specific nation—before, anyone was welcome—save for a ban on prostitutes and convicts in 1875.[4] When it was over, many Chinese went home. Those remaining retreated to places like San Francisco. The Chinese population there reached some 30,000 by 1900.

The anti-Chinese hatred was followed by an attack on the Japanese in the first two decades of the 1900s, mostly because they were buying or leasing farms. In 1907 President Theodore Roosevelt invited the mayor of San Francisco and members of the city's school board to Washington in an attempt to stem the anti-Japanese rhetoric. Historian Carey McWilliams said it was "as if the president had invited the ambassadors of a sovereign power to meet with him for the purpose of negotiating a settlement of an international dispute."[5] To try and quell anti-Japanese moves by California, the United States and Japan reached a "gentleman's agreement" in 1908 in which Japan agreed voluntarily to stop the emigration of more laborers. In 1913 President Woodrow Wilson sent the U.S. secretary of state to Sacramento to ask that California not restrict Japanese land ownership. Despite this effort, an overwhelming majority of the legislature voted to ban anyone "ineligible for citizenship"—which meant the Japanese—from owning land. "Californians thoroughly enjoyed this . . . sense of power," said McWilliams.

That power was bolstered on November 2, 1920. Upset with the Japanese who got around the law by buying or leasing land in the names of their citizen children, an 85 percent majority of voters favored Proposition 1, banning the ownership of land, or even the leasing of land, by Japanese nationals or their children who were American citizens. The initiative was later upheld by the U.S. Supreme Court.[6]

In "California—White or Yellow?" an article on the "threat" of Japanese land ownership in the 1921 edition of *The Annals of the American Academy*, Marshall De Motte, the chairman of the state Board of Control, said the Chinese Exclusion Act was the answer to "California's first race problem. She had to settle it and she did so in her own way." De Motte concluded: "It is utterly unthinkable that America or an American state should be other than white. Kipling did not say 'East is East' of the United States, but if the star No. 31 in Old Glory, California's star, becomes yellow, West may become East. . . . Californians, to a citizen, will see that the star of her glory shall not grow dim or yellow."

Noting the high Japanese birthrate, John S. Chambers, the state controller, predicted that "by 1949 they will outnumber the white people." In 1924 Congress passed an act that cut down on all nonnorthern European immigration, but also excluded the Japanese.[7]

THE LEGACY OF ANTI-ASIAN MOVEMENTS

The only Asian in the 120-member California legislature during Martha Escutia's first term was Republican Nao Takasugi. (California then had three Asian congressmen.) Takasugi's parents came to the United States in 1903 and ran a grocery store, Asahi Co. Inc. in Oxnard. They were forced into a relocation camp during World War II. Unlike many of those interned, the family did not lose the store and all their possessions. A Latino couple, Ignacio and Emma Carmona, ran it in their absence, taking only a salary. When the Takasugis were released in 1946, the Carmonas turned the store back over to the family. Nearly 50 years later, they were still friends.

Takasugi believes America's attacks on Asians have had long-term effects—and these attacks may explain the low voter turnout among Asians, the least significant voting bloc in California. "The Japanese American population," Takasugi said, "bounced back from their World War II experience." But, because of the internment, he added, "they are reluctant to put themselves in a public light." Asked if the situation against Asians could ever get as bad as in World War II, he said, "I don't think it will happen again." He paused, before adding, "There's always that possibility occurring." But like his colleague Martha he feared this time it might be Latinos who bear the brunt of scapegoating. [Though later he would oppose affirmative action.] "The Latino groups, many remember [the Japanese internment] 50 years ago. They also know what happened was not out of military necessity, but racism and economic jealousy."

ASIANS IN CALIFORNIA TODAY

Hundreds of thousands of Asians arrived after the national origins quotas were abolished in 1965. The speedy growth surprised some, but a natural force that had long been suppressed was finally released.

Almost 40 percent of the Asians in America live in California. In north Orange County, there is a freeway exit for "Little Saigon." San Francisco is still the destination for many, like Maria Ha's family. The city has more Asians than any other large North American city—211,000, who make up 29 percent of a population that is less than half white.

Maria was never subjected to overt racism of any sort growing up. But at her high school a palpable tension belies the apparent calm.

The tan and blue exterior of Lowell High School takes up two city blocks behind a row of pine trees. One sunny spring day the halls were cold from a chill that blew off the nearby Pacific. It was moments before the end of the class period. Outside Room 334, the science and math resource center, someone had taped an article with the headline, "U.S. Workers Putting in More Hours to Stay in Place, Study Shows." The clip was well-thumbed. The students know all too well that only the most energetic will succeed. It was hard enough to make it this far. A complex ever-changing scoring system was used to admit each year's freshman class. When Maria entered, the school looked at 7th grade scores in arithmetic, English, and social studies and 8th grade science scores, and it administered a test much like one used for college admissions. The top score from these three sources was 69, which means a perfect "A" average.

Admissions were also influenced by a court order to desegregate San Francisco's schools that came out of a 1982 lawsuit brought by the National Association for the Advancement of Colored People (NAACP). As a result, no ethnic group can constitute more than 40 percent of the student body. At Lowell, this means the top scores required of each group vary. In effect, students of each ethnicity compete among members of their own group. Chinese Asians must score at least 66. Whites have to get 59, and Latinos and blacks each 56.[8]

If admissions were based solely on ability, Chinese Asians would make up well over 50 percent of Lowell's student body. Whites are now the second largest ethnic group, at 17.3 percent, and Filipinos are third, at just under 10 percent. This regulated diversity was apparent when a bell rang and doors burst open. The corridors filled with the school's 2,600 students. Immediately startling was that they were utterly segregated socially—black youths with other blacks, Asians with Asians, whites with whites, Latinos with Latinos. Cluster after cluster of monoethnic groups walked the halls. A stranger would guess there are four distinct student bodies, and therefore great tension, but students and administrators say there is virtually no racial conflict. The segregation is "natural," largely based on an affinity for one's own kind, not animosity toward others.

This separation is not limited to Lowell—the same self-segregation is found at high schools and universities throughout the state. The splitting is not absolute, but for each case of different races mingling, there seem to be a dozen where they are quite separate. If students do not mix when they are young and presumably more open, one wonders how they will relate to other races when they grow older. As California and the nation become more diverse, is "natural segregation" the inevitable future?

In 1991 this trend caught the attention of the administrators at the University of California at Berkeley. "The Berkeley undergraduate students report pressures to socialize and affiliate with 'one's own kind,'" said a study of this natural segregation. "Blacks, whites, Asians, Native Americans and Chicano/Latinos tend to affiliate, study together and socialize in relatively homogeneous groups."[9]

There are no historic parallels for this development. With integration, blacks and whites were mixed in schools, but one or the other formed a dominant culture. In California, there are many schools where no ethnic group is more than 25 percent, and the separation is often codified in ethnic clubs. At Lowell there are a host of clubs, but no white ones. At Silver Creek High School in San Jose, however, white students, whose population had shrunk to 17 percent, formed a club like those of the blacks, Cambodians, Chinese, Filipinos, Asian Indians, Latinos, South Pacific Islanders, and Vietnamese. When interviewed, blacks said they feared the white club would become a supremacist group, but the most prominent act of the European American club its first year was to hold a lasagna dinner. Silver Creek school officials express concerns that the young people have not formed a united student body, but for most students, apart from the few ethnocentric activists, the separation seldom has political overtones.[10]

At a coffeehouse near Lowell, across Highway 1, Maria explained there is no anger or overt tribalism at the root of the clustering. "It's usually Asians hanging around Asians and Caucasians around Caucasians," said Maria, a shy girl with a round face. "I don't know why, it just happens that way. I mean, you have more in common with them or something. I remember when I was in middle school, I was with lots of different types of people. When I went to Lowell, I met a lot of people that were similar to myself, and I just got real friendly with them."

Even though she associates mostly with Chinese Asians, Maria said she had no use for the special clubs. "When I was a sophomore I joined the Chinese club. But that was totally boring." She said its meetings consisted mostly of gossip or inane conversation. Yet she does speak Cantonese with her friends.

"I like speaking Chinese," she said, adding she's careful not to use it when there are other friends present who only speak English. "It's mostly gossiping and stuff like that."

Maria had heard about the tension over ethnicity at Berkeley. She said she did not have the time or the inclination to get involved with any of it. She knew more hard work would be in order that fall, especially with Berkeley's huge undergraduate classes. But she liked competition. "If I don't have competition, I won't do as well. It just gets me going—I have to beat that guy."

Maria was uncertain of her major. The previous summer, she had an internship as a clerk at the hospital of the University of California at San Francisco, and it sparked a possible career interest. She was also thinking about biochemistry or business.

Her sister is only seven, but the family is making plans for her. "I'll probably have to support her for college," Maria said, certain by then that tuition will cost far more than her sister can earn to pay for it. The summer before Maria entered Berkeley, she worked at two jobs, the San Francisco internship and stocking shelves at a grocery.

THE DIVISION AT BERKELEY

On Maria's first day at Berkeley in 1993, the campus's Sproul Plaza was crowded with student groups vying for members. There was the Committee for Korean students, the Korean Student's Association, the Oakland Asian Student Association, the Filipino Academic Student's Services, the Chinese Student Union, the Asian Business Association, the Society of Hong Kong and China Affairs, the Taiwan Forum, the Chinese Student Association, the Center for Racial Education, the Asian Student Union, the Multicultural Interracial Student's Association, the Raza Recruitment and Retention Center. Outside her Chemistry 1A class Maria said, "I have no time for lunch." She then rushed off to another class. Most days, she would be in class nonstop from 10 in the morning until 4 in the afternoon. Maria would spend most of the first year at Cal in her room studying. "It's like going into this tunnel," she said. She did well, but had wanted to do better. Deciding to major in molecular biology, she took physics, chemistry, math, biology, plus English and an American cultures course that is part of Berkeley's multiculturalism curriculum. And she continued to hold a job.

In the eyes of many whites, Maria was a typical Asian student. She worked very hard and took little time out for fun. White students, when speaking privately, complain that Asian students work too hard, are not well-rounded, are strict academics.

Some whites refer to Berkeley as the "the University of China," said Bob Laird, director of the office of undergraduate admissions and relations at Berkeley.[11] Asians make up 41 percent of the class that will graduate in 1999, compared with 22 percent in 1985. At the University of California at Irvine, which some whites call the "yellow campus," Laird said Asians are 54 percent of the class. At Berkeley and Irvine, affirmative action has kept down the Asian numbers. The biggest affirmative action boost was given to blacks and Latinos, but some whites benefited as well.

"If we just admitted based on academic scores," said Laird, "the school would be 95 percent white and Asian American. Of that group, more than half would be Asian."

There is a reason why there are four times as many Asians at Berkeley than in the general California population, and it is not because they are smarter than whites or blacks or Latinos—the reason is rooted in culture, family structure, and the ambitions of some parents. Referring to this intellectual pressure, one Chinese Asian said the Chinese are the "Jews of Asia." Some Asian leaders caution that the focus on Asian achievement feeds what they call the "model minority" stereotype. They argue all Asians are not rich and successful.

A report by the Asian American Studies Center at UCLA found that the poverty rates among Asians in Los Angeles, San Francisco, and New York were twice as high as for whites. For each Asian household earning more than $75,000, there's one making less than $10,000. Chinese, Indian, and Japanese Asians are the most successful. In California, 77 percent of the Cambodians and Laotian immigrants were on welfare two decades after they first fled their homelands. Nationwide, 30 percent of all Asians were on welfare.[12] Nevertheless, other figures cannot be disputed: Asians divorce less than any other group, have the lowest rate of teen pregnancy, the highest median family incomes. Asian homeless are rare, and Asians do place higher academically at many schools.

This work ethic was at the heart of the debate in California in 1920 that led to the anti-Japanese land initiative. University of California Professor Elwood Mead wrote at the time, "In order to compete with the Japanese, the American farmer . . . must sacrifice rest, recreation and the giving of time to civic interests or the development of the higher life of a community. Only by devoting all of the energy of himself, his wife and children to the hard task of making a living, can he pay the rent and do the other things necessary to withstand the rural competition of the Japanese."[13] Mead cited farmers who quit in the face of the challenge. He did not see virtue in the Japanese work ethic. Seven decades later, the Center for Immigration Studies put a modern spin on this reactionary view. It argued that the best and brightest Asian professionals have flooded the United States to take a disproportionate share of the top positions in computer science, engineering, and medicine. The center sees a "three-tier racial distribution topped by Asian professionals, with non-Hispanic whites as a middle tier, and blacks and Hispanics in the lower tier."[14]

Some whites at UC Berkeley who grumble that there are too many Asian students will at the same time complain about affirmative action that has enabled some blacks (really only a handful, because Berkeley is just some 6 percent black) and Latinos to attend. This two-way argument is confusing: on one hand it implies that high school academic scores alone should rule who gets into the university; on the other hand it says so many Asians, especially those of Chinese heritage, should not be admitted solely on merit. These whites do not want *too* much credit given for ability and hard work. As in so many aspects of the cultural change affecting California, the logic in the debate is seldom consistent.

Maria is neutral. But two of her Lowell High School classmates spoke bitterly about the affirmative action given to whites and others, which they saw as limiting the numbers of qualified Asians; many Asians at Berkeley agree.

The controversy over admissions has sharpened because of the rapid change in the ethnic makeup of the state's universities. For most of its history, Berkeley's student body was composed of the sons and daughters of California's white middle class, whose tax dollars built a premier public university system at the nine UC campuses. It provided a Harvard education—or better, depending on one's view of Harvard—for a Wal-Mart price.

But times changed. In 1978, when California voters passed Proposition 13, the ballot initiative that rolled back homeowner's property taxes, the university was besieged by budget cuts mandated by the legislature.[15] By the early 1990s the system had amassed a nearly $1 billion deficit, and there was a 124 percent increase in tuition over a period of four years. Between 1990 and 1996 annual UC fees jumped from $1,624 to $4,409. In 1959, 65 percent of Berkeley's budget came from the state, compared with 41 percent in 1992. Laird, the admissions spokesman, wonders whether a majority of white voters have lost interest in the institution because they think it is not serving them. Whites form just 30 percent of the class of 1999 at Berkeley, down from about half in the early 1980s.

"I worry about California as a viable society," said Laird. "California is taking that parsimonious 'me and mine' attitude. I don't think we can live in gated communities and control the other 80 percent of the population. It won't work. I can think of places where that approach has failed."

There is a burgeoning demand for education among nonwhites. California's higher education officials estimate that by 2005 students in the state's three-tiered college system will have risen to 2.7 million; they numbered 795,000 in 1989.

"We turned over heaven and hell to take care of the baby boomers," said Patrick Callan, director of the California Higher Education Policy Center, a think tank working to shed light on issues surrounding the state's higher education system. "Now that we've got, instead of the baby boomers, Latinos and African Americans, the idea that we become smaller and more elite is a disaster for our society. I don't think there's any way we can become a more inclusive society if we have a more exclusive higher education system."

Berkeley has long been a driving force in California's economy; the investment returned to the state by its graduates has helped California compete. Nonwhite students will have to continue this role as whites become a smaller fraction of the workforce. Berkeley Chancellor Chang-Lin Tien knows about the value of an affordable public education for immigrants and minorities: he came to the United States in 1956, an immigrant from Taiwan whose family first fled the Japanese in World War II and later the communists. Given the growth of minorities in California, he said, an affordable Berkeley is more vital than ever. "Coming from a minority, disadvantaged background," Tien said, "I feel if we lose this, we lose everything for our society."

PROPOSITION 13

Proposition 13, which economically starved the University of California, came just as the share of minorities in California's population was increasing; in 1970 California was 78 percent white; by 1980 this figure had fallen to 67 percent. The tax rollback that benefited white voters came right about the time minorities had grown to account for over 30 percent of the state. This may be more than a coincidence if one looks at theories about white tolerance of minorities in their midst.

In *American Apartheid: Segregation and the Making of the Underclass*, sociologists Douglas S. Massey and Nancy A. Denton trace the emergence of "hypersegregation."[16] The authors cite a Detroit survey that reveals the amount of cultural change whites will tolerate before they flee. It found that "when the black percentage reached 21%, half of all whites said they would be unwilling to enter, 42% would feel uncomfortable, and 24% would seek to leave. Once the neighborhood reached about one-third black, the limits of racial tolerance were reached for the majority of whites: 73% would be unwilling to enter, 57% would feel uncomfortable, and 41% would try to leave."

At half black, almost two-thirds of the whites would leave. Yet blacks prefer a 50-50 racial mix. This level of tolerance was termed the "tipping scale" by Berkeley instructor Joon Kim, who used the book in a course.

The Detroit study did not look at polyethnic residential racial attitudes, but another study by UCLA sociologists Lawrence Bobo and Camille L. Zubrinsky, though not exactly parallel, gives some understanding of the situation in California. The authors cite a survey of 1,869 Los Angeles households that, not surprisingly, found,

"Blacks are unequivocally at the bottom of the preference hierarchy and whites, just as unequivocally are at the top." [17] Asians said they disliked living near blacks far more than did whites: 46 to 34 percent. There was a hierarchy of residential preference. Whites were the most popular neighbors, followed closely by Asians "with ratings of Hispanics quite close to those found for Blacks." In other words, most residents, regardless of race other than their own, would first prefer to see an Asian neighbor, followed by a Latino, and lastly a black. Whites were the most popular potential neighbors among nonwhites.

In Dana Point, the backlash took off when Latinos reached one-third of the Lantern Village's population. At the state level, the scale tipped in the 1970s, when nonwhites hit one-third of California's population. It is a partial explanation, beyond basic antitax greed, for the collective refusal by white voters to pay for services. Proposition 13 was a stealth law, comparable to the anti-Japanese land law and other punitive measures all rolled into one.

But Proposition 13 further benefited whites, according to L. Ling-Chi Wang, an ethnic studies professor at Berkeley. Wang said that with Proposition 13 homeowners enjoyed vastly reduced taxes. At the same time, their homes continued to shoot up in value. As immigrants poured into the state, whites began "selling these homes to new immigrants at outrageously high prices—and then split. We have the immigrants coming in mostly from Latin America and Asia and the people who are leaving the state are mostly white. The closest analogy that I can draw is the white flight of the Sixties from the cities, because of school integration, crime. Now, in the Nineties, the white flight is actually out of state." The whites who remain, Wang said, "continue to strangle government, to prevent government from investing in the infrastructure. It's a very dark picture." He shook his head. "We might as well place the state university in the state prisons. That's where all the money is going. I think the California higher education system is being dismantled very rapidly. It's a real tragedy that's unfolding."

Wang had anecdotally noticed that white islands were forming, just as I had found studying census data. He views them as control centers, where whites vote to serve their own interests, and wonders how long this can last:

They will continue to hang on and to reap as much benefit as possible before they get the hell out of here. If we don't change the political leadership fast enough for the minorities who want their future to be in California, we will become a third world country. I see [us] racing against time. I just think that the sooner that minorities get into the power structure, the better chance we have of doing something about the future of the state.

Minorities, however, are not moving quickly into the political arena. While Latinos vote in small numbers in relation to their proportion of the population, the Asian vote is equally minuscule. Though Asians outnumber blacks by one-third in California, they are the least politically active ethnic group, forming the smallest segment of voters among the four major race and ethnic groups— 4 percent on average. Latinos and blacks, which combined make up as much as 17 percent of the active voters, are likely to vote Democratic, and thus their smaller fractions have more power to swing elections and counter the white suburban vote. The Asian vote, however, is fragmented between parties.[18]

"You look at San Francisco," Wang said. "It's about 711,000 people, and the [number of] registered voters is slightly over 400,000. I would say that maybe about between 40,000 and 50,000 Asian Americans [are registered]. And then when you look at these 40,000 or so registered voters, they are basically split three ways: Democrat, Republican, and a growing number who decline to state. The Asian American population is very bifurcated. Half of them are middle-class and upper-middle-class, the other half lower-class."

In addition to splitting party allegiance, Asians are so geographically dispersed that they do not form solid voting blocks in districts like Latinos, blacks, and whites. Moreover, the bulk of Asians are simply apathetic and do not vote at all.

"There's a very complex historical and contemporary reason," Wang explained.

Most of the Asians who are here come from countries that have no political participation. Given history, the only time that Chinese peasants come into contact with the government is [for] two things: when they come around to the village to collect taxes, and the other time when they come around to take away your sons.

All they want is to have shelter, three meals a day, be able to bring up their children. The Chinese endure hardship. They work hard, rarely complain. It's only when you strip away even these most minimal living standards that they rebel. That's where the genius of Mao came in. He discovered how to work the peasants. It was the peasants who led him to victory in 1949.

Thus far in California, no democratic version of Mao has surfaced to turn Asians out at the polls.

Despite San Francisco's long-standing Asian presence that dates to the Gold Rush, no Asian had held a seat on the 11-member San Francisco Board of Supervisors until 1973. George Chinn was appointed by Mayor Joseph Alioto, but Chinn lost an election nine months later. Three other Asians were appointed but never won election. It was not until 1994 that the first Asian was elected in the city—Mabel Teng.

Many reasons besides low voter turnout account for the failure of Asians to gain power: funding mechanisms of the two political parties tend to lean toward whites, and the at-large election process has diluted the Asian vote; there has been no heavily populated Asian district from which to elect a member. District elections tend to create more opportunities for minorities. But opportunities for whites to help Asians are repeatedly squandered, Wang said. When Frank Jordan became San Francisco mayor in 1992, his first appointment to the Board of Supervisors was his goddaughter, a white woman.

Wang pointed out that the anti-Asian bias extends to state politics. Pete Wilson was criticized by liberal Democrats for nominating only white men to the 18-member Board of Regents that runs the University of California. The Democrats said any more such nominees would be dead on arrival. So when two openings came up, Wilson named conservative minorities—Lester Lee, an immigrant from China, and Ward Connerly, a black developer who later championed the dismantling of affirmative action in the university system. When the state Senate voted on the nominations, Lee lost. Lee was the first regent who failed to win confirmation since Leland Stanford in 1883. Later that same day, Connerly was unanimously approved.[19]

"There's racism involved here and I'll tell you why, and I'm not

just name-calling," said Wang. He explained both men were conservative Republicans, which Democrats should have expected, but
that "none of the liberal Democrats could bring themselves to cast
a vote against a black." It was easier to vote against an Asian. "My
point is that we don't count in the state of California."

Wang noted another seemingly minor area of intolerance: store
signs, especially when in Korean or Chinese. In small to midsize
cities, these signs are usually written in both English and Spanish
or Asian characters; in the largest cities, however, it is fairly common for store owners to forgo English translation. Some find this
offputting, but the message does not seem to be "white people not
allowed." Open wallets are not turned away. Proprietors just do
not expect much business from other quarters. Yet in Monterey
Park, the city of 60,000 east of Los Angeles that is 56 percent
Asian—the only Asian majority city in the state—the town's leaders, the majority of them non-Asian, tried to ban Chinese-language
signs.[20] They also tried to halt the donation of a large number of
Chinese-language books by the Taiwan government to the local library.

The same kind of outrage is not expressed over Spanish signs.
Asians also fare worse than other ethnic groups in bearing the
brunt of jokes in bad taste. Typical is a prank played by KKXX-FM,
a station in Bakersfield, a city in the oil and farm country at the
south end of the 300-mile-long Central Valley. Both Bakersfield
and Fresno to the north have seen an influx of Asians. Fresno has
35,000 Hmong, the largest population outside of Laos. Others,
such as Asian Indians, have bought markets up and down the Central Valley; some Sikhs own farms, and it is not uncommon to see
turban-headed men driving tractors down the road.

To promote its morning "zoo-format" talk show, KKXX-FM in
early 1992 played a cut from a show in which the white female deejay called a young white girl.[21] The deejay instructed her to hang
on while she telephoned a local convenience store picked from the
phone book. As the phone rang, the deejay told the girl to ask if
"Abdul" was there—the point of the prank being to prove that all
markets are owned by Asian Indians with this name.

The merchant answered the phone, saying "hello" with a heavy
accent.

"Is Abdul there?" the listener asked.

The store owner paused. "Hello?" he said again.

"Is Abdul there?"

"This is Abdul," said the owner. The deejay screamed with delight. "Yes!" she said.

It is difficult to imagine the same station playing a similar "joke" on a black store, using, say, the name "Leroy."

ASIAN CULTURE VERSUS OTHER CULTURES

Two points must be kept in mind when looking at Asian culture. The first is that the very nature of the term is so broad as to be almost meaningless. Asians are far more diverse than Latinos. There are vast differences between Cambodians, Chinese, Filipinos, Indians, Indonesians, Japanese, Koreans, Vietnamese, Thai, and others. Unity cannot be assumed. In 1991, for instance, Chinese Asian architects and engineers in San Francisco wanted to block Asian Indians from being considered a preferred minority category when bidding for city contracts.[22]

The second point is that there are two types of Asians, no matter what the point of origin. One is wholly Westernized. On the telephone, they sound white—in person they act white. The other is very Eastern—they are new arrivals, or have maintained the old culture into the third generation. The overt politeness of the Japanese is well known; honor is valued at all costs, even in times of stress. It is common in Japan to see both drivers in a car accident apologize for being wrong. Some Chinese Asians are also very reticent in the presence of whites; they are almost maddeningly deferential.

Iris Chang, a writer living in Santa Barbara, said that the actions of Chinese Asians around whites "drives her crazy." Among themselves, she said she has often found great division and argument. All it takes to quiet things is for a white to enter the room. Berkeley Professor Troy Duster notes that for some Asian women in the classroom, the ultimate undermining of respect would be to challenge the professor. Duster says one has to change the notion of "aggressive brightness," in which the students deemed best are those who leap to offer answers ahead of others in the class. Duster said if he had not changed his teaching views to accommodate the cultural differences of Asian women, he would not be "delivering education in any substantive way."

Whenever I spoke to Maria, she was shy, not quite as reticent as some of Duster's Asian students, but more of the Eastern world. There was a line she would not cross. She would meet only in public places and would not allow her parents to be interviewed. Iris Chang was not surprised that Maria sheltered her family and friends. Iris, a third-generation Chinese, said the cultural bifurcation is common among newcomers and sometimes extends into subsequent generations.

Adaptation is not always easy. Iris's cousin, Bernard Chang, was familiar with the "banana complex—Asian on the outside, white on the inside." A young doctor whose parents had come from Taiwan, he grew up in a very white area of Los Angeles. His parents forbade the speaking of Chinese in their Brentwood home, and he had gone to the elite Pacific Palisades High School.

"I felt more comfortable with Caucasians than I did with Asians," he said. "I was around Caucasians at school; I was like one of maybe two Asians. All of my friends until college were Caucasian." He was not sure which culture he belonged to, and this sent him into a period of introspection, in which he found some peace.

For many Americans, however, Asian culture is synonymous with the images of Chinatown: the crowded streets and cramped apartment buildings; the back alleys with occasional patches of graffiti in Chinese characters, strangely beautiful, but for all one knows could say "Die Yankee pig."

Maria lives amid this un-Westernized environment, but many Asians are like Bernard's parents who head straight for the white suburbs. Maria's parents are friends with one such family in the Bay area suburb of Concord, and their way of life confuses Maria.

"Usually after a few generations, a lot of people become, like, whitewashed," Maria said. "I got offended last time I was visiting my Mom's friends. They have young children and were speaking English to them. They say they hate speaking Chinese. [But]I think if I grew up in the suburbs, I would be like that. I tend to be between it all. I go into little groups, but I cross over. When I grow up, I would like my children to take Chinese. It's good to be bilingual. I feel it's better to have heritage other than like white, Western views."

Yet she allowed that she has irreversibly changed.

"I've already lost a lot of traditional ideals," she said. "I don't think I'm like a typical Chinese girl anymore. Moving away from home, that wasn't accepted. Now, my mom doesn't care about that. My Mom's family was a family toward men—they favored guys. I really disagree with that. I don't want to keep that tradition. There's always a lot of Eastern ideas still in the Asian community. I think Confucian ethics come into it: you work hard, you don't cheat, you do everything right, get a good education. I hope I keep some of that stuff. Not all. Some people keep the best."

In many white cultural islands, Asians are the largest minority. These Asians present one of the dichotomies of California's mix of cultures, given the state's hateful past toward Asians. Even as white voters separate themselves from minorities, there is also great acceptance of Asians. Personal columns in the weekly newspapers in the Bay area and Los Angeles reveal a fair number of black and white crossovers, but these are eclipsed by Asians seeking whites and vice versa. Iris, for instance, is married to a white man, and her cousin Bernard is married to a white woman.

One theory offered by *Sacramento Bee* columnist Dan Walters, who has written about cultural change in California for many years, is that the state has evolved into a prototype of America's have and have-not society. Many Asians belong to the "have" group, and because California is divided along class lines, whites and Asians find much in common. Both have similar values toward work and family. The hope is that given economic clout, two widely different cultures can coexist and thrive. The bad news voiced by Walters is his fear that many blacks and Latinos will sink lower into an economic abyss, separated even further from the white–Asian overclass.[23]

Maria ended the 1993–94 academic year at Berkeley with a 3.8 grade average. She continued to hold a job and was talking about going to summer school so she could graduate early and not incur more debt. She had switched to optometry—she could complete her entire education in 7 years, versus 10 for medicine. She had no time for any student groups. "I was mostly in my room, for the midterm and the finals," she said. She found herself living in a small world. As at Lowell High School, most of her friends were Asian: "All my friends are from Lowell. There's over a hundred students at Berkeley from my year. I know around 20 or 30 of them, and that's my little social group. It's like when I already have friends, it's hard for me to go out and open up."

PART TWO

7

The New Wedge

The period between 1993 and 1994 was as pivotal as previous an-tibrown waves in which the state shaped national policy. The groundswell of anger against Latino immigrants echoed across the country, just as the virulence against Asians had done earlier. California became the seedbed for the immigration backlash, which was rapidly followed by the revolt against affirmative action. One would lead to the other.

Many on the left in 1993 dismissed as ludicrous the possibility that California could come down so harshly on Latino immigrants. They felt the state was simply too liberal. This was the view on college campuses and among leaders like Martha Escutia. But most optimists either did not know the state's long history regarding race matters or thought it was ancient history with no bearing on the present.

Critical ingredients were present to fuel the xenophobia. As in the past when the state erupted against nonwhites, the economy was rotten. The state was mired in a recession, mostly because the defense industry, which had long made California recession-proof, was reeling from cutbacks in the aftermath of the Soviet Union's collapse. The East-West power struggle had been good to the state. In the last half of the 1980s, one-fifth of all defense contracts went to California, for an infusion of $120 billion. Even though inflation was checked, a house that sold for $120,000 in Orange County in 1980 was worth $300,000 eight short years later.

But by 1993 the good times were a distant memory and Governor Wilson was on hand to blame. He sunk to the lowest approval rating of any California governor in 30 years—just 15 percent of the public gave him good marks, according to the California Field Poll.[1] With just one year until he faced reelection, Wilson had to do something. Like many politicians, he had used crime to appeal to voters fearful of violence—"getting tough" was hardly a new approach. California had begun a prison-building spree, and record numbers of inmates were behind bars. Immigration was a possible target.

Wilson had raised the issue in 1991 when he blamed immigrants for "taking" services. But his message was largely aimed at the federal government from which he wanted more money for the state's share of immigration, both legal and illegal. Wilson's pollsters could see the large mass of worried and angry white voters in California's suburbs.

Any politician who assailed immigrants risked losing votes among Latinos. But in California you could win without the entire 8 to 10 percent of the active Latino electorate. Contrary to the hopes of Chicano activists, the community is quite conservative—some Latinos dislike illegals, viewing them as competition. Nor would Wilson be harmed by black and Asian voters. There is little love lost between working-class Latinos and blacks, who compete for the same jobs; Asians are so politically diverse that many would certainly go for Wilson. Multicultural California is split not just along white–other race lines, as any astute politician knows.

What did Wilson have to lose? In 1993 his approval rating was so low that one poll showed him 23 points behind Democrat Kathleen Brown, who would challenge him in 1994. Brown, the daughter and sister of two of the state's former governors, was the heir apparent to the Brown "dynasty."

The risk was that by using immigration Kathleen Brown and progressives could charge Wilson with racism. If this stuck, it could alienate a significant number of whites, Nixon's predicament when he used busing as a wedge issue. Wilson had to walk a narrow line.

There was also the matter of Wilson's personal beliefs. Ronald

Reagan followed deep ideological lines throughout his political career. Wilson bent with the times. When he was a state assemblyman and mayor of San Diego, he was known as a moderate and even liberal Republican, when that was what was needed to win an election in the 1960s and 1970s. For nearly his entire political career he had supported affirmative action. Reagan's ideology was at least consistent, said John Whitehurst, a campaign spokesman for Brown. "He gave the same speech in 1976 as he did in 1984." By the 1990s, Wilson had shed the San Diego moderate Republican label and was rapidly growing more conservative.

Martha Escutia's seatmate John Vasconcellos was, like Wilson, elected to the assembly in 1966. He witnessed this change. He said Wilson was "among the most progressive of the freshman Republicans in my class." But by the time Wilson returned to California after his stint in the U.S. Senate, he was different. Vasconcellos thinks Wilson's rightward tilt came in 1991, when Otto Bos, his 47-year-old communications director, died of a heart attack. "With Bos by his side, he was magnanimous. With Otto not at his side, he has people around him who [have] him inclined to be mean."

Wilson had surrounded himself with other former Nixon and Reagan people and their influence was strong. One of them was George Gorton, whose Republican roots date to 1972, when Nixon emissary Jeb Magruder recruited him to be national college director for the Committee to Reelect the President. Gorton pushed Wilson to hit hard on immigration and other issues.[2]

Others saw Wilson's shift to the right earlier. LaQuita Robbins, one of his first affirmative action hires in San Diego, where she worked in the Human Relations Commission, saw this in 1972. The Republican National Committee abruptly switched its convention from San Diego to Miami because of the fear of antiwar protests, among other reasons. Wilson took the decision personally, said Robbins. Susie Davenport, another of the city hall minority hires, said, "He was angry. He figured that the liberal Pete that we knew was no longer going to [get him] where he wanted to go. Minorities simply could no longer help him accomplish his goals."

Whoever the real Pete Wilson was, in early 1993 it was clear he was in trouble. Without something definitive, he was going to lose the governorship. It may have come down to simple survival, the same thing that motivated Arkansas Governor Orval E. Faubus in

1957 when he defied the federal government on desegregation. Faubus was the fairly liberal son of a socialist. He had never before used race as in issue, but he invoked it as a maul to shore up support from angry hill whites when he refused to allow blacks in white schools. It worked—he became the first Arkansas governor to serve more than two terms—even though the state was shamed when President Dwight Eisenhower had to send in federal troops. "Survival is the first law," Faubus later told an interviewer.[3]

On August 9, 1993, Wilson plunged into Faubusian—if not Faustian—politics. In a Los Angeles press conference, he announced that illegal immigrants were the root of the state's problems. In an "open letter to the president of the United States on behalf of the people of California," Wilson said illegals were bleeding the state dry. He called on Congress to pass a Constitutional amendment denying citizenship to the children born here to illegals and to repeal federal mandates requiring states to provide for health, education, and other benefits.[4] His message was carried the next day in a full-page ad in the *New York Times*. He continued his attack in the following days, calling for the use of troops to keep out Mexicans. Martha Escutia went into a frenzy. Immediately after the announcement, she paced around her Sacramento office sputtering about his arrogance. She recounted his demand that Mexicans be allowed to cross the border to pick crops when he was a U.S. senator in 1986. "After all," Martha said, "he was the one that was arguing that agribusiness needed a source of cheap labor. He assumed from the very beginning that the reason they came here was because of jobs. Now in the 1990s he's saying that they come here because of public services?"

In interviews with the press Martha and other Democrats reminded the public that when he was a U.S. senator Wilson had literally invited some of the very people he was now blaming—as many as one million of them. Wilson responded by publicly asking Democrats to "kiss my rear end."[5] Within a week, his approval rating shot up seven points, to 22 percent.

Wilson may have played the savvy politician, responding to deep emotions in the electorate, but he was also shaping California's approach to its new multicultural society.

THE FAILURE OF PROGRESSIVES

On the eve of Wilson's attack, Eddie Cortez, the mayor of Pomona, was driving his pickup truck when he noticed Immigration and Naturalization Service agents questioning some Latinos. Cortez had heard complaints about citizens being roughed up in raids and picked up because of their skin color. Some, like him, were third-generation American citizens. Before he could investigate, the INS agents pulled him over and threatened to arrest him and throw him in the van with the others. Only after he proved he was mayor did the agents back off.[6]

When the story of Eddie Cortez reached Sacramento and the assembly's Latino caucus, Martha and her colleagues plotted a strategy. To them, Cortez's experience was a possible key to the future for their Latino constituents—or themselves. If a conservative mayor elected on a law-and-order platform could be harassed, any of them was vulnerable to heightened racism.

The Latino caucus's immediate goal was to convince the leadership of national Latino groups and other progressives that a battle with national implications was about to begin. But when Martha and her chief of staff Suzanne Wierbinski contacted these groups, the two were ignored. The threat just did not seem that imminent. At this point in 1993, Proposition 187 had not yet been announced and Wilson's attack was in its infancy. Both immigration and affirmative action had cropped up over the years, but the attacks were easily beaten back. Both across the nation and in California, Democrats managed to kill reactionary bills in congressional and legislative committees.

Progressive groups' complacent disregard of California's rising xenophobia would prove catastrophic. But a bigger problem was the way the coalition of left groups, progressives, and Democrats had stumbled before the Republican racial-based onslaught since the 1960s. In *Chain Reaction,* Thomas and Mary Edsall outline "the unintentionally cooperative role" that the national Democratic party and liberals played "in shaping presidential politics to the advantage of the GOP."[7] It was as if the Democrats were working to drive away working-class white voters.

The Edsalls cite liberals' pursuit of policies such as busing to achieve school integration. Most whites did not like busing and polls showed that blacks were fairly evenly split on the issue. Also liberals were unwilling to deal honestly with poverty and race. The Edsalls point to Daniel Patrick Moynihan who authored the 1965 report "The Negro Family: The Case for National Action" when he was an assistant secretary in the Department of Labor. The report was savaged by liberals and black leaders because in it Moynihan argued that the decline of the black family had to be dealt with if civil rights were to advance. (Donald Northcross would struggle with the same problem almost three decades later.) Though not termed "politically correct" in those days, the harsh criticism showed that it was impolitic to discuss the crumbling black family structure; the debate was ceded to conservative writers such as Charles Murray, who became a Republican darling in the 1980s and 1990s when he attacked the welfare state and the intelligence level of blacks.

What happened in California following Wilson's announcement became a textbook example of the continuing failure of progressives to respond to the Republican domination of race as an issue. But in their defense, they were faced with a new situation in a new society: never before had racial politics been played out in such a culturally diverse environment. In most of the country, the black–white racial political division was difficult enough to cope with. California's multiple race and class society is vastly more complicated, and it is easier to divide and conquer than it is to unite. This fact alone made combating Wilson difficult.

The Latino caucus also had to contend with the apartheid-like voting of whites. Liberals had to get nonwhites out to vote, or somehow appease white voters attracted to Wilson. The former would take years of organizing, and the latter seemed impossible in the short term; such a feat would have to counter two-and-a-half decades of bungling by those opposed to Republican race baiting.

Martha and the other handful of Latino leaders faced an impossible task, and they had to act fast. The Latino caucus emerged from their meetings with a 13-point plan that relied on education and reason. In part, the plan called for stiffer penalties for smugglers of illegals, stepped-up enforcement by the INS against visitors who overstay visas, and increased enforcement of existing labor laws.[8] The caucus hoped these measures would allay white fears. It was their best shot, and they unveiled it at a press conference two weeks after Wilson's announcement.

THE DISASTROUS PRESS CONFERENCE

There was a large media turnout for the unveiling of the Latino lawmakers' plan in Room 1090, where statehouse press conferences are held. Martha and her fellow Latino assembly members stood on the stage, lined up awkwardly behind Richard Polanco, the senior member of the caucus. Martha fidgeted beneath the bright television lights.

Polanco read from a carefully crafted statement:

> We do not believe in open borders, we do not support noncitizen voting rights, we do not support illegal immigrants receiving welfare, which is already prohibited by federal law. We need proposals that are well thought-out, and that are realistic. We need to curtail illegal immigration and ensure that these efforts do not translate into discrimination against people of color.

When Polanco finished, Martha told the reporters how her grandfather had come to pick crops as an invited guest worker. Then as now, she said, Mexicans came for jobs, not welfare. She said enforcement of existing laws would be enough. (At that time, under the supposedly tough employer sanctions approved with the 1986 immigration reform act she had helped influence, *no* employer in Los Angeles had yet been busted under its provisions.)[9] Immigration laws were not being enforced, Martha said, and there were enough measures on the books. She noted pointedly that Latinos were not the only illegals: in 1991 alone, 320,000 other people, many European, overstayed visas.

"If you are rich, you hop on a plane and overstay your visa illegally," Martha said. "If you are poor, you cross a river. I beg of all of you to please start analyzing the issue from a more balanced perspective."

Martha's argument made perfect sense, and other speakers repeated her views. The last comments came from Cruz Bustamante of Fresno, who had won office in a special election—he was the eighth and newest member of the Latino caucus and the first to be elected north of the Tehachapi Mountains that separate Los Angeles and southern California from the upper two-thirds of the state. Bustamante's story was similar to Martha's—he was the son of farmworkers who had worked hard and sent him to college.

He spoke kindly of illegal immigrants. "They come here to provide themselves a better lifestyle," he said, his voice hoarse from a cold. "But in doing so, they're providing all of us a better lifestyle. I think we have to as leaders somehow separate the emotional from what is actually taking place. I don't think that by automatically closing off the borders, that's what people really want. I think what people want is something that is fair."

His voice grew stronger as he told how hard immigrants work and how they are vital to his district, a Central Valley farm center. "In the area that I represent, we could not conduct business without the immigrant. It's on the sweat and the hard backbreaking work that they do—that none of you do, or ever will do—that picks those crops, that provides food."

Bustamante continued the agricultural lesson, eliciting laughs when he informed the reporters that the fruits and vegetables do not originate inside their local grocery: "They come from an area that you basically put a lot of water on and you put a lot of prayer into the land, and you put people on the land who are willing to do the backbreaking work to put those products on trucks that eventually get to those supermarkets. We all benefit."

"Can I ask a question?" one reporter said.

"Yes sir."

"It seems like you're trying to have it both ways. On the one hand, you say [we] shouldn't have an open border and we should keep illegal immigrants out. On the other hand, you're praising what they do. So which is it? Should they be here or not?"

Other reporters murmured agreement.

"What I'm telling you, sir, is that my district cannot exist without a flow of people."

"Illegal people?" the reporter asked. "Should they be here in the first place?"

Martha stared straight ahead poker-faced as her colleague stumbled deeper, but Polanco and Assemblywoman Hilda Solis looked stricken.

"There is a dichotomy," Bustamante said. "There is something that is both sweet and sour in terms of the issue. It is something I believe that we have to make allowances for people to be here, to be able to maintain the standard of living. So am I trying to have it both ways? Yes. Absolutely."

Reporters gawked. Bustamante was not being political. He was not playing the game. He was being honest.

This was cause for a united assault. Bustamante probably would have preferred being in an Amazon swimhole with a hoard of predatory fish.

"People should have a right to come here illegally—is that what you are saying?" one reporter asked, rising above the blast of questions.

Bustamante, now sweating, grew testy.

"I'm telling you that people have a right to immigrate to this country."

"Legally or illegally?"

"I would prefer legally."

"But you would accept illegally?"

"My district requires it."

"Requires it? What do you mean?"

"Have you ever been on a farm, sir? Have you?"

"Yes."

"Then you understand basically what takes place on a farm. You understand there are people who have to work on that farm to produce the product. Those folks do not come from the welfare rolls, as some think they should. They do not come from our colleges."

Someone called on Polanco to clarify his original comments. Polanco stuttered—he said Assembly Speaker Willie Brown would first make a statement. Reporters laughed. They waited to see how this master of spin handled the evolving disaster.

"I represent an agridistrict," Brown said of his San Francisco district, stepping into the glare of the klieg lights. There was laughter. "Many apartments in San Francisco have grow lights." More laughter. Brown made a few more jokes, and then grew serious. He said the Democrats were going to counter the ill-founded immigration proposals by pushing asset forfeiture as a means of stopping illegal immigration. If someone is caught hiring the undocumented, they would lose the farm or hotel. This announcement came as a surprise—it had not been planned.

Brown suggested that the state might confiscate the Matterhorn if Disneyland used illegal immigrants to work on it. The Walt Disney Co. at the time was being targeted for a $394,840 fine by the INS for violating laws requiring the documentation of a worker's immigration status, though the company was not accused of hiring illegal workers.[10]

"My guess is they would never use undocumented persons if [they] had to forfeit the Matterhorn," Brown said. Then he addressed Chinese immigration: "Instead of simply stopping those ships midocean or wherever you stop them, take the boat! I've been interested in owning a boat for years."

Reporters chortled.

"The whole concept of asset forfeiture says if you are engaging in those kinds of activities, you ought to be penalized and you ought to pay the supreme price. It will be other than this one African American and these several Latinos up here; I'm telling you, you'll see a whole lot of white folks up here when you start talking about asset forfeiture."

The 13-point plan had been blown to pieces by Bustamante's bumbling and Brown's surprise announcement. As an afterthought, Brown said the debate was reaching the "ugly side" and he implored the press to educate the public on its complexity.

"You're going to reduce those politicians to the simplistic nerds that they are on this issue," Brown said in a reference to Governor Wilson without using his name. "And when that happens, those simplistic nerds are going to simply disappear and start some other thing that simplistic nerds do to get reelected."

It was foolish to assume reporters would translate the message or would have time or space to mention that Bustamante's position was a mirror of Wilson's 1986 views. Out of the two dozen or so journalists at the press conference, just one—from the *California Journal*—got the deeper story.[11] The television that night and the newspapers the next day contained nothing of the caucus members' response to Wilson. The stories showed only confusion, Bustamante's stumbling, and a hastily announced proposal.

The caucus never meant to float the idea of asset forfeiture. It was an arrow in the quiver of the Democrats with which to threaten Wilson's business friends with punishment; the possibility of such a bill might make Wilson back off if he persisted with his immigration attacks.

Brown shot the arrow early and in haste. And like most hastily shot arrows, it flew wild. Big business would never allow the bill through. The one constant throughout history is that business has never been at the center of combating illegal immigration. Yet within days the bill started on its course through the legislature, where it later met its death.

At the bungled press conference, the Latino caucus lost any chance of controlling the immigration debate. From that point on, Wilson owned the issue. Before Wilson made illegals the center of his campaign, the anti-immigration sentiment was largely a local political issue, limited to places such as Dana Point. Now his attacks made national headlines. And California's U.S. senators, both of whom were Democrats, tried to out-Wilson Wilson. Barbara Boxer called for National Guard troops at the border. Diane Feinstein wanted a border-crossing toll to pay for increased enforcement.

WHO WILL DO THE WORK?

Assemblyman Cruz Bustamante's burst of frankness may have been unwise, but he got at a truth few Americans want to admit. Cheap immigrant labor built the nation. American business of the last century wanted black slaves to pick cotton, Chinese labor to build the transcontinental railroad, Eastern Europeans to work in the coal mines and in the steel mills. In the computer age, it still wanted underpaid brown-skinned people to pick crops, clean hotels, run the back of restaurants.

Not long after the Latino Caucus's press conference, Bill Shepherd had his own opinion about what should be done to fill low-wage jobs—change the work ethic of America's youth.

Two weeks earlier, Bill said he was in Madison, Wisconsin, doing consulting work. "I felt something strange, and then it hit me. There were no minorities. It was very European. It felt so strange. It was unimaginable. When I went to a hamburger place, everyone who worked there was a young white kid. In the hotel, the maids were white people—people who speak English. You order a burger and fries, and you get it. If young people are able to do these jobs in Wisconsin, why isn't it true in Orange County?"

Because Mexicans now have these jobs, Bill said they have low status: they are seen as "Mexican work." For whites and blacks, these jobs are seen as beneath their status.

"The biggest argument I've heard is we have to have these people because they do jobs other people won't do," Bill said. "I haven't accepted that. It's reversible."

Bill's solution is to limit welfare and to change the American attitude toward work. He feels many Americans have grown lazy. It is a good point. Why aren't whites and blacks rushing to fill jobs out in the fields, or making beds in Dana Point's hotels? Bill's idea, however, conflicts with a long history of the views of Americans toward "undesirable" work. It is common to think that in a time past, before welfare and the New Deal, the virtue of hard work was inherent in all Americans. But history contradicts this.

In a 1929 article in the *North American Review* about Mexicans in the United States, University of California professor S. J. Holmes quoted a labor contractor saying, "I have been an employer of labor for many years, running as high as 20,000 per year for farm operations. If I had to depend upon the class of white labor I have had experience with, I would quit tomorrow. . . . These editors and sob sisters who are talking about Los Angeles being full of unemployed Americans who could get work if it were not for the Mexicans never tried to recruit a threshing crew or fruit pickers among them or they would be singing in a different key." [12]

With the exception of the Dust Bowl migrants who came a few years after Holmes wrote this, the bulk of American citizens have never been willing to do stoop labor. It is human nature to move up, not regress. For those who insist that white Americans from the lower class should simply accept their fate and work these jobs ignores a very basic trait of the American capitalist system—the imperative to move up economically. A mantra of the middle class is that one's children will do better. It is also human nature to look down on "inferior" people. In the South of slave days, dirt-eating hill whites felt above blacks. When blacks moved north, blue-collar whites could feel superior, even if their position was only marginally better. This dynamic occurs elsewhere. In southern Mexico, illegal Guatemalans are hired to work the coffee plantations and are paid less than the local Mexicans, who view them as a caste below.[13]

One could argue that if we paid higher wages for field and hotel work more Americans might be willing to take these jobs. But in the case of farmwork, we would have $2 tomatoes and sugar at $5 per pound, a situation that consumers would find intolerable. Perhaps Bill is correct, Americans have grown more lazy. But until those who are most vocal about getting rid of immigrants themselves are willing to do the work they do—or pay more for food and services—nothing will change. The day that unemployed investment bankers or even blue-collar workers enter the fields or make hotel beds is the day that Americans will have any moral argument to seal the borders.

Six months after California voters approved Proposition 187 to keep Mexicans out of the state, the Nisei Farmers League of Fresno, which represents 1,000 farmers, urged the U.S. Congress to pass a new Bracero program to bring in more Mexicans.[14] The growers conceded that half their present workers were illegal and that there was a surplus of labor, but they feared the immigration backlash would harm them in the future. The farmers were derided. Martha wondered out loud if it would not be more honest if America just admitted it needed cheap labor and brought back the Bracero program to legally import Mexican nationals, as had been the case when her grandfather came. At least some control would be in place. And it would be more honest than our wanting their labor while we attack them for coming.

THE BACKLASH GROWS

Some Republicans had long pushed bills in the legislature to combat immigration. These bills often came from Orange County members who seemed to go out of their way to antagonize Latinos. (In 1988, for instance, Assemblyman Curt Pringle was in a close race and under the guise of a fear that illegals would swarm to the polls to throw out Pringle, the Republican Party posted uniformed "poll guards" at 20 voting locations supposedly to ensure there was no fraud, but Latino American citizens were intimidated and some did not vote.)[15] The Republican bills that targeted illegal immigrants always died, unable to break through the Democrat-controlled committees. But many Democrats felt the heat of Wilson's rising poll numbers, and suddenly, several bills were poised to make it to the floor of the assembly.

The first, which came to the floor exactly one month after Wilson's press conference, having passed the state Senate, would require proof of citizenship to obtain a driver's license. Martha went into the assembly that morning knowing the odds were stacked against her—some in the Latino caucus had switched their votes in favor of the bill. In fact, Latino lawmaker Louis Caldera was its main sponsor in the Assembly. This development was made more bitter because Caldera is the cousin of Leo Briones, Martha's fiancé.

The driver's license bill happened to be preceded by a measure that would give state recognition for a holiday in honor of César Chávez. "César Chávez was our Gandhi," Martha said to the chamber as she introduced the bill. She said he fought for equal pay for the Latinos who pick the crops the nation eats. "He's alive in my grandfather," Martha told her colleagues. "Every time I see my grandfather who is dark-skinned, who has Indian features, who has white hair, who came here to pick the crops, I think of César Chávez. Please vote for this bill." The measure passed 42-23, along party lines, with Republicans in opposition. Caldera introduced the driver's license bill, and in a sharp departure from the Latino caucus, said he supported it as a wise alternative that would "help enforce our immigration laws." He tried to counter the negative reaction to his favoring the bill by adding that he essentially supported SB 976 because it might help forestall a more serious racial backlash.

Martha responded. In a low voice, she countered that the bill was dangerous because it was a first step in what could be a rash of bills that would do nothing to stop immigration while fueling xenophobia. She said undocumented persons would continue to drive without a license, endangering others. Why not ensure they were licensed? "This bill does nothing to curb illegal immigration. In our false search for true immigration reform, we are opening up a Pandora's box. And let me tell you, look at the bottom of Pandora's box. Perhaps now we'll have to show residency in order to use public parks. Will we have to show residency to use museums?

Guess what, members. People do not come to the United States to drive a car. I am ready to discuss illegal immigration reform, but let's keep our intellectual integrity. Immigrants such as my grandfather come here to work. If there is a demand, there will be a supply. It's a very simple economic theory that's at work here. Do you remember the movie, *Field of Dreams?* When Kevin Costner was told, if you build it, they will come? The same thing applies here. If you hire them, they will come. But for immigrants . . . it's not coming to a field of dreams, but to a field of nightmares."

Her voice trembled. "I think our country right now is treading on thin ice. Voting for this bill is going to lead us down a slippery slope and at the bottom of that slope, members, we have big brotherism and race discrimination. Discrimination, because in the final analysis only people who look like me, and speak like me, will be asked to show proof of residency. I cannot help the fact that I have dark hair, dark eyes, and I'm Latina. I cannot help the fact that I speak with an accent.

"I sincerely believe that our society will be judged by how we treat our most vulnerable and our most disenfranchised. And frankly, as a rookie legislator, in my first nine months here, I don't know whether we are at the apex or at the decline of our civilization, by the targets that we are choosing. Last year the target was welfare mothers. This year the target is immigrants. Members, when are we going to stop target practice? Let me tell you what kind of a house we're building here by passing SB 976—we are building a house of cards! It's going to tumble down on us! I urge a no vote."

As Martha's voice trailed, the chamber was silent, rare in a place that usually resembles recess at a sixth-grade schoolyard.

Others spoke, including a Republican who called Martha's fears of discrimination "bogeyman arguments." The last speaker was Martha's seatmate and supporter John Vasconcellos. He made a bitter observation about the changing demographics. "The state before long will be no white majority. I say the sooner the better. They may treat us better than we've treated them."

Willie Brown, standing beneath a life-sized oil painting of Abraham Lincoln, called for the vote. There were 53 for, 13 against.

As Martha left the assembly chambers she said, "It's the beginning of the end." The gate had indeed opened for other bills aimed at cracking down on Latinos and immigrants.

NATIVISM

The debate over illegal immigration as defined by Governor Wilson and other California conservatives has a historic ring. Besides the West Coast anti-Asian agitation in the 1870s, there was also later animosity toward white immigrants. After the turn of the century, in the "Americanization" movement, those with British, German, and French roots reacted against southern and eastern Europeans. Prior to 1890, the bulk of immigration was from northern and western Europe, but after this date many came from the other regions of Europe and from Japan. In the Immigration Act of 1924 Congress froze the ethnic composition of America by setting quotas on nationalities on the basis of their numbers in the United States in 1890. Thus Italian emigrés were cut from 40,000 to 4,000 a year, the Japanese almost to none. Yet many could continue to come from the United Kingdom.

The mood leading up to the 1924 act is reflected in an article in the July 1916 *Yale Review* by Henry Pratt Fairchild, who wrote, "The hyphenated American . . . is a man without a country, because he is a man with two countries, to neither of which does he adhere completely. . . . [E]very Greek coffee-house or Chinese restaurant bears testimony to the presence of people who cannot or will not conduct their lives on a strictly American basis." [16]

There was widespread fear that in time of war nonnorthern European immigrants would not be loyal Americans. Many adults did not learn English, resided in ethnic enclaves, and communicated in their native tongues. (There were some 1,200 foreign-language newspapers in the nation.) [17] English-language newspapers were filled with words like "human vermin" and "canned-good befoulers . . . prison birds, revolutionists and potential if not actual assassins" to describe these "undesirable" immigrants. [18] One article decreed that Polish immigrants would never learn to speak English or join American society.

The Americanization movement was a powerful force for conformity. Local school boards created night classes in English, and social pressure was applied to eradicate Old World customs; July 4 was transformed into "Americanization Day."

In 1993 anti-immigration proponents were quick to compare the current backlash to these earlier nativist sentiments. They said that opposing Mexican immigration was not now racist because 70 years ago whites instituted restrictions against fellow white immigrants. It is true that simply being against illegal (or legal) immigration is not inherently racist. But as with other aspects of race, some unique factors make contemporary California nativism different.

The Americanization movement was racist, even though it was whites against whites. (Poles and other eastern and southern Europeans were considered another "race" by Americans.) But beyond this oversight by contemporary immigrant-bashers, the California xenophobia toward the darker-skinned Mexicans takes on a different tone because of the proximity of the border.

Whites are aware (in concept if not name) of the belief in *Aztlán*, which posits that the land California occupies was once part of Mexico. Even if only a small number of Latino activists believe Aztlán should be returned to Mexico that is enough to cause whites to fear Mexican immigration in ways that the old British stock in 1924 did not fear Poles or Italians. Those Poles and Italians were also seen as invaders, but they did not have any cultural claim to New York or New Jersey that predated the arrival of whites. In the scheme of world history, the 150 years that the United States has laid claim to California is not all that much time. And Poles and Italians came on ships that could easily be stopped. Mexicans can walk here. Also, many Poles and Italians returned home after earning enough money in the United States to live out their lives in their native lands. Whether or not their children remained, most eastern and southern Europeans grew more distant from their heritage because the old country was so far away.

Mexico is not that distant. With the two nations sharing a 2,000-mile land border, it is much easier to travel back and forth. There is less motivation for Mexicans to abandon the old country because it is so close. Many Mexicans have not become legal and yet have not returned home. After half a century in the United States, Martha Escutia's grandparents were not citizens. Her father Raul, who only became a citizen to vote for Ronald Reagan, explained he has always felt part of two worlds. "Morally, I am Mexican. I have always been very proud of my origin." The complexity of emotion is difficult to explain, he said. Raul still contemplates once again living in Mexico. He is a man with two countries that he loves equally. "I don't like anybody insulting Mexico. And I don't like anybody insulting the United States. Why? I cannot deny my roots. And I cannot deny the fact that this beautiful nation took me in her arms."

The proximity of Mexico, along with the complex emotions of those such as Raul, make many white Californians believe that those who come from Mexico will never become part of their society. But to see Raul (who is very light-skinned) walking down the street and to talk with him, one would hardly imagine that he was not a native-born American. This does not register with some whites who view the third world nation to the south as an invading force. And many whites forget that American culture is a powerful dynamic, and that the vast majority of the children of Mexican immigrants succumb to a de facto "Americanization" process.

What is really happening is that the two nations are still dealing with the outcome of the Mexican-American War, and even the way North America, Central America, and South America were colonized. The Europeans' greatest success, it must be recalled, in terms of creating countries as white as their motherlands, occurred in sparsely populated stone age regions, such as Australia and temperate America north of Mexico, where a relatively paltry one million or so indigenous Americans lived before contact. In these places, whites were able to take control, utterly, either by killing off or conquering the natives. In the lands south of the current U.S.-Mexico border, however, this was not possible. This was the most populated region on the continents; it was home to an estimated 12 to 25 million people in pre-Columbian times.[19] Even by the brutal standards of the day, it was impractical to kill off millions of dark-skinned peoples, which is why Latin America retains much of its Indian character.

In 1819 Simón Bolivar, the liberator of South and Central America wrote, "It is impossible to say to which human family we belong. The larger part of the native population has disappeared. Europeans have mixed with the Indians and the Negroes, and the Negroes have mixed with the Indians."[20] The debate over what it means to be "Hispanic" has been ongoing. It reached the U.S. census, which is considering changing this group from an ethnicity to a separate racial category.

Even as the conflict between Latinos and whites takes place north of the border, Mexico has not established its identity. There is plenty of racial stratification in Mexican society. Television newscasters have lighter skin, advertisements show white-looking people and use race in a way that would cause revolt in the United States. One television ad for a paint company featured a black man and the line, "They're working like niggers to offer you a white sale."[21] Indians are not served in some restaurants, and they are not found in high political or administrative office. Black American businessmen report that Mexicans do not like working with them. Ricardo Ovilla, Martha Escutia's Chamula Indian grandfather, had *"moreno"* written on his exit papers, which meant he had dark skin.

As in the United States, darker-skinned people in Mexico are less likely to have jobs. Two-thirds of the Indians over the age of 12 are unemployed, and most of the rest who work earn less than lighter-skinned Mexicans.

These issues will surge north of the border as Latinos grow to an unprecedented size in American society—when they become the largest minority group after surpassing blacks sometime after 2010. There will likely be a growing friction between Latinos and all groups in the United States, as presaged by the backlash that began in California in 1993. Will Latinos become the new blacks? Or will they be in the middle on a scale of racial hate, with blacks at the bottom; the next tier up being the *morenos,* who are a little darker; and the lightest-skinned Latinos being indistinguishable from whites?

8

Conservatives

The rising pitch of the immigration debate in 1993 emboldened the extreme right. In a high school in Rancho Palo Verdes, a wealthy community south of Los Angeles, the White Aryan Resistance distributed a flyer carrying a diagram of a pregnant Mexican woman who had a pregnant fetus with a burrito for a placenta. The caption said: "This remarkable medical revelation just in! . . . Finally, an answer to the age old scientific mystery, 'how do Mexicans manage to reproduce so rapidly?'. . . Research has now revealed that their female offspring are actually *born pregnant!*"

The flyer presented other hateful comments, including the question: Was the white race extinct? Other less strident but more influential whites were spreading racially inflammatory material. Republican Assemblyman William J. Knight in early 1993 had distributed among fellow Republicans at the Capitol a ditty written by one of his constituents in the white flight island of the Antelope Valley desert north of Los Angeles:

> *Everything is mucho good.*
> *We own the neighborhood*
> *We have a hobby—it's called breeding.*
> *Welfare pay for baby feeding.*[1]

The poem, purposefully ungrammatical, continued, "Thanks, American working dummy" and

> *Write to friends in motherland,*
> *Tell them to come as fast as can.*
> *They come in rags and Chebby trucks,*
> *I buy big house with welfare bucks.*

As the poem went on it showed the immigrant's house packed with 14 families until

> *Finally, white guy moves away...*
> *We think America damn good place.*
> *Too damn good for white man race.*
> *If they no like us, they can go.*
> *Got lots of room in Mexico.*

The ditty was a rare exhibition by a state Republican leader, the closest any California official came to openly purveying the kind of language used against the Chinese and Japanese between the 1870s and 1920s. Knight, who called the poem "interesting," was surprised that anyone found it offensive, but after the ditty was publicized, Republicans did not make this mistake again. Most, especially Governor Wilson, stuck to coded rhetoric. He never mentioned the state's growing polyethnicity, and he did not have to, because the message came through in the same way Nixon's language about busing appeased whites otherwise squeamish about appearing racist. When Wilson opened his salvo against immigrants in 1993, for instance, he stated: "It is hard not to sympathize with and even admire illegal immigrants in their struggle to come to a better life. But it is also no longer possible to ignore or accept the magnitude of their success in achieving illegal entry . . . or its costs to the American people. We can no longer allow compassion to overrule reason."[2] When he attacked illegal immigrants for taking services, he sounded moderate, praising while damning them. The message resonated with tax-paying Californians on two levels: they were supposedly footing the bill for foreigners, and the message struck a chord with whites who did not like the way their society had grown nonwhite and more like the third world, even if the roots of some Latino families dated to California's pre–Mexican

War days. Prior to Wilson, resentment over cultural change was only murmured; Wilson legitimized fear of immigrants and helped make illegal immigration a national issue. Newspapers everywhere ran with stories.

Even before Wilson went on the offensive, energy ricocheted between the Right and the Left. Some Chicano activists at UCLA had gone on a long hunger strike to press their demands for a Chicano studies department, and this helped fuel debate that the state was being "taken over" by another culture. But after Wilson's August 1993 press conference, both sides became turbocharged. One afternoon that August, when the hate was arcing between these poles, I was driving out to Riverside to interview the first of two major southern California anti-immigrant groups. I flipped on the car radio to KPFK-FM and heard a report of a riot in progress in East Los Angeles. Jesus! Looking for a spot to make a U-turn I heard Laguna Park, its former name, mentioned—and I realized the news bulletin was a replay of the broadcast of the 1970 riot, after which Rubén Salazar was killed.

As I pulled up at the home of Susan Tully, president of the Citizen's Committee on Immigration Policy, the station was interviewing people who had been at Laguna Park that day. One man told of his World War II veteran father, a "superpatriot," who hit a cop with a brick. The man said *La Raza,* the people, must once again rise up against the *"gabacho* pigs" in the face of Governor Wilson's attacks, to finally create a greater Aztlán that was the dream of the first Chicano activists.

In Tully's backyard, facing a horsebarn and the dusty channel of the Santa Ana River, I sipped iced tea. Without knowing what I had just heard on the radio, she launched into a complaint about the Aztlánistas. "All this diversity, it's a big mistake," Tully said of the UCLA hunger strikers and their demand that their culture be studied. "It focuses on what divides us, not what makes us the same. We think we're the only ones in the world that can mix all these groups and live happily ever after, that we can cut out hundreds of years of hate between groups. It's not going to work. It's never worked before. You're asking for a miracle." She said that even if it works in California, the state is unique. "Let's face it, . . . we've had an ethnic mix for a long time. But what about people in Iowa or Oklahoma? It won't work in Iowa."

Tully until recently had been a code enforcement officer for the Orange County city of Orange. One of her tasks was to study an apartment complex that was the focus of many complaints. There were 263 units in the building. She found an average of 25 people per two-bedroom unit. That meant there were over 7,500 people in the building. Just like Bill Shepherd in Dana Point, Tully wanted Orange to pass an ordinance limiting occupancy. But the courts in a case from nearby Santa Ana ruled that the state-mandated allowance of 10 people per one-bedroom unit was permissible.[3]

At the time of her 1991 study, she took a lot of heat, and she said it eventually forced her out of that job. "Everybody who was talking about immigration was called a racist," she said. She felt that now, in 1993, California society was waking up to the problems and the racist label would no longer stick.

"Ten years ago, we were talking about the migrant farm worker, the guy coming up to work and send money back. Now they're coming with no intention of going back. It's not just José coming to mow lawns and send money back to his wife. José is now bringing his wife."

She understands why they come. Tully once rode along with a U.S. Border Patrol officer who busted a family that did not even have diapers for their children.

"They had nothing. Your heart goes out to the people who are just seeking a better way of life. We do have an obligation to help Mexico develop. I'd rather do that than say all you people come here and become my problem. I'm willing to give money to my church to build houses in Mexico. But I'm sick to death of my own child competing in the classroom for a decent education."

That evening, I sat poolside with Nancy C. Thomson, the head of the Citizen's Committee on Immigration Policy, at her home in Orange. A committee paper stated that "multiculturalism has proven unworkable in reality and should be avoided in America."[4] She handed me a packet of material taken from college campuses that their group found offensive. One flyer was of an angry Mayan warrior pointing, like Uncle Sam, and saying: "Who's the illegal alien, PILGRIM?"

Thomson once went to a council meeting about a job center that was proposed for Latino day laborers. Supporters had packed the chambers with Mexican nationals, outnumbering residents. "I thought, this is how cities are taken over," Thomson said. "We are afraid of them, not them of us."

Thomson and Tully both expressed confusion and frustration. The women were self-described housewives who became active after witnessing the changes in their communities. It would be easy to label them as racist as Assemblyman Knight or the Aryan flyer distributors, but it is not that simple. Opposing unlimited illegal immigration does not automatically make one a racist. A country has a right to control its borders. Both women were serious in their convictions, and they raised a lot of good points. Somehow, however, legitimate concern about immigration was being turned into the worst kind of hate against Latinos.

SAVE OUR STATE

Governor Wilson's attack on illegal immigrants to bolster his campaign against Democrat Kathleen Brown was not enough to propel the backlash against Latinos. That took an Orange County resident who had decided to act after hearing Wilson's press conference on August 9, 1993. Ron Prince had long been angry about illegal immigration. On August 20, 11 days after Wilson launched his salvo, Prince set up a table in front of a Vons Supermarket in the Orange County city of Huntington Beach, trying to interest people in fighting immigration, but few signed and he saw little hope for change in acting alone. A few weeks later, Prince was still upset. "I thought, 'something has got to be done.'" Prince considered using the state ballot initiative process, in which citizens could shape policy by collecting enough signatures, to put a measure before the voters to bar illegal immigrants from public services.

A precedent had been set in 1986, when California voters passed an initiative declaring English the state's official language. That had been in the good times when immigrants were not being attacked. He figured his chances were even better now. He talked with Robert Kiley, a political consultant, and a few days later they met with Harold Ezell, who had been the Western states' chief of the Immigration and Naturalization Service during the Reagan years. A larger meeting was planned.

On October 5, 1993—two months after Wilson's press conference—10 concerned citizens attended an all-day meeting at the Center Club, a members-only restaurant in Costa Mesa. Two key people were there: Republican Assemblyman Richard L. Mountjoy and Barbara Coe, the cochair of the largest anti-immigration group in the state, the Citizen's Committee for Immigration Reform, an umbrella for a number of grass roots organizations, including the two run by Susan Tully and Nancy C. Thomson.

The group agreed to Prince's plan for a ballot initiative. The first name for the initiative was "Save Our Streets," but over the following weeks it evolved into "Save Our State" (SOS).

SOS would prohibit undocumented children from public schools, with school districts having to verify immigration status of each student; it would bar public health or social services, except for emergency medical care, and hospitals would have to report suspected illegal immigrants; it would require police to verify the legal status of arrestees; and it would make the manufacture of false documents a felony with a five-year prison sentence.

The group recruited front men—"star names"—to be the authors of the measure: Ezell and Alan Nelson, also a former INS official. To get the measure on the ballot, they needed the signatures of 384,974 registered voters by the qualifying date of April 22—a near-impossible task for a group with almost no money. They vowed to rely on volunteers.

The SOS endeavor was not unlike other racial outbursts in California history. The closest voter-initiated parallel was Proposition 1, passed in 1920 to bar the leasing or sale of land to the Japanese. Proposition 1 probably helped set the stage for the internment of Americans of Japanese descent during World War II. Proposition 1 was an overreaction to white fears about the Japanese "taking over" their state.

SOS was not so drastic. It did not forbid Latinos to own property. But it was as extreme as modern times would allow. Current laws could control illegal immigration, as Martha had argued when she opposed the drivers' license bill in the assembly.

The SOS group's prospects seemed so dim that only several articles showed up in the state's newspapers about the initiative between that fall and the following spring. It was easy to dismiss Prince and Coe's group, the California Coalition for Immigration Reform, as a marginal organization of no consequence. One monthly gathering of their group at the Fullerton Savings & Loan in Garden Grove brought out 46 people; all but two were white.

Martha Escutia knew nothing about SOS in those days. When told about it, she and other Latino leaders dismissed the initiative's chances. Nobody felt such a measure could possibly get enough signatures to make the ballot. By December of 1993 Martha thought the xenophobia had eased because Wilson's attacks against illegal immigration had subsided.

In this period Martha and other progressives made a big mistake: they assumed that California was too ethnically mixed and tolerant for SOS to have any appeal. How could a state as socially liberal as California spawn a racial outburst? Many either did not know California history or believed that the state had changed.

Part of Martha's lack of concern was based on her meeting with an emissary from Governor Wilson just before she went to Mexico on vacation with Leo Briones. The envoy told her that the governor wanted to cool his anti-immigration rhetoric. There was talk of a deal.

While in Mexico City, Martha and Leo visited Chapultepec. Martha stood at the edge of the wall where the *Los Niños Heroes* jumped. She looked at the jagged rocks far below and shuddered.

After they returned, I asked Martha if she trusted Wilson's emissary. She said maybe the truce was not real, but that she would try to work with him. "I think crime is going to take over as an issue this year," she said.

INSIDE SAVE OUR STATE

Latino leaders' reluctance to see SOS as a threat is understandable. SOS supporters had to overcome monumental obstacles. They did not finish the draft of the initiative until November 8, 1993. The ballot language was not approved by the state until January 11. They had 100 days to gather 384,974 registered voters' signatures, seemingly not enough time to make the 1994 ballot. An army of volunteers, many of them members of Ross Perot's United We Stand America, set up tables in front of supermarkets. When it was clear they would not make it, conservatives donated money and the SOS group paid $150,000 to professional signature-gatherers. Assemblyman Mountjoy gave $43,000.

At the end of the 100 days, Save Our State—later to be named Proposition 187, coincidentally the California Penal Code number for homicide—had collected some 600,000 names. The surplus would cover the inevitable disqualification of signatures that were illegible or otherwise not valid. Four days after those signatures were approved by the California Secretary of State, Ron Prince and Barbara Coe were laughing together in a booth at a north Orange County coffee joint.

Coe, 59, had a head of white hair and a perpetual cigarette dangling from her lips. Prince sat stiffly wearing a dark suit and a narrow tie. *Nation* writer Elizabeth Kadetsky later called him "vampirishly charming," a precise description.[5] He and Coe were delighted at the major headaches they were causing for everyone against them—the liberal-left-media-Democrat-Republican-big-business axis.

"Republican money likes cheap labor, so they're not opposed to limiting illegal immigration," said Prince. "The Democratic power structure likes cheap votes."

Coe said of their success, "The timing for all of it was perfect."

Yet that spring morning in 1994 they were still largely ignored by the media, a situation that would change within days. Prince was feeling disregarded, and he felt the media was showing a liberal bias. The *Los Angeles Times* did not come to their press conference announcing the initiative's approval, which made it the equivalent of an unheard tree falling in a forest. Prince saw foes everywhere. His group had filed 32 formal complaints with the Santa Ana Post Office for tampered mail. Who were the culprits? "Our enemies in the Santa Ana Post Office." Authorities should raid the Post Office to ferret out illegals, Coe added. (The Postal Service later ruled the complaints unfounded.)

In recent weeks, Latino leaders had finally awakened to the threat of Proposition 187 and hastily mounted a counterattack. Upon mention of this, Prince smiled broadly. He vowed their foes would not stop them—the wording of the ballot language was carefully chosen, and the words "Save Our State" made prominent. SOS would spend no money for advertising, he promised.

"They are depending on the public being really, really stupid,"

Prince said. "I'm counting on people's intelligence. Our strongest plus is that anywhere from 25 percent to 50 percent of the people who go into the voting booth on November 8 will not have paid attention to any of the advertising. What they will do is read the title of the initiative and make up their mind at that moment."

Not long after Prince made this assertion, the California Field Poll found most Californians had not heard of the measure—which was not surprising because the media had virtually ignored it. But when the pollsters read the initiative, 67 percent of those called were in favor, indicating support across the political spectrum. Governor Wilson was fueling the cause. The emissary who had come to Martha Escutia promising that Wilson would soften his stand did not deliver: Wilson welshed big time. Not long before Proposition 187 qualified, he ran the most devastating television advertisement yet in his campaign against Democrat Kathleen Brown: grainy black-and-white footage of a "banzai run," dozens of Mexican nationals storming border checkpoints. It showed brown hordes streaming north. In a voiceover, Wilson said, "I'm suing to force the federal government to control the border. And I'm working to deny state services to illegal immigrants. Enough is enough."

The ad went on to say, "Kathleen Brown thinks differently. She supports continuing state services to illegals and says illegal immigration is not a cause of problems in California. Where do you stand?"

One would have assumed Prince would embrace Wilson, but he bitterly lashed out at the governor as a phony opponent of illegal immigration. Prince was angry because Wilson was alternately hot and cool in the early days when SOS was gathering signatures. Wilson either had delayed endorsement for more impact or only plunged in to support SOS when it was clear he needed to careen right.

Prince saw nothing racist in the ballot initiative. He said he was motivated to fight immigrants because he was ripped off for $1 million by an illegal Canadian.

Few in the media were looking behind the scenes of SOS, and one of the rare investigative articles was published a few months later in the *Los Angeles Times*. In some first-rate reporting, *Times* staffers Gebe Martinez and Doreen Carvajal, with help from Matt

Lait, found court records that disputed Prince's account of the "Canadian" illegal immigrant.[6] They wrote that the Canadian was legal and quoted Prince saying that the figure was half a million dollars, in contradiction to what Prince told me. The money, from a complicated construction deal gone sour, was far less—a bankruptcy court showed it was about $70,000 and that Prince settled for less than half. Prince explained to the *Los Angeles Times* that the "Canadian" was not the illegal immigrant he had referred to in other media interviews, but he would not say who that immigrant was. Harold Ezell, one of the two official authors of the initiative, apparently did not even know where the SOS headquarters was because Prince did not want anyone to know, including Ezell. Prince also feared his enemies' wrath, and he refused to say where he was born, where he lived, or where he worked.

He argued that the incident with the Canadian proved that there was nothing anti-Latino about SOS. "We find it kind of interesting, since we're consistently being accused of racism," Coe said. "Yet we have one specific race that is demanding that their culture have the total focus, if you will—they will react very overtly if those demands are not met, including the destruction that occurred up there," she said referring to the UCLA Chicano hunger strike and a minor riot that occurred when students took over an administrative building.

A few months before, three simultaneous hunger strikes like the one at UCLA were announced. One was out of state, the other two at Santa Barbara and Stanford. Outside my Stanford window, four students occupied a blue plastic hut set up amid the Canary Island palms, planning to starve until they were given a gender-inclusive "Chicana-Chicano" department. Even liberal white students quietly muttered that they were offended by the heavy-handedness and the charges of white racism that flowed from the microphones. At the same time, a group of Chicano students at Berkeley marched to have University Avenue renamed "César Chávez Avenue."

Conservatives such as Prince and Coe saw the universities hammering at their hive with a baseball bat. This made them work harder.

"I think it is absolutely ludicrous," Coe said. "This is our country, our language, our history. This is an outrage that these people should demand not only that we reverse [the] cultural teachings of our nation, but that we pay for it."

She and Prince saw the cultural conflict leading to an exodus of whites from California. "The outflow of Americans from California—American refugees from California—are in the tens of thousands if not hundreds of thousands right now," Prince said. He added that people are getting out of California "while the getting is good."

The conversation then took a decidedly strange turn as they started to talk more deeply about conspiracies and the prospect of violence—their voices tinged with excitement.

"I am sure you are well versed on this: there will either be a massive outpouring of people from California into other states, or you're looking at total violence," Coe said. "We went to a lot of the gun shows to do signature gathering and this is where you have loyal, hard-core Americans who are not going to budge an inch. I saw a man go to one booth and he ordered $3,000 worth of ammunition. He ain't going anywhere. He's going to stay in his state and he's going to defend it.

"Now, we're looking at either a massive outpouring of these people, and this is the very, very frightening part. The rumor is out, and I've had feedback both from northern California and the Los Angeles–Ventura area: the word is among the pro-illegal organizations—particularly La Raza, which is the militant side of it, MEChA [the acronym of a student activist group], et cetera—that if SOS passes, that's the fuse. And they will light it. For violence. They will take their history back.

"The second thing is the reports. I just started getting the first few, a little here, a little there, and a few implications hither and yon, is that in Mexico, the explosion is just about there. It's going to blow. They're already talking about the massive invasion into the United States of refugees. There is no way possible the Border Patrol could control it. The only way to control it would be with firepower from our military. Nobody anticipates that Clinton will allow that to happen. We are looking at a true flood, a deluge if you will."

At that point, Coe invoked the rhetoric of the extreme right that fears the United Nations will use unrest in Mexico as an excuse to invade the United States and set up a one-world government.

"They got a game plan; it's all there, okay? You can take this as doom and gloom, alarmism, and the whole ball of wax if you want to, [but] some of this data I have, there are reportedly 43 dissident camps ready—I'm sure you've heard all of this—in the United States, for people like Ron and me. At least they're ready for us."

Prince nodded.

"It is interesting," he said, "to think they would put us in camps for being radical centrists. However it isn't just the gun shows where we're hearing this kind of talk, it's in front of the supermarket, it's at the swap meet, it's everywhere you go. Because there is such an extreme frustration that nothing is being done to protect our country. If they are not going to do anything about it, then we don't have a government. If those people aren't going to obey the laws, why the hell should we?"

Few Californians knew that the ballot initiative's leaders believed the United States might fall under the control of a world government that would build 43 detention camps to house those fighting illegal immigration. No mainstream press interviews revealed their beliefs, not even in the *Los Angeles Times*. (The *Nation* did report that Christian fundamentalists as well as a state senator tied with the white supremacist Christian Identity movement had given substantial amounts of money to SOS. But relatively few California voters read the *Nation*.)[7]

One reason for the lack of in-depth coverage is that Prince and Coe were smart enough to keep themselves in the background. Most newspapers had interviewed Nelson and Ezell, who did not even know where SOS headquarters was.

Even though the media was failing badly with the story, Prince feared what might happen if this situation changed. In late April Prince warned his troops to beware of the press. At a meeting of supporters he said the media would compare them with the "beginning of ethnic cleansing" or would say that "we're going to start our own Hitler Youth Group." He cautioned them to speak carefully, not to "slip" with any racist comments.[8]

Initially, when the SOS backers were feeling jubilant but were ignored by the press, they planned a rally called "United We Stand at the Border," to be held in conjunction with Ross Perot's group in August 1994. Coe predicted a turnout of 50,000. But in May, as the number of stories in the press grew after the initiative was approved for the ballot, the event was abruptly canceled. SOS did not need the attention and the event might come off as appearing racist, as well as provide an opportunity for a clash with anti-SOS foes in front of the cameras.

WILSON UPS THE ANTE

Governor Wilson sued the federal government in early 1994, charging that illegal immigration was taking $2.3 billion from the state each year in prison, education, and health costs, and that it was a federal responsibility to help. His opponents countered that the immigrants paid taxes and contributed to the economy.

Wilson predicated the 1994 state budget on this federal money, even after President Clinton dismissed any chance of sending it. Wilson could not lose. When the $2.3 billion did not come and the state was short the same amount, he could say the state budget was ruined because of illegals, further driving the wedge home.[9]

As Wilson gained power over the immigration issue, Republicans in the east grew worried about their California counterparts pinning so much animosity on Latinos. This was a strategy that worked in the short term but might have adverse long-term effects. In late 1994 former Republican cabinet members Jack Kemp and William Bennett voiced their opposition to Proposition 187 and accused Wilson of chasing Latinos away from the Republican Party, a repeat of the mistake at the turn of the century, when the party attacked immigrants and pushed several generations of Irish and Italians to the Democrats.

Blacks were not part of the Kemp-Bennett warning: they had long since been written off to the Democrats. Latinos, on the other hand, presented incredible opportunity, because after 2010, they would be the largest minority group. In Florida, Cubans were already proving valuable to the Republican Party.

The joint Kemp-Bennett statement said Republicans had grown "pessimistic, angry and opposed. . . . The anti-immigration boomerang, if it is unleashed, will come back to hurt the GOP."[10]

Kemp and Bennett knew long-term demographics. But Wilson knew Californians. He said, "They are two guys who live in Washington. It's clear they've lived there too long." Of course, he was saying they were out of touch with *white* voters in California. Wilson was betting on short-term results, but also that Latinos would not become politically active. But in the long term, Wilson is wrong. Latinos can be a powerful force in future politics, as demographics and the history of other immigrant groups strongly suggest. If Democrats learn from the Proposition 187 debacle, a Latino power base could be incorporated into the party to give it a winning edge, just like the one provided by the Irish and Italians early in the century. It is not so much that Democrats have to learn to meld the campus Chicano activists with white suburbanites. The Democrats can make many mistakes—not organize in Latino communities, assume Latinos will automatically come their way—but one of the biggest would be to focus on the so-called Chicano leaders. Most Latinos are as far removed from Chicano politics as white suburbanites. Latinos and white suburbanites are quite similar in their attitudes toward work and cultural "values."

By 2010 when California develops a population that will be 40 percent Latino, it could provide a Latino political power base to the nation in the same way that East Los Angeles gave birth to Latino enfranchisement in California. The prize is not just the state's 54 electoral college votes, but a model for Latinos in other states to follow.

PROGRESSIVES FUMBLE

Public sentiment ran strongly against an open border. And, as Martha Escutia and the Latino caucus should have learned a year earlier at the bungled press conference, a response based on a slow educational process was doomed. Opponents would have to stage a careful campaign. But errors of the kind made by the Latino caucus in their early reaction to Wilson only multiplied as Democrats floundered through 1994. It was not enough for Democrat Kathleen Brown to call Wilson's television ad showing the grainy pictures of illegals invading California "dangerous" and "divisive" as she sought to unseat him. Brown told one interviewer: "We have to address [immigration] in a responsible and tough and smart fashion. People come here for jobs. Let's prevent them from coming by beefing up the border, going after employers who give them jobs."[11]

However accurate, this sounded soft. Perhaps the answer was a counterinitiative, like the asset forfeiture proposal that would seize the property of those who repeatedly hire illegals. Martha was opposed to forfeiture because she felt it could create worse discrimination—employers might simply not hire anyone with dark skin to avoid risk. But the alternative was a right-wing initiative that could have far worse implications. Those against Proposition 187 had to give something—the status quo was not acceptable. Otherwise, Prince and Coe's proposition would harvest a lot of voters not sold on United Nations conspiracy theories. Prince had said that a counterinitiative was his worst fear. A tough alternative would send the message that the state should not punish the little people, but the big boys who were making money off them, and by extension, the average citizens who also benefited from the cheap labor. It is important to remember that SOS would not stop immigration—it would just punish those here—and more would continue to come as long as there were jobs.

Instead, opponents played into Prince's hands. One day after I met with Prince at the Orange County coffee shop, I ran into Leo Briones, Martha's fiancé, on the same plane to Sacramento. Leo, a political consultant and veteran of many campaigns, said he was bidding on the anti-SOS public relations contract. He had many ideas of how to run the anti-SOS television campaign.

Leo's television spots would show the "faces of immigrants"— famous and not-so-famous. One would feature a Latino, the son of illegal immigrants, who died in Vietnam having received the Medal of Honor for saving his unit. "The ad will say that if his parents had not migrated, their son would not have been a hero, he would not have died for his country—America."

Leo said that the anti-SOS forces could build coalitions. He counted on Republicans and Libertarians against big government, citing an *Orange County Register* editorial that morning that railed against INS immigration busts.[12] And running opposite Prince, he counted on voters to see through the racism and do the right thing. To ensure that voters knew the initiative was racist, he wanted to hit hard on this angle.

During the flight, Leo said whites were being swamped and there was nothing they could do to retain power. "This is it. The last stand. It's California, the world," he said of the shrinking white presence. He did not mean this as an Aztlánista. A clue to how it will work lies in something he heard the previous year at the National Association of Hispanic Journalists meeting in Albuquerque. Mexican novelist Carlos Fuentes said, "We can survive if we can accept them as us and us as them."

We fell silent. The green squares of Central Valley farms passed below. Half Dome in Yosemite rose like a broken jaw. On the other side of the plane, the Pacific stretched beyond the coastal ranges. There was a lot of real estate between Los Angeles and Sacramento, the distance equal to that between Boston and Baltimore. In terms of creating community, as Donald Northcross was trying to do, or surmounting the hurdles that Leo wanted to jump to combat Proposition 187, it seemed an impossible state in an impossible country.

Leo never got the "No on 187" contract. Part of the reason was that leaders did not want to take Leo's hard line against racism. The ads that ran emphasized that if Proposition 187 passed, the federal government might withhold $15 billion in education and Medicare funds from California because the initiative violated federal privacy laws.

It was not exactly a catchy campaign to which moderates would rally. And the first press conference was not held until August, some two months before the vote. The Democrats were committing suicide for the Republicans.

9

Progressives

From the 1960s on, a small number of Latinos, Asians, and blacks were setting themselves apart culturally in ethnic theme houses on college campuses. At the same time, tens of thousands of whites were moving behind gates and walls, quietly isolating themselves in wealthy enclaves such as Dana Point.

By the 1990s these two worlds—the gated retreats and the culturally separate enclaves—were two opposing phalanxes in Wilson's battle plan, which was using voter fear about California's changing culture to help him win reelection. He was betting on proving the impotence of campus activists and the strength of the frustration and anger among the large mass of white suburban voters.

Wilson was going to expand the wedge issue, which had been aimed primarily at blacks. Richard Nixon opposed school busing and talked tough on crime; and Ronald Reagan later attacked a plethora of liberal programs that were largely perceived to be helping blacks. Some Latino and Asian campus activists seemed blind to the notion that the same tactics used against blacks could be turned against them. While this seems obvious given the power of race as a wedge in American politics, it is understandable that the campus groups felt they had strength. When they protested, college administrators almost always bowed to their demands. This led some writers and conservative politicians to overstate the influence of a relatively small number of students. The Right assumed the ethnocentric activists had power—but that it did not—to change American culture. The mistake of the Right was to equate the noise of a small number of activists with clout. If the Latino caucus's hastily arranged response to Wilson's attack against immigrants in 1993 was merely bungled, these students were being self-destructive. They made the same mistakes that Democrats and progressives had made in the 30 years of racial debate.

ALIENATING WHITES

In early 1993, before Wilson announced his attack on illegal immigrants, some 70 Berkeley students—a mix of Chicanos and Asians—stormed California Hall, the campus administration building, demanding that ethnic studies programs be expanded.[1] The students wanted additional courses that focused on their cultures, and they held the building for seven hours, until police maced and arrested many of them. A week later, 150 students stormed the faculty club. In May at UCLA, a mob demanding a Chicana and Chicano studies department smashed the windows of the faculty center, causing $50,000 in damage.[2] A month later five Chicano students and a professor began a hunger strike.

"We either get a department of Chicano studies or we will die here," said Professor Jorge R. Mancillas.[3] The newspapers and television were filled with images of the weakened strikers and their chanting supporters. The strike ended when the administration caved.

The new ethnic studies hires at UCLA would be made amid severe cutbacks across the University of California system. State funding for prisons was escalating and now equaled what was being spent on higher education. A prison guard with a high school education earned $44,000, which was $10,000 more than the income of an average public school teacher and even more than that of a tenured associate professor at a public college.[4] The prison budget was going even higher—many more guards needed to be hired—and amid the recession, the state had to make cuts somewhere. Education was a target.

Just as Maria Ha was about to enter Berkeley, the budget cuts hit, and some 335 courses were dropped. The graduate programs in art, drama, and library science were eliminated. At UCLA, five professional schools were slashed, the faculty was decimated by salary cuts and buyouts: Berkeley had 9 percent fewer teachers.

This pruning was just a start. Days after the UCLA hunger strike ended, the state legislature considered a budget bill proposed by Governor Wilson that included a $138 million cut in the University of California system. This would ensure a tuition increase of $995 for Maria in her sophomore year. Democrats and student lobbyists were pushing a compromise, a reduction of "only" $88 million, which would push tuition up by $630. Even the lower figure would hurt Maria, who was already working as hard as she could to save money for school.

A serious problem facing educators was the ethnocentric activism. As the legislature began debating UC's funding, the most prominent images in the public eye in the previous weeks were the Chicano hunger strikers at UCLA and the Berkeley takeover. It did not matter that they represented only a few hundred protesters, a mere thimbleful of the nearly 166,000 students on the system's nine campuses. Image was reality. The impact of these protests cannot be underestimated. An Orange County Republican group published a brochure that asked, "Is this not an effort to promote racial tension, violence, hate crimes, etc.?" The group decried that the Chicano radicals were being supported at "taxpayer expense."[5]

Elo Carrillo, a staff person for the still-forming Chicano studies program, answered the phone during the strike. "There were so many hate calls and threats," she said. "They said, 'You don't belong at the University of California. You're all illegal aliens, go back.' The phone would never stop ringing. I think for every 10 good calls I got about 200 bad ones. I would cry. They would leave me shaking."

Militant ethnocentric actions create resentment across party lines. When Khalid Muhammad of the Nation of Islam spoke at Howard University, for instance, he blasted Jews and praised a black gunman who killed six commuters on a Long Island train. "I am going to bite the tail of the honkies," he said. Later, the United Negro College Fund—which had nothing to do with the event— was deluged with letters from people saying they would no longer contribute: the letters painted all black colleges as breeding grounds for anti-Semitism.[6]

A further problem was created by the University of California Regents, the controlling body run by 18 Republican appointees. In the early 1990s the regents secretly voted to give a $2.4 million retirement package to outgoing University of California president David Gardner. When the deal was exposed in the papers, it unleashed a hammerstorm of criticism. State Senator Tom Hayden took out a full-page advertisement in the *New York Times* saying that 1,700 UC administrators were paid over $100,000. Each year there was an annual ceremony for raising the salary for the UC president, who earned more than the president of the United States.[7]

It was a bad case of lingering 1980s greed. The argument was that salaries had to be competitive with private industry, but many UC administrators were so narrowly specialized that they could not land a comparable job outside academia. Hayden also went after professors' salaries and teaching loads.

All these things made the university an easy target for more cuts. In the summer of 1993, the assembly hearings on the budget stretched into the hot Sacramento evenings. During one of the night debates over university cuts, Democrat Delaine Eastin scolded the Republicans.

"My grandparents somehow were able to build a fine UC system," Eastin said. She added they made a lot less money than people today, especially the 80 politicians in the chamber. "They did so because they had something most in this room give lip service to— something called values. We should be having a conversation about building up our higher education."

Orange County Republican Gil Ferguson, who sat behind Eastin, pulled a hankie and with no small amount of burlesque, dabbed his eyes, laughing. Many other Republicans laughed with him. Ferguson's performance played well with the typical older white and conservative voter in his southern California district upset with the cultural activists. Many were wealthy enough to pay more for tuition or could afford to send their children to private universities.

A vote call was made. Assemblyman John Vasconcellos had the last word for the chamber as he pleaded for reason: "I've been attacked by my own people, more than by Republicans. I stretched myself and my conscience," Vasconcellos said of the concessions that were made to the Republicans. When the vote was taken, Martha was on his side, but the budget was defeated 44-32; two-thirds, or 54 votes were needed.

In late 1993 the legislature compromised on the size of cuts, and Maria's tuition went up "only" $630. She paid more for less that year—over $12,000 for all fees, room and board—and her sister in grade school, studying hard to make it into Berkeley, would pay even more for a lot less. Amid all this, Maria was too busy studying to even notice the Asian and Latino activism.

ETHNIC ELITISM

According to a member of the Asian Student Union named Ed, the students stormed the Berkeley administration building that spring of 1993 to correct what he and his fellow members saw as an imbalance in the way the university funded the study of ethnic groups. Ed agreed to be interviewed six days before the assembly began the budget hearings that would decide the fate of the tuition increase.

He talked cautiously in his cramped office on the Berkeley campus with his back to the open window, from which poured the sound of traffic on Bancroft Way, explaining that when the ethnic studies program was established in 1969, four groups were included: blacks, Chicanos, American Indians, and Asians of Asian nations. He wanted an *Asian American* studies program. After the takeover, he and other student leaders met with Chancellor Chang-Lin Tien. Ed spoke cryptically about the intricacies of the dispute, then suddenly stopped the interview.

Ed then said: "Have you thought of having an Asian American student talk to other Asian American students? That's the only way you're going to get anything."

I asked what he meant.

"There's a broad distrust of whites. I am not saying you are distrustful," he said. He smiled. "But they might not see you as legitimate. If you want to get the story, you should have an Asian American do the interviews for you."

"I want to understand," I said.

"Someone from the outside cannot write about it."

"Are all whites looked at as being bad?" I asked.

"There were some white students in the takeover. They were looked at as being patronizing. These are white students who want to do the 'ethnic thing.' They're not being accepted. It will be difficult for you to approach [Asians] and have them trust you. There's hostility toward outsiders."

He said the reason was that many Asians discover their "Asianness" for the first time at Berkeley. He came from Riverside, east of Los Angeles, and he only identified with his ethnicity after he came to school. "I know a lot of Asians who come from white suburbs, and this is the first time we have gotten together as a group of Asians."

When he was asked if a white outsider could learn anything by accompanying him to some events, he said no.

"I want to spend time learning," I said.

"I don't want to be seen around you. I will be considered an informant."

Ed's reaction was a precursor to stranger receptions to come. When I went to see Elaine Kim, a Berkeley Asian studies professor, she threw me out of her house after I had barely asked two questions; her stated reason was that my questions were too simplistic. She offered no other explanation; it seemed I was not "inside" enough in the Asian community for her to talk with me.[8] A student ran a database search on my work to determine my political bent before he would talk to me. I was deemed liberal enough, though he harshly criticized my choosing to write about Maria Ha in a magazine article. He felt she was not "activist" enough to represent the kind of Asian he wanted to see in print. Another Asian student only agreed to meet me after the intervention of a black graduate student I knew. The Asian Student Union representative's suspicion and exclusion of whites from his cause was indicative of the power the ethnocentrists felt in 1993. Some of them were going out of their way to estrange whites.

Alex Wierbinski, a graduate student in history who is the brother of Martha Escutia's chief of staff, Suzanne, told of walking across the campus during the 1992 Columbus quincentenary when some students used the milestone to protest 500 years of European occupation. "An Asian American student handed me a [flyer] say-ing the Berkeley history department is ethnically biased, a white male bastion—blah, blah, blah—they're teaching lies," he said. "I read it and I walked back to the guy and I said, 'Have you taken a history course here?' He said no. I said 'Do you know what you're passing out?' He said 'Yeah.' I said you haven't seen the change in historical studies. This is a lie. He said 'You're a *white man!*' I al-most hit him, I swear to God.

"I don't like the patronizing way they deal with me as a white person—not as a student. See, what they're doing is they're isolat-ing themselves and making it impossible to reach out and get a broad-based coalition, a consensus for political action to moderate the ills in our society. Instead of looking at a general context and saying what's best for everybody, they're saying what's best for my narrow political agenda. They make it harder for other people to move forward and find—not a liberal or a conservative—but a common-sensical way to do anything. In the meantime, the situa-tion for everybody has declined."

Alex is angry that no group has mobilized to combat lofty tu-ition increases, but instead a small number choose to fight for the right to study ethnicity.

"I don't see any fucking Polock department," said Alex, who is Polish. "We are seeing a power push by minorities, especially at UCLA. If I tie myself to a post and threaten to starve myself to death, will I get a Polish Studies Department? I don't want a Po-lish department. If you want to study it, you can find an institution that specializes in it. If you want to study Filipino culture, then why did you come here? If you're coming here, appreciate the ideals of liberty in an American context.

"I believe a lot of them will find failure. There will be disen-chantment, cynicism, the group that is more radical will fall out, just like white radicals in the sixties did."

OLD-LINE ACTIVISTS

Even if they were not wanted in some racial circles, 1960s-vintage white revolutionaries were busy in post-riot Los Angeles, at the various trials that consumed the city for several years. They were also active in 1994, trying to inject themselves into the Latino high school movement against Proposition 187. They were at the trial of the men accused of beating trucker Reginald Denny at the start of the Los Angeles riots. Denny, who is white, had been nearly beaten to death by black men who had pulled him from his truck.

It was a sluggish news day in the broadcast and print pressrooms on the ninth floor of the Los Angeles Courthouse. Both pressrooms were being trolled by plaintive revolutionaries of the white and Latino variety, extolling their spin on the riots. A man came through and passed out a magazine, *New Visions of Aztlán*. A white gave away a flyer called "Refuse & Resist." The flyer was vintage 1960s and referred to those arrested as the "LA4," saying the riots were a rebellion that was an appropriate answer to long-standing abuse by the police, as well as racial and economic tyranny. In part, it said: "The 1992 Los Angeles Rebellion blew away the stultifying atmosphere of yellow-ribbon fascism . . . following the Gulf War. . . . Unlike the rebellions of the '60s that were more easily contained, the Los Angeles Rebellion was multinational." On the pressroom video monitor trial witness Gabriel Quintana told in Spanish what happened that day Denny was beaten along with five other motorists and two firefighters. Quintana worked in the cash register cubicle at a Unical gas station. When the attackers were finished with Denny—rescued by black residents—they smashed Quintana's booth. Quintana had not exactly been embraced by the black looters as a comrade in a multinational rebellion: he was whacked bloody. A video showed him bleeding and dazed, lurching to the ground as the looters merrily stole cigarettes.

The revolutionary hopefuls had left the pressroom by the time Quintana testified. They and some on the left used the words "rebellion" and "insurrection" in place of "riot" every chance they could. But they were not having much luck finding buyers. They wanted to mold the postriot environment into a revolutionary spirit, but they were merely quaint holdouts in a world that had moved beyond them.

But at least the white communists exuded enthusiasm, even if they were doomed never to succeed. There was little of the same 1960s vigor on the Latino left; only bitterness remained. At the time Martha and the record number of other Latinos were sworn into the assembly in 1992, I tracked down longtime Chicano activist Raul Ruiz. Ruiz snapped pictures outside the Whittier Avenue bar the day Rubén Salazar was killed, and his documentation was published in the magazine *La Raza*.

When Salazar was slain, there was just one Latino in a higher state office. Now there are many, but Ruiz was not cheered by the political success of Martha and the others. A professor in the Chicano Studies Department at UC Northridge, he was critical of Latino politicians but stopped short of calling the new legislators *vendidos*, or sellouts.

"They don't really deserve to get elected," said Ruiz. "Those who benefit from the struggle are not grateful for the sacrifices of people who gave their lives, like Rubén Salazar. We do have some representation now. But in many ways the community is worse off. I'm much more impressed with the way [black officials] serve their community. Everybody criticizes those crazy Chicanos. They should say 'I am a Chicana.' Often those who struggled the hardest are forgotten, and the little princesses and royal family members get these things bequeathed to them."

Ruiz seemed to be referring to California Assemblywoman Diane Martinez whose father is a member of Congress; many believe she ran on his coattails. Martinez herself was resentful of even being associated with the seven Latinos in the assembly. "It's really very difficult to stomach to be treated as one of *los siete*," she said. "I think that is all journalistic racism. It sounds like we're running in a gang. We're all very different. Yet we're lumped together as Latinos. How many generations do I have to be in America?"

There was little sense of camaraderie among progressives with the larger cause. Ruiz disdained Martinez and others. Martinez did not want to be identified with her fellow Latino lawmakers, who had experienced even wider splits. The infighting had reached legendary proportions, the boring details lost to arcane slights suffered long ago. At the same time, some Asians did not want whites. Some white communists were still preaching for workers to throw off their chains. Other liberal whites such as Alex Wierbinski felt alienated and angry. There was little unity at a time when it was most needed. If Latinos alone could not come together, how could the larger progressive community?

BLACKS AND JEWS AND LATINOS AND
PROPOSITION 187

Despite the factionalism, the Latino caucus created a political action committee to fight Proposition 187. Martha was the treasurer. A few days after this committee was formed, some 3,000 young men from an American Legion boy's group swarmed the state Capitol grounds. All visible boys were white and wore identical T-shirts. Martha was in her office, staring out her window. Across the courtyard was the office of Republican Assemblyman Richard Mountjoy, who had donated critical money to the SOS cause to pay people to gather signatures. About 10 American Legion boys were clustered around his desk.

"Look at those Nazis in there," Martha said facetiously of the youths gathered around the conservative legislator. "I ought to go over by the window and talk Spanish."

She had already raised $600,000 for the anti-SOS campaign. She hoped for a much larger war chest. Martha spoke confidently, but then she worried that the Right ruled the issue, with no room for give and take.

"Wilson has gone so far to the right on this and same thing with the SOS people," Martha said. "The farther to the right they go, frankly, the farther to the left we go, almost to the point where there's no basis for rational discussion. There's maybe 25 percent of the really hard core crackers that Wilson's counting on. My concern is to keep moderate Democrats within the fold. We're trying to coalesce with other groups and my job is to bring in the Jewish community."

Martha hoped that some Jews would see the domino effect: if the rights of one group were assailed, it could open the door for attacks on others. Martha was probably correct about Wilson's base of hard-core conservatives, but the progressives' message thus far had not reached the moderates. At the time Martha was named treasurer of the "No on 187" campaign, Leo Briones's bid for the public relations contract had not yet been rejected by the committee. The anti-187 forces could have run hard-hitting commercials, exposing the beliefs of Ron Prince and other SOS proponents. Had progressives waged a smarter campaign, they might have broken the cycle of past racial outbursts when small groups of California extremists got a majority of citizens to adopt their policies such as the anti-Japanese land law of 1920.

In early 1994 Martha struggled to align Latinos with other ethnic and racial groups. Asians were so politically split that it would be difficult to rally much support. She focused on blacks and Jews, but worried about support from blacks. (There was no frontal attack against affirmative action at this time, and no one could see it coming.) Martha did not think blacks saw a domino effect, that they might suffer worse racism if it were tolerated against Latinos.

"I hear that mostly from the Jewish community. They're the ones that understand that," she said. Martha added many blacks dislike Latinos, seeing them as economic competition. They believe that "if the black male is unemployed, it's because some Latino took his job. I disagree with that. Juan Garcia did not displace the engineer from Rockwell. There are far more numbers proportionally of blacks in middle and upper management than Latinos. Nobody is displacing anyone here. We're only talking here about really cheap, cheap jobs that frankly people don't want to do."

A further problem was that Latinos were not being taken seriously by Democratic Party leaders because of their relatively low voter turnout. "The Democratic Party, which is controlled by liberal whites and African American communities [doesn't] understand the impact of Latinos as a block vote," she said.

But no rainbow coalition formed around Proposition 187. Despite all the talk of unity among "people of color," liberal whites were the Latinos' strongest allies. They were the most outspoken and fought the hardest. The silence from blacks and Asians about the Latino-bashing was conspicuous. And the Jewish community never rallied. Martha had berated a Jewish assemblyman for not strongly denouncing the bashing.

"You should know how I feel—because you know what happens when you tolerate this—it's evil," Martha told him to no avail. Not long after this, Martha spoke to a group of blacks in Los Angeles and the reception was *very* cold. In the state capital, the situation was different. Black leaders were against Proposition 187, but an article in the *San Francisco Chronicle* said these leaders were not reaching their constituents.[9] The article said that unlike civil rights leaders, they could no longer count on the united support of black voters. Polls showed blacks split, yet at least one black leader denied this.

"In the legislature, the Latino and black caucus works closely together, the issues are very similar," said Marguerite Archie-Hudson, the black assemblywoman representing Watts. "The press would like to make the war," she said of the *Chronicle* article. "We have to hang together."

Much of the tension between blacks and Latinos was due to the influx of Latinos into former black strongholds. Her district, once almost all black, was roughly half Latino. Archie-Hudson said blacks were moving out of areas like Watts as they gained economic status, just as Jews had left East Los Angeles.

"It's a continuing part of the natural migration. Latinos are going to take over their communities. We celebrate that. It may appear that African Americans have a fight with Latinos and Asians. That's symptomatic of people at risk. Everyone is worried the last piece will go to somebody else. Our task as leadership is that we have to remind them that the last bone is not going to go to someone else. If this state is going to go forward, we have to work on this."

But it is hard to imagine she would find agreement from a large number of unemployed blacks in her district. Nor with some Latinos, such as Xavier Hermosillo, a Republican talk radio host and conservative activist who was a cofounder of N.E.W.S. for America, the acronym standing for "North, East, West and South," because Latinos are now spreading everywhere. Hermosillo is best known for his declaration that Latinos are taking over California "house by house, block by block" and that Americans should "wake up and smell the refried beans." [10] He had picketed job sites after the Los Angeles riots protesting that there were too many blacks and not enough Latinos being hired. He also led other protests against blacks having too many government jobs.

"Blacks . . . are very angry at Latinos, especially recent Latino immigrants because they view them as taking black jobs," he declared. "They despise seeing Latinos standing on streetcorners looking for work . . . because they're too damn lazy to go stand on their own corner. When you go to the bottom of an off-ramp in Los Angeles, you see Anglos and blacks with a sign that basically says give me money. You see Latinos selling you something. It's our entrepreneurial nature. It's part of our culture."

During the UCLA hunger strike, Hermosillo negotiated behind the scenes, and it angered him to see black students involved with a Latino cause. "What bothered me was the African American influence on these kids got to the point where they started wearing Muslim scarves in front of the media. We put an end to that shit real quick. College students are young, idealistic—'We're all brothers, we are the world, you know.' The old *veteranos* were going 'Fuck you man,' because 20 years of coalescing with blacks didn't get us a damn thing," he said of Tom Bradley's years as mayor of Los Angeles. "I think blacks have cleverly used Latinos. 'We'll help you, stick with me buddy.' And they haven't helped us a damn bit."

THE HUNGER STRIKER

It's easy to say how the black radicals of the 1960s helped play into the hands of George Wallace, Richard Nixon, and Ronald Reagan as these politicians framed the race debate. One can say the same thing today as ethnocentric activists engage in self-destructive actions that benefit Pete Wilson and other Republicans. The sense of powerlessness leads to a rage that dooms the very people who have been disenfranchised. It is a negative feedback loop that seems beyond solution—without leadership and organization.

It is not much in vogue these days to acknowledge the roots of the frustration that blacks such as Donald Northcross have experienced. He had the weight of several centuries against him. As Don says of the fallout of the slavery-cotton South, "This system is like you break a man's leg, then you blame him for limping. Why don't you just walk like me? Jimminy cricket, you can't keep up? You know, you deliberately broke my leg, and now you've forgotten that. You seem to have forgotten that you are responsible for the condition that causes me to limp."

The argument can be made that Don and other blacks should just get over the wrongs of the past. They happened a long time ago, this reasoning goes, but Americans have little sense of history and the sources of the anger that drives students to smash up buildings on the UCLA campus and then go on a hunger strike. Slavery has ended, but we are just a generation removed from the sharecropping system that replaced it. It is a problem that transcends blacks and reaches other ethnic and racial groups. How does one get over the anger when the conditions that cause it are still with society? Latinos were not enslaved in the United States, but the semifeudal farm labor system in which many are employed is not history.

Joaquín Ochoa, one of the six hunger strikers at UCLA, grew up picking strawberries and harvesting raspberries for $4.25 a box in Watsonville, a farm town just inland from Monterey Bay. Historian Carey McWilliams accurately defined the situation in California's farm centers such as Watsonville when he wrote, "Farm labor is California's 'peculiar institution' in much the same sense that chattel slavery was the South's peculiar institution. Today as yesterday, the farm labor problem is the cancer which lies beneath the beauty, richness, and fertility of the valleys of California." [11]

Written a half century ago, McWilliams's words apply today. This farm economy is ruled by a largely white and Asian overclass that employs an underclass of Latino workers who are kept in place not with sharecropping agreements, but the threat that machines will take over the work, or that it will be given with lower pay to fresh arrivals from Mexico. It is a precarious existence that goes on in the coastal valleys and in dead-end Central Valley towns with the names of Orange Cove, Hallwood, Firebaugh, places where there is a stratified world of Mexican workers, landowners, tiny trailers, big houses, and endless rows of crops and orchards.

The situation is even harsher in Watsonville, for the Mexican workers live in public housing, shacks, and rundown trailers in dusty patches set back from the road, amid many giant new houses set like spaceships between the berry fields, with gates blocking the driveways. These suburbanites commute to jobs in San Jose and the Silicon Valley, and they have turned Watsonville into an elite, faux-country, suburban enclave. In McWilliams's day, this contrast of wealth and poverty did not exist. These suburbanites are not part of the feudal order, but their existence shows Mexicans how much of the American dream they are missing out on.

In this environment, Joaquín grew up angry as he picked strawberries and raspberries and planted flowers. By the time he made it to high school, he had been expelled from four elementary schools. Then he was kicked out of high school. His grade point average was 1.8. It looked as if he might spend the rest of his life in the Watsonville fields, just another *cholo* destined for a bad end. Among Joaquín's circle of friends, to aspire to be assistant manager at Pizza Hut was a job that offered unimagined status.

He credits his grandmother's influence for changing his course. "The light turned on. I studied day and night." He was nothing one would expect from an *Aztlánista,* given the descriptions offered by right-wingers, or even pictures in the papers. He was serious, intense, and shy.

When Governor Wilson launched his 1993 attack against immigrants, Joaquín was 21 years old and was about to graduate from UCLA with two degrees, taking as many as six classes during the summer breaks. "I was always tenacious," he said. "I never laid down for anybody." He learned many things at college, one, that it was just as much a "dog-eat-dog" world as the one in the fields. He also learned about history, got caught up in Chicano activism and the desire for a department to study Latino culture, as had long been the goal of the Chicanos.

"This is something we've been asking for for over 20 years, nicely, and we got denied for over 20 years. It's a legitimate field, yet we've been denied for racial reasons."

UCLA Chancellor Charles Young was unreceptive. After the students smashed up the faculty center, the issue seemed dead. There was talk of escalating the battle by starting a hunger strike, but no one wanted to go that far.

"I said come Monday, I'll be out there." He invited others to join him. "I did what I did for the future generation."

When the hunger strike entered its twelfth day, Young agreed to most of the striker's terms. Departmental status was not granted, but a quasi-separate unit was created called the César Chávez Center with four core faculty members. Joaquín had lost 18 pounds by the time the strike ended. Now he wondered if they shouldn't have starved for a few more days to have won more professors, more funding.

"We had the brass ring in our hand. We felt our community was coming to power. I thought what we got was a lot. Some of my friends say it's just a little stepping stone."

When asked if he feared the hunger strike alienated whites, he shrugged. "I don't think we've really faced up to the reality that there is going to be that backlash. We have to deal with that." Then he noted that Latinos are on a climb—they are now some 40 percent of the Los Angeles population and will nearly reach the same percentage statewide by 2010.

"What are you going to do about it? We're going to be here, we're going to be a force. Whether people want to accept it or not, that's the reality. It's like we're taking over L.A. now."

He said that contrary to conservatives' beliefs, the ethnic studies departments are popular. In the previous year, 2,000 students went through the various Chicano studies courses; most were overenrolled. "I think a lot of people are sticking their nose into it, seeing what it's about. We have to have an understanding of everybody."

Months later, in 1994, when the attack on Latinos had intensified and the Proposition 187 vote approached, Joaquín visited the site of the hunger strike, pointing to where the 50-some tents were set up in a park in the heart of the campus.

During the strike, banners were everywhere. There were pictures of Ché Guevara, dancers, a sacred circle with sage burning, statues of the Virgin Mary. Other groups—Filipino, black, Japanese, and Korean—set up tables. It was called "Cal-Mecca." Now students call it Placita Aztlán, the home haven. For one moment, there was unity, a sense of purpose. But it seemed distant in the face of Proposition 187, as support from other ethnic groups crumbled.

"I think everyone was engulfed by this Utopia that was created," Joaquín said as he wandered amid the trees of the now-quiet park. "They thought it would last forever and that everybody would get along. But it's kind of regressed back to where it was before . . . they went back to their own world, we went back to ours."

He walked across the lawn of Placita Aztlán and looked back at the site of the high point of his life. Over a coffee he talked about the anger he harbored through most of his youth. "My Mom says, 'Why do you hate people so much?' 'I don't hate no one, just people who give me a bad time because I'm Mexican.' She says 'Oh no, you must do something to them.' I don't think I was mad at any particular race, I was just mad at the unseen. A lot of people let those barriers get the best of them. That's when you hear we have got to be separate entities, you know, *chicanismo,* we got to solve our own problems. That's when you start getting that hatred. That's the dangerous part.

"At school I always talked about Watsonville. After the strike, when I went back, it didn't click. Something was different. It hurt me. You say I'm going to go back into my community and help, but once you succeed, you're seen as a sellout."

Is he viewed as a *vendido?*

"I've been called it. So I say yeah, I'm going to make 'Forbes Top 20' and give millions back to the community. They always say no, you get into that system, you can't do that. They'll stop you before you get up there. I say I'll be the first. I don't want to be rich. I want happiness. What do I want out of life? A roof over my head, food to eat.

"People have said, oh, you are living the American Dream. You know what? It's exactly that, a dream to me. I'm still looked at a little funny in certain areas. It's like you are torn between these two places. Sometimes it takes me going back home and looking at the fields I used to pick in. The American Dream paints the picture for everybody, yet it comes at a high price and not everybody can pay for it. Some people don't even get to touch the painting. They stay in the ghettos, they stay in poverty. Some white people are angry at the system too. They're just still workers too."

WHITE LIBERALS

Even though the actions of ethnic activists grabbed the most headlines during the early days of the backlash against nonwhites, liberal whites maintained a backbone of support. In the state assembly, it was often white liberal members and their staff who spoke most forcefully. Suzanne Wierbinski, Martha Escutia's chief of staff, is typical of many white liberals. Suzanne, a Berkeley graduate confined to a wheelchair from a teenage auto accident, sees the multicultural backlash as a test for progressives. She disagrees with those who say the Left is dead. It will have to re-create itself because it has been going on autopilot for so long that it has lost sight of its roots. In the short term, Suzanne said progressives have got to return to organizing. "The Right is taking people who are already politically active. They are picking away at the moderates, the dissatisfied liberals, Democrats, whatever they are called." Liberals need to cultivate a whole new voting base by working groups such as Latinos—not through slick television campaigns, but old-fashioned community organizing.

"Too many times, the Democrats think, okay we'll register 6,000 people. That doesn't mean 6,000 people are going to go out and vote. Okay, you have 6,000 more Latinos, 6,000 more Asian surnames. That's all you got. But social and political development needs to be cultivated."

Part of the job of the Left will be education. She sees the California backlash against changing culture as part of a larger test in the continuing development of America. "People think once you've passed a constitution, we're all one great big country," she said, shaking her head. "We haven't totally resolved the Civil War. And who knows if this country was founded on the idea of the diversity that it has become? It was basically built [as] a white European culture. What does it mean to be an American, what does it mean to care for everybody within the society? What we have not decided in this country, what does it mean to be a group of people."

Like many progressives, her optimism is coupled with a dark side.

"The advancements, technologically and socially, have separated us," she said of California's suburban society. Even without cultural change, Americans would be confused and isolated.

"Then with the influx of new cultures, we don't know where the hell we are, or where we're going. We're in a transition. How do we find that connectiveness that binds all of us together? The problem is, people like 3-second sound bites and want 30-second solutions. There ain't 30-second solutions. You have to work from the ground up. You can't just work from the top. I'm a real optimist. I really think people are good and basically want to do well. It's hard for me to truly realize that there are people out there who don't give a shit."

She pointed to Tito's Yugoslavia. With the end of the Cold War, his multicultural union fell apart.

"The minute it ended, they were out of there. Are we doing the same thing? Are we legislating unity? If those laws were not there, what would happen?"

10

Orange Curtain

As the immigration debate intensified in late 1993, no one in Dana Point yet knew about the looming Save Our State ballot initiative. Immigration was a local issue. Only one of the whites active in Lantern Village politics belonged to any of the myriad state and national anti-immigration groups. And even as local tensions continued, there were no hate flyers, no shouting in public. Dana Point is not that kind of place. "Everything's under the surface," Rosalyn Williams, Bill Shepherd's neighbor, said before one city council meeting.

Dana Point and south Orange County are typical of places in California outside the circles of the activist right and left. For every instance of hot conflict, at the UCLA or Berkeley campuses, or of whites shining their headlights on the U.S.-Mexican border fence to drive back immigrants—there are numerous environments like Dana Point. This does not mean underlying passions were not strong or that Wilson's message was not getting through to the Dana Point whites, or that things could not yet erupt.

On October 15, 1993, a little more than a week after the 10 key people met to craft Proposition 187, south Orange County blew apart. The attitude toward illegal immigration in Dana Point and several surrounding cities suddenly became one of overt fear.

It was a Friday night in San Clemente, the town immediately south of Dana Point. Steven Woods, a 17-year-old high school student and nine of his friends had attended the school football game. After the game, they drove several cars to the beach to listen to music before going on to one of several parties.

One member of Woods's group was at the far end of the parking lot where some Latinos were gathered; he approached them and said "We're San Clemente." The white youth wanted to know if they knew of any parties, but the Latinos thought they were being provoked: the San Clemente Varrio Chicos were a rival gang. The kid returned to his friends and suggested it would be wise to leave. The whites told police that when the Latinos came toward them with baseball bats and chains, they sped to the exit.

The three cars headed straight for the Latinos, who told police that they feared being run down. They began throwing things from the back of a truck: rocks, logs, beer cans. One object shattered the car window on Woods's passenger side; a microsecond later, a paint roller sailed through the now-open window, the metal rod piercing Woods's skull.[1]

Woods lingered in a coma for a month, then died. Racial charges and countercharges flew: as a result of the killing, community meetings were held in San Clemente and Dana Point. In San Clemente, whites demanded they "take back" their town. Latino leaders said the white kids provoked the trouble and that the youths arrested that night were not gang members. This denial angered Bill Shepherd. He saw a lesson in cultural differences.

"You see something like the Steve Woods incident . . . what's the response from the families and the Latino community? 'Oh, they were bothering us, it's racial to call them gang members, they were victims, we didn't do it.' There's all this excuse and victimization."

Bill contrasted the death with an incident in north Orange County the year before, when four Asian youths from well-to-do families killed a fifth member of their group, Stuart Tay, when the others feared he was about to snitch on plans to rob an Anaheim computer shop.[2] "The four other guys that he perpetrated the crime with, they panicked, assassinated him, and buried him in [a] backyard. The response of the families of those Asians was, we're ashamed, our sons have dishonored their name.

"I think it's a very important distinction between the way those two cultures handled the same kind of event. Both were atrocities, both kids were more than likely guilty, and yet you have one culture that's consistently portraying itself as a victim—whatever the rationale is to say it wasn't my fault—to the other culture which talks about honor, family name, being shamed. Even though it's a horrific crime, there's something to be said for that kind of response."

In the wake of the Woods's killing, Bill decided to run for one of the three vacant seats on the Dana Point City Council. The death was not the sole reason he wanted to run, but it was the latest incident in a long list of changes in his community that prompted him to do something more. The number-one item on Bill's agenda would be crime, "a zero tolerance for gangs, drugs and graffiti. If it looks like, walks like, talks like it, stop it and harass it." Bill wanted to use a "multidisciplinary approach" to go after the problems of blight that he felt led to crime; he wanted to see a team of police, code enforcement officers, public health and fire officials who would "go block by block, combing each property." They would hold property owners accountable. He said there would be results within three months.

"We need to find creative ways," he said. "As long as it's legal, let's do it."

Many things were not legal. For instance, the city had looked into an occupancy ordinance to limit the number of residents per dwelling, but they were blocked by the recent court ruling that had stopped the city of Santa Ana from doing the same thing. Other tools had yet to be explored, such as a street parking permit system that would limit each unit to two cars.

Bill threw himself into his city council campaign, and the town suddenly sported many of his fluorescent orange and blue signs. He carried a message to the rest of the community that crime was encroaching—and something had to be done before it was too late. He wanted to coordinate antigang efforts with San Clemente and other nearby towns. "At best we'll displace it, but at least we'll displace it far enough away that maybe it will stay away for a while. We can't go directly to the problem and say you can't have 15 people in one apartment. We can't get to the disease, so we work on the symptoms."

Was he singling out immigrants?

That would be "political death," he said. "You immediately get called a racist." Of course, the real point of Bill's plan was to get at Latinos who were not obeying the law or adhering to the cultural values of the whites. Bill repeated his belief that he did not mind the presence of Latinos or any other racial group so long as they conformed to local laws and standards. "I don't think that crime is a racist issue. I think it just goes to my personal sense of self. Unfortunately, [racism] is a very easy accusation to make." Curiously, in the coming months, he was not attacked from the quarters one would expect—Latinos—but from some local white Libertarians. Several Libertarians referred to him and Lantern Village members as "brown shirts" for their actions in fighting blight and gangs. And he received anonymous phone threats.

Bill was deeply disturbed by the accusation that he was a brown shirt. He expresses the dichotomy of many California whites: they can be very accepting and still be reactionary. This can be found in whites elsewhere, but it is more acute in California because whites live in "islands" like south Orange County. Some whites who have left the Los Angeles polyglot and its crime and drive-by shootings feel surrounded in south Orange County, their fear ratcheted up when Steve Woods is killed in their backyard. They believe their island is surrounded and perhaps about to be invaded. Their fear is mixed with an acceptance of blacks, Latinos, and Asians. Saying all whites who vote for Pete Wilson are closet Wallaces is a ruinous assumption of the Left.

An illustration of this split personality can be found in the redwood country of California's north coast. In one community is a mix of pagan worshipers, marijuana growers, retired lesbian cops, Earth First! activists, hippies, musicians, survivalists, rock-ribbed old-time ranchers straight out of the cowboy West of 1880—all who more or less get along. One can belong to a religion that worships pigs as God. No one is interested in interfering with what you do on the other side of your property line and the same respect is expected in return. On the rare occasion when transgression occurs, people can turn very ugly very fast in a way as extreme as their lifestyles. It is a way of dealing with things rooted in the Gold Rush frontier. If your pigs escape and eat the neighbor's garden, the pigs, Gods or not, will be shot dead.

While this western brand of liberalism (or Libertarianism) is most pronounced in the wilds, it is found in the state's suburbs. In Bill's neighborhood, many white residents only grew worried when their "lines" were crossed. The Latino or black or Asian who buys the $500,000 home next door to these same whites will be accepted so long as they mow their lawn and do not otherwise offend the sensibilities of the neighbors. It was not until poor non-whites moved in and brought "problems" with them that things turned nasty.

ANOTHER WHITE'S VIEW OF RACE

The killing of Steve Woods energized many Dana Point whites who wanted the city to more aggressively prevent crime. A few months after the Woods killing, a woman with long reddish hair came to speak to the city council. Diane Harkey held up a copy of that day's newspaper, with an article about 15-year-old Angela Wagner, a San Clemente High School sophomore who had been found murdered in the parking lot of a south Dana Point apartment complex near Diane's home.[3] (Wagner, ironically, was a friend of one of the white kids on the beach when Woods was killed, though Wagner's death was not gang-related.) There had also just been a drive-by shooting in a town just east of Dana Point.[4]

"I know Mayor Curreri doesn't like this issue because of the racial overtones," Diane said. She paused before adding, "I don't think this is racial."

She said she had seen signs of gang activity in the oceanfront park in Capistrano Beach and was afraid to walk there.

"We have been thinking about moving to a gated community. I don't want to do that. I don't think you can build walls around yourself. We need to take a more proactive stance on crime. The guard gates aren't going to help us."

A few days later, Diane stood at her window, pointing to the beach below where she recently faced two black men who stared her down. She also pointed to the railroad tracks and told how she sees Mexican hobos riding north. "I don't blame them for coming. If I were them, I'd come too. I don't mind if they come to work. I just want them to obey our laws."

The gang members she saw on the beach and the Latinos involved with the Woods killing were part of the world she knew existed in Los Angeles but felt could not be tolerated in Dana Point.

"I don't think people in Dana Point are racist. What we had primarily here before were hard-working Mexican Americans and Mexicans. Over the years, especially as the economy went down, the mother and father both started working, and this led to gangs. It's amazing how fast this multiplied. In the last two years, suddenly the gangs are here."

Why, Diane asked, is it racist to dislike kids who do bad things? When she was a child in Los Angeles and went to a multiracial high school, the good kids were accepted and no one liked the bad kids. "They were *cholos*," she said, using Mexican slang for dead-end kids. "They were low class. That's what we've got in Dana Point now. I don't care if you're white, black, brown, or purple, trashy people are trashy people."

Diane grew up in the Baldwin Park area of Los Angeles. In high school, she dated a Mexican man; his sister was her best friend. Diane, who is white, joined the Mexican service club, and she used to cruise Whittier Boulevard in East Los Angeles with her Mexican friends. Later, when she became a banker, she sponsored a young Vietnamese refugee for citizenship. Yet it troubles her that the United States is so generous to immigrants. "It would be nice to say okay, land of plenty, but the plenty is running out. I hear a lot about egalitarianism. Don't we realize that it calls for decreasing everyone's standard of living to be egalitarian? Somebody is paying for that—it's been me. Quite honestly, I'm not willing to do that. How can we keep paying?"

Diane and her husband had worked hard to afford their home. It is not in a gated area, but the neighborhood is not easy to get to, with just two access points and the steep bluff on one side. Like Bill, she was active in her neighborhood community association. She was also concerned about Lantern Village, because she and her husband own rental units there.

Diane not only saw cultural change in her neighborhood, but on a college campus. She was about to graduate with a degree in economics and political science from the University of California at Irvine. When her daughter was born in 1986, she quit a 16-year career as a bank vice president, promising herself that she would go to back to college when the girl was old enough.

Diane, a Wilson supporter who would attend his 1994 inauguration, was puzzled and amazed by what she found at the university.

"They all stayed together. They had the Chicano club, and the 'this' club, the 'that' club—ne'er the twain shall meet. What really saddened me was that nobody got together. I would be the first to admit that the European race has had a superior claim on everything for the last hundreds of years," she said of the domination of the world by white Europeans, through colonialism and economic domination.

"But there's such a lashing out—it's not changing anything. When I grew up, the melting pot was the deal. Now, you've got to have your tribe. I have empathy. I know what they're trying to do. But you've got to deal with yourself first. What's wrong with becoming part of a group? If you go back and trace roots, we're all alike, we've just been in different climates for a while. So what's the deal? Assimilation helps us all. Assimilation is what you need to do all throughout your life to get along with people. I mean, I went [to college] with people who were 20 years younger than me. Talk about the ultimate outsider. I had to become a student. Otherwise, I would have walked around alone. Because I was 42 at the time, I was the pal to everybody. I had black friends, I had Asian friends. I enjoyed them all.

"There's people that would sit back and complain rather than get out and work. Economically, these people aren't moving anywhere. Why? Maybe you're spending so much time worrying about your fences that you're not making any strides. And if anyone of their own breaks out of the group, they're looked upon as an Uncle Tom. It's very hard to leave your group. That's one way that I progressed through my life. I was able to leave my group. There's nobody I have maintained contacts with from high school. The only people I maintain any contacts at all with are my own family. And even those people I've broken from. Other than to talk about the past, we don't have a lot in common. But I never looked back. It's sad remembering the fun times, but then you've got a life out here. There's nothing wrong with that."

ON THE STREETS OF DANA POINT

One sunny Saturday afternoon not long after Bill announced his candidacy for the city council, he drove his black BMW to an area near Diane's house. He and John O'Hara, a former neighbor and now his campaign manager, were going to knock on doors to drum up support. The neighborhood, adjacent to San Clemente, consists of funky flat-roofed bungalows as well as some grander homes. They began working a street called Calle Naranja.

"Naranja," said John, "I think that means orange in Spanish."

"Really?" Bill asked.

Bill wore a white shirt, open at the neck, an ubiquitous ballcap, loafers. His first pitch set the tone for the 35 houses that would follow.

"Hi, I'm Bill Shepherd and I'm running for city council," he said as he held up a campaign flyer. "Would you take a few minutes to read it over, when you get a chance? My number-one issue is crime. I'm for a zero tolerance policy. Do you know the Lantern Village area? When I moved here eight years ago, it was a nice place. But it's gone down. [This elicited nods.] The police arrested 10 people down my street for drugs, and they found a .357 magnum in the place. Last December, that girl was killed down here on the beach. I decided to get involved because if we don't stop it, it will spread to other parts of Dana Point."

At one yard near Sunset Park, they were greeted by a dog. A blond and tanned woman in her late thirties pruning a hedge put down her shears.

"We get them hanging out there," said the homeowner, pointing to the park and the place where Latino youths were starting to congregate—but she never said the words Mexican or Latino. "And we call the police. Sometimes the helicopter comes. We don't want to let it get started."

"You can't let it start," said Bill. "How has the police response been?"

The woman shrugged. "They come pretty fast." As for the kids in the park, she added, "we never see them, but we find the needles. They must do it at night. Our kids play over there in the day and it's okay. And they come with spray paint. My neighbor goes over right away," the woman said, pointing next door, "and sprays over it."

At another door, a woman in her fifties said, "I haven't worked in six months. And I want to work. All these illegal aliens are taking the jobs. I can't get a job."

The woman added that she sees Mexicans walking up her street at night, something that never before happened. This scared her.

"I'd like to see the city hire an INS officer," Bill said.

Even though the Save Our State ballot initiative had since qualified for the ballot and would be voted on in six months, there had been little mention of it in the newspapers. Not one person, including Bill or John, knew about it.

After three hard hours of walking and talking, Bill's pitch still sounded fresh. Over and over, residents mentioned crime they associated with immigrant gangs. Another big issue was the Headlands, the last undeveloped fragment of Dana Point shoreline. The owner wanted to build a hotel and preserve part of it, while the opponents wanted it all to remain pristine—but the city had no money to buy the land.

"I'm very concerned about it," said one woman of gangs and crime. Then she asked about Headlands. Bill gave the middle-of-the-road response that the city cannot afford $120 million to purchase it. He favored a scaled-down hotel and houses.

"But with the hotel, they will need employees, which will lead to more overcrowding in the Lantern Village," he said. "There are solutions—maybe we can bus the workers in."

As they drove away, John said "I think we got 30 to 40 votes, and that's a conservative number."

A few days later, there was a fund-raiser for Bill at a restaurant overlooking the Dana Point Harbor. Yachts rocked gently in a rising tide outside the window. An American flag graced one wall and a table held a bowl of red, white, and blue tortilla chips.

Bill worked the crowd, which included councilman Mike Eggers, who was leaving office, and Mayor Judy Curreri. Inside the open door of the kitchen all the visible workers were Latino. Out front, all but one of the servers were white. The only nonwhite worker scurrying to serve hors d'oeuvres was Alma Valladres. In her job as a public health nurse in the 1970s, Judy had helped Alma's mother as she struggled to feed her children after the family arrived from the state of Morelos, south of Mexico City. Now 23, Alma served Bill and Dennis Vlach before vanishing into the kitchen to restock the tray. Bill told the 40 people in the room how he would reduce crime in Dana Point.

ALMA'S STORY

Alma grew up in Lantern Village on the Street of the Amber Lantern, in one of the crowded apartments that worried Bill. She lived with her three brothers and mother, a single parent who worked as a housekeeper. She was six when her mother brought the family to Dana Point. Much less crowded then, Alma could run through the undeveloped brown hills. Her mother stressed the need to work and the need for education, but after Alma graduated from high school, her academic career proceeded on an uneven course. At the time of Bill's fund-raiser, she was working double shifts while attending Saddleback College, a nearby two-year school.

Alma understood that she belonged to two cultures. Several times, her mother had taken her and her brothers back to Mexico. She was impressed by how much stronger families were there, but the poverty repelled her and made her thankful her mother had come to El Norte.

Alma had recently visited San Diego with a guide from the Student Organization of Latinos, a school group known by its acronym SOL, Spanish for "sun." They toured the grand murals and learned of Aztlán.

"He explained to us about the murals, why there is a red hand and a black hand holding each other, because the whites wanted the Mexicans and the blacks to basically fight each other," Alma said one day before she started her shift at work. "The reason they don't get along is here comes the white man and tells them, 'You're not going to get anything.' It's like there's a piece of meat, so they fight for that."

Alma had taken great interest in Latino culture and agreed with much of what she had heard at college. But for all of her focus on Latino culture, she was very Americanized in manner and dress and speech. Typical of many youths who identified with the Chicano

movement, she straddled two cultures, but was much more American than Mexican. Yet though legal with a green card, she was not
a citizen: she qualified under the 1986 federal amnesty, but was
not sure she wanted to go through with naturalization. Alma now
lived with a roommate in an apartment on the Street of the Blue
Lantern but was thinking about moving back to Mexico. She dis-
dains the materialism and shallowness she sees in American culture,
the oddness of people living behind walls.

"The reason they go gated is because they feel safe. And they
want to go higher, because they want to feel above. To me, they're
afraid to realize the truth. The truth that we are all human and we
all have to stick together. But they don't want to be equal. They
want to always be a little bit above. Everyone here is so much into
real estate. I mean they're just so much into their money. In high
school, if you don't have the car, the biggest car, you basically
don't have friends.

"I don't want to live here anymore. They don't care if you're
human or not. The only thing they want is this area to look nice.
Even though it looks nice on the outside, but when you get into
the places, you know it's not that nice."

Without knowing what Diane Harkey had said, Alma countered her belief that it was important to cut oneself off from one's
past. "You look at our culture, Indians, they are super tight. People
from America, they're not tight. Their families are not important.
As soon as they turn 18, they want to split. They want to put their
parents in a retirement home. Did you forget that when you were a
baby, your mom changed your diapers? They only think as an individual, as a one. We think as a whole. We're all in a circle, we all
combine. You can't have just for you only, because you'll be stuck
with you and you only at the end."

Americans, she said, are so willing to experiment with things
like drugs and sex, but are unwilling to learn about other cultures.
She wishes the whites would learn the best parts of Latino culture.
She was not advocating a separate society in the United States, just
an incorporation of the best of both worlds.

"Like say we grabbed somebody from here and we took them
down to Mexico and they saw what Mexico was, they would come
back with a totally different outlook."

Her view of the United States? "This is heaven, it's hell. The devil is right there in front of you. The devil to me is those people who are trying to get illegal aliens out of here. If you think about it, if you get them out of here, you're stuck with nothing. If this law does go by, a lot of places, they're going to go right out of business. I know ours totally will. These guys work so hard for nothing."

THE PREACHER

Three Mexican men walked up the Capistrano Creek channel, shouldering road packs. They disappeared in the dust beyond a patch of bamboo while Christian Pedersen finished with a customer. By day, Pedersen was an auto mechanic. By night, he was a minister who wandered amid the bamboo canes to help immigrants and held services in an old carpet store with walls of bare studs in south Dana Point.

"I need my car today!" demanded the customer, pointing to his Mercedes. Pedersen explained that he was waiting for a part to be delivered. As this older white man stormed off, a weathered campesino materialized in the creek channel, framed by the open door of Pedersen's shop. Pedersen, himself an immigrant from Peru, looks very European, but speaks with a Spanish accent.

"They're just trying to find some jobs. They move a lot. I talk with somebody, and I don't see them after two weeks."

Many, Pedersen said, are really quite "innocent." They don't become fully Americanized, but become something else. Some immigrants take on the worst aspects of life here; they get caught up in materialism and acquiring money.

"They just want to work, work, work," he said as he wiped grease from his hands. Some men work two jobs, and the mother works as well. "This is superficial. The kids are going without love. The lifestyle here is faster. Over there, you take the bus. Here you need a car. Here you go 100 miles per hour. There you go 40 kilometers per hour, which is a lot slower."

For the new arrivals, work is not easy to come by. In fact, his own business was down 50 percent from the previous year.

"They get very depressed. Families get problems because the husband drinks too much, because of no jobs. They have this type of machismo. They are too proud to ask for help."

For those employed, the kids are often left to fend for them-selves. "It is tough and they join gangs," he said. "Why? Because they don't have love. The parents are not there when they want to say something. When a little boy goes to play softball, no one is there. Both the mother and father are working. They are so busy they leave the children with the television. The girls believe the boys who tell them they love them to sleep with them. Then they get pregnant. Then the parents kick out the daughters, 16, 17 years old."

The kids do cause a lot of crime, he said. He often repairs cars with windows broken from burglaries. "I see it getting more and more violent. What can we do? What I do, I pray, and try to do the best I can."

COMMERCE

The Marina Ranch Market—the first Mexican grocery in Dana Point—opened its doors in early 1994 at the base of Bill Shep-herd's street. Opening day was a festive scene of balloons, Mexican music, the store filled with spices, tortillas. Amid the crowd of Spanish-speakers came one white man, later another; they anx-iously inspected the store and left without buying anything.

At a recent council meeting, one white man had muttered about the market. "Everything's turning Mexican." He bitterly said he was going to get a burro and start selling things from a wagon. When the market owner, Vince Grillo, a Spanish-speaking Italian who immigrated in the 1950s, later heard this, he said the Latino presence cannot be ignored.

"They're here," Grillo said. "The Anglos are all moving out. You see, it's too late. I don't blame them for feeling the way they do. When they [Mexicans] move into an area, property values go down. They fix their cars on the lawn, they think it's Mexico. The Mexican people are set in their ways. The city didn't want a Latino market here. I told the inspector it's not our fault they're here. You built the apartments that made them move here. We just opened the market to take advantage of it."

At a convenience store in adjoining Laguna Niguel, a white businessman came in looking for a copy of *La Opinion,* the Spanish-language newspaper. They were sold out—usually it was gone by 9 in the morning.

The businessman said the paper was the perfect medium. His company had an ad in that day's paper, the second one it had placed. The first ad attracted 35 Spanish-speakers to his sales pitch, which led to eight big sales. He told the store owner that he'd learned to speak Spanish. "They like to buy when you speak their language," the store owner explained.

"It's what we call a laydown," said the suit with a smile.

THE NEW IMMIGRANT

In early 1994 activists gathering signatures for the Save Our State initiative were rumored to have been at a supermarket in the south part of Dana Point. A newsletter supporting SOS used a picture of Steve Woods's skull impaled with the paint roller.

Amid the growing concern among Latinos, Hermandad Mexicana Nacional, the national Mexican brotherhood, a group that promotes immigrant rights, decided to hold a meeting at Our Lady of Fatima Church in San Clemente to discuss the initiative. About 30 Latinos showed up. The woman running the meeting asked those present to give their immigration status.

The first man to speak said *"Soy un mojado,"* I am a wetback, which brought chuckles. The group was a mix of the documented and undocumented. A woman from the Mexican brotherhood lectured in Spanish, saying that in not too many years Latinos will be the state's majority race. She said they would have to become citizens and vote. She emphasized the United States was not like Mexico, where one party dictates.

"It's important for all members to participate," she said, adding that even those here illegally needed to get politically involved, such as getting citizens out to vote. "The discrimination is against everyone, the residents, the *mojados.*"

A young couple came from Dana Point with their baby girl. Both were illegal. The father, Antonio, held their daughter and said they came to the meeting because he could not understand why so many people hated them.

A few days later, Antonio sat in his family's sparse apartment.

The living room had a small television on a pedestal. There was a large worn couch, its stuffing exposed, and an old coffee table. The only wall decoration was a macramé hanging with the word "Guatemala" embroidered upon it. Antonio had come alone from Acapulco six years earlier, at the height of the employment boom in Dana Point. He got lucky and worked hard—after he landed two jobs, he brought his girlfriend from Mexico.

"I come here first, working hard, one year. I went to pick her up," he said in English, a language he was desperately trying to learn.

The family shares the two-bedroom apartment with another couple, who also have a baby girl. They split the $960 rent. Antonio works two jobs, 14 hours each day. One job plus part of the second pays the rent. The remaining hours take care of food and other bills—barely. He felt it was worth the extra rent to live in Dana Point because it is a safe neighborhood.

Life in America is expensive and Antonio wanted to better himself. He enthusiastically told about an "American" and Latino man who had come to his home the day before. They offered him a job selling real estate. To work for them, he would have to attend real estate school, at a cost of $3,400. The men told Antonio they would pay the tuition if he produced four families who bought homes.

"Maybe when I have experience for this job, I can quit with my other jobs. I think it's okay, because the other guy told me, he brought four families and he don't pay anything. I like this job because you know I can relation with different people, and I can speak more English, I can learn more . . . you know, about life in the United States. What do you think about this?"

I suggested he proceed slowly. But Antonio did not want words of caution. Antonio repeated that he needed to earn more. He complained that so much of his money went to pay taxes.

"When you buy milk, you pay tax. When you pay rent, you pay tax. We pay taxes. A lot of taxes. When you get a check, they take out. I make 400 dollars, they take 50 dollars. They think we don't pay taxes," he said of the anti-immigrant organizations who said illegals take services without paying into the system.

But don't they take some services?

"She has medical, but she born here," Antonio said, pointing to his daughter. "She's American. She's citizen. Lot of people take service, but I think maybe two in ten people. Lot of black American people, black men, they get lot of service—and a lot of American people, especially American womans with children. I think they can work because they speak English. I don't know why they have welfare. It's not fair. They think every Mexican, every Spanish people, is bad."

Antonio showed a ticket he received from an Orange County Sheriff's deputy. He was stopped on the Street of the Golden Lantern for a faulty brake light. The cop went over his car and told him he needed new tires. Other Latinos interviewed said police harass them. (This, it seems, is a means of keeping the pressure on, letting them know they should not get out of line.) After the Steve Woods killing, the cops in San Clemente began photographing the Latinos they stopped.

"I never had problem with the police because I'm always in my house, on the job, sometimes I go to the park with my family, restaurant sometimes," Antonio said. "I think if you not a bad boy, you don't have problems."

THE POWER STRUCTURE

When I first visited the local sheriff's station in Dana Point City Hall, Officer Joe Homs outlined a recent crime year in which they had three murders, three rapes, 232 vehicle burglaries, 181 residential burglaries, and 108 commercial burglaries.[5] Almost none of this crime occurred behind the gate-guarded areas. Did he have a racial breakdown on arrests?

"We won't touch that," Homs said.

Instead, he said: "It took L.A. a long time to get where it [is]. Orange County is heading that way."

I asked how far behind they are from Los Angeles.

"I say 20 years, if we don't start addressing the gangs."

He paused. "It's not the gangs, it's society itself. We know how to put people in jail. The jails are full. The problem is—it is a social problem. We need jobs. If people are working, they're not going to hang out drinking on street corners. I spent two days in Los Angeles during the riots." He was part of a team sent to assist local cops guarding a Watts Safeway. "Going up there and seeing what goes on, how they live, I felt I was in a totally different world. I don't want to say another country, because I don't want to disrespect different countries. It was another world."

To understand how much crime was or was not being committed in the Lantern Village on a typical Friday night, I wanted to see the sheriff's patrol at work. I asked permission to ride along—which most departments routinely grant to the press and interested citizens. Officer Homs arranged it, but the day before, Homs called to say his boss wanted to talk with me.

I went back to City Hall on the Street of the Golden Lantern, to visit Lieutenant Paul Dennis Ratchford. He was shaking his head as I walked through his door. The answer was suddenly no. He asked what do you want, what are you going to say? I said I simply wanted to see what happened.

Wrong answer. Ratchford smiled more coolly than any southern cop. He said whatever happened on the ridealong could inflame either the pro or anti-immigrant factions. And "there's the 'L' word," he said—liberal. I was not going to see them do anything unless I was really pro-police. He offered a bone: send clips of my past police reporting and a letter and he might reconsider.

Ratchford's response was typical of a much wider suspicion in the power structure in Dana Point. Warmth and candor are not exactly the response when one questions too deeply how things are run in a wealthy enclave where the tax base is derived from Latino labor. The reaction is not much different from California's Central Valley farming centers, where the rulers of the local order conspired with agribusiness to control the workers, especially anytime there was talk of a labor union. For years, agribusiness was the biggest employer of Latinos. It was common to see men with wads of cash at the end of the season on the passenger trains heading out of Mexicali, fresh from field work, heading back to their homes and families deep in Mexico. In the 1980s, the work shifted—labor in hotels, sweat shops, and on suburban lawn crews surpassed farm work as the biggest employer of Mexicans. Now that the jobs were for the full year, many more were remaining and bringing their wives, instead of seasonally migrating. Often, the wives worked as well.

The same kind of feudal order exists today in the suburbs, but it is a more subtle form than was seen in the old farm centers. The suburban Latinos of Dana Point are making beds and washing dishes, not picking peaches or melons. They are kept in line by police who take their photographs or cite them for balding tires. The police merely act out the wishes of the ruling order—the hotels, the town leaders—which does not want things stirred up. When the city of Dana Point conducted a study of who works in the town's restaurants and where they live, overwhelmingly the answer was Latinos and Lantern Village. The report, finished just before the council election in which Bill Shepherd ran, was not released.

Other facts are guarded. When I went to the City Hall, located in a fake New England–style office and shopping center and asked how much tax revenue the hotels raised, a secretary called up on her computer the $36.5 million figure that the hotels grossed, but in the middle of giving me the breakdown that 80 percent of this money was generated by the two biggest hotels, with the vast bulk of it—some $20 million or so—coming from the Ritz-Carlton, her boss stopped her.

"We don't want that to get out! You can't use it!"

When I went to Dana Hills High School to talk with a woman who works with gang kids, I was stopped because I had not gone through bureaucratic channels. I was quickly hustled into the office of Al Rios, a vice principal. "I just came from South Central L.A.," Rios said of his last job. "I've dealt with the most violent and bad kids. And here I am in paradise, and I'm dealing with even more violent and bad kids." I asked if he was joking. He shrugged, then quickly cut off the interview.

When I wanted to interview the managers of the two big hotels, my phone calls were not returned. Only when I sent registered letters politely requesting a meeting did I get a reply. The Ritz-Carlton people were never available when I was in town. At the Dana Point Resort, I met with Cheri O. Abbott, the personnel and training director.

Abbott was *very* tense, even though she brought out many good points and it was obvious from what she said and from what Latinos told me that the hotel treated its workers quite well. She said the hotel was careful about checking papers—Abbott said they do not hire the undocumented. "From the viewpoint of the law, they have every right to be working here. We're really talking about jobs that no one else wants."

Whites almost never apply for these jobs, said Abbott, who was born in Huntington Park, in what is now Martha Escutia's assembly district. Abbott had to think hard about how many whites had applied for dishwashing and room cleaning jobs.

"Maybe two," she said after a long pause, in a period of 15 months. Few blacks and Asians show up, either. Their entire workforce is 42 percent minority, and about 35 percent of this is Latino. If not for Latinos, they would have no workers in the basic positions, she said. The hotel employed about 100 Latinos in these jobs, most of whom lived in Lantern Village. She said that many work two or even three jobs. "When they come in for work, they are as ready to go as anyone else, even though they've already put in eight hours somewhere else," she said.

Were American citizens of all races lazy? Abbott would not comment on this, but she did say that many Latinos have been with the hotel since it opened, which is unheard of in the industry. Abbott was so nervous that she almost did not mention that the hotel sponsors free English classes for those who want to advance themselves.

"It starts early in the morning, so they've got to catch a bus in at maybe seven o'clock, so they're here an hour and a half before they start work. And that's two days a week," she said of the 24 Latinos who'd signed up.

Many whites point to the hotels as a magnet for Latino migration, but some are a bit hypocritical, for some hire Latino gardeners and nannies. Even Pete Wilson and his first wife Betty hired an illegal immigrant maid in 1978 and never paid her Social Security taxes. One white woman in Dana Point who hired a Salvadoran nanny said she had tried to hire American citizens, but could not find anyone who satisfied her.

"I mean you don't leave your child with anybody, documented or un-, unless you know that they're going to take care of her. I tried to hire a nanny, I put ads in for a regular person. I got this one lady that was older, but she was just hostile. And then I got another lady that wanted ten dollars an hour." So this woman hired the Salvadoran and helped her become legalized when amnesty was offered.

THE LINE IN THE (BEACH) SAND

In the months after Steve Woods's murder, south Orange County whites were tense. Some spent their evenings not watching television, but tuned into police scanners, as one imagines settlers in darkened log cabins listened, rifle in hand, for the cracking twig outside. One described a report on the scanner of a woman who was mugged the previous night by three Mexican men at an upscale shopping center. This middle-aged man who lived in a $500,000 house vowed this would never happen to him—he carried a gun in his car.

Talk of moving away is a common mantra. Outgoing Dana Point Councilman Mike Eggers considered leaving, but he said there's nowhere to run—the problems are everywhere. "You got to stand and fight," he said. "You've got to draw a line in the sand. People have saved for years to move here. By God, they want it to be as secure as possible."

Of all local officials, Mike was the most outspoken against immigration. His day job was as the local staff member for Republican U.S. Representative Ron Packard. Packard had long been against illegal immigration, and Mike had pushed the issue in council meetings, with little success.

"There's three women," he said of several fellow council members. "One is a public health nurse. The other was a nurse. And the other one is a teacher. By nature of their jobs, it's 'Let's be warm and fuzzy.' But you can't solve gang problems with the warm and fuzzy solution." Between the San Clemente and San Juan gangs, Dana Point has long been considered neutral territory. But, Mike said, "my fear is that Dana Point will become a battleground between the two."

In this environment, many voters were ready to punch their cards for anything they thought would fight crime. But their frustration did not help Bill Shepherd. In June 1994 he lost the 12-way city council election by 134 votes: he came very close and was far ahead of most other candidates, but the battle over the last remnant of undeveloped Dana Point coastline dwarfed other issues.

Bill's message about crime resonated in the gate-guarded

neighborhood of Monarch Bay, where he won half of the 341 ballots cast. He was angry about losing and he did not like the direction the city issues were taking. But he continued working harder than ever to fight the problems he found.

What the future holds in Dana Point is hard to say. Radical cultural change is not out of the question, said Robb Steel, the city's economic development coordinator, who had just left a job with the Los Angeles suburb of Azusa. He said that in 1970 Azusa was around 80 percent white. By 1990 the town was 35 percent white. Most flight occurred when minorities—mostly Latino—hit about one-third of the population, the apparently critical number that sets the "tipping scale" into action, in which whites flee. By the time Steel was hired to help Azusa's economy, whites in power wanted him to maintain their culture—long after their majority had fled. He said there was even talk of outlawing additional Mexican restaurants.

"They wanted me to bring in the kind of businesses they used to have. But I told them it was like trying to bring in Mexican restaurants when [Mexicans] were just 10 percent of the population."

Parts of Orange County are like the Azusa of 20 years ago, Steel said—but with one critical difference, the ocean. He believes some areas will become largely minority, but because Dana Point is an affluent coastal community, it will be difficult for low-income minorities to expand into the richest areas with ocean views. Mike Egger's line is drawn in beach sand: the ocean neighborhoods will keep out all but the wealthy—except for small pockets like Lantern Village. Steel said natural barriers will stop the expansion. He co-owns a rental unit in San Juan Capistrano and became concerned after he bought the property when nearby apartments filled with poor Latinos. But railroad tracks and a highway between those units and his building stopped the barrio's spread. "Housing is at a premium," Steel said. "They won't get too much beyond that."

11

The Campus and the
Suburban Ghetto

In the 1980s the percentage of whites in the undergraduate population at the University of California at Berkeley declined. There were many more Asians, along with smaller numbers of blacks and Latinos, mixed in with a student body that by the class of 1999 was only one-third white. Students were clustering along racial lines. School officials decided to find out how much enmity was or was not behind the broad new racial mix. For 16 months, 22 Berkeley academics conducted 69 focus groups with students of different ethnicities and races to produce the most comprehensive look at multicultural interaction on an American campus.

When an interim report was released in 1990, major newspapers, television, and overseas media picked up the story. Conservative writers such as Dinesh D'Souza seized upon the word "Balkanization" to describe the stark separation the report found among different campus groups. Much to the dismay of Troy Duster, the report's principal author and director of the Institute for the Study of Social Change, the debate by some in the media framed multiculturalism as either good or bad. There was no middle ground.

When the final report came out in late 1991, it emphasized neither extreme, arguing that a new racial and cultural dynamic was emerging.[1] It was neither Balkan nor separatist, nor a return to the so-called melting pot: it was something new. The media virtually ignored the report, in part because it is easier to focus on a story with two opposing positions. Meanwhile conservatives could not believe that multiculturalism is anything but divisive.

"There's nothing but trouble—this is the theme of the multicultural attack," Duster said. A bearded, intense man who used his hands as he spoke, he was passionate about the importance of the report's message and the attack by conservatives on the interim version.

"This is ideological, unempirical, and as mindless as the notion that multiculturalism is everybody together, sharing each other's food and dance and thought. Both positions are transparently stupid. It plays into the subterranean, not-so-hidden nostalgia for a period that never was. The period in which there was peace, people from different races—Asians and blacks and Latinos—simply got along with each other, with white people. I haven't found it.

"What you do find historically is that one group is able to dominate with law, tradition, access to resources, then lay claim to peace. So the Fifties are the prototype of the peaceful period. Hey, it was the golden era—for middle-class whites. The sixties break out because some blacks and some portion of the white population looked around and said wait a minute, there was peace in the fifties, but what's the cost?"

In the 1950s it was easy for whites to dominate culturally. Society outside of the South was mostly white, with very small numbers of nonwhites on American campuses.

"Our white students feel this loss of what could be called unnamed privilege," Duster said. In the 1950s and even 1960s, nonwhites were so small in number that they had to blend in with the white students. Nonwhites faced two choices. "They could either 'assimilate,' try to be more acceptable in language, dress, and behavior, or they could go off in their little corners and do a real 'black thing,' or a real 'whatever thing,' and become marginalized and never be admitted to the mainstream." Now, he said, students do not have to make this choice.

"We have a freshman class of 41 percent Asians. You got all

kinds of choices you couldn't have had when you're only a [small] percent of the population. You can form clubs that relate, you can form clubs that don't. You can have parties which are mixes, you can have parties which are not."

Duster said that on the surface, a black like him might look at Asians and see them "clustering," when in fact they are congregating along the lines of their Korean or Chinese or Japanese heritage. Or there are class divisions. But other races outside the scene simply see a monolithic Asian group. Duster pointed out that even whites separate along class or religious lines, but no one notices. Clustering among blacks and Asians and Latinos is more visible, at least to whites.

Duster wishes the public stage was not dominated by those who insist on a "binary version of multiculturalism—either it's a terrible thing, or it's a wonderful thing. You get the ideologues who are arguing get rid of it, let's go to one nation. Or another ideology which says there's only one way, down this path called La Raza, or African-centricity, we must be the Cherokee nation, otherwise we can't learn."

Conflict between groups is "the nature of the world," he explained. "But you can see this as healthy, not pathological. If my premise is right, fighting over resources maybe levels the playing field. It's called 'interest group conflict,' a time-honored idea in western political thought, when people with different interests get together, carve out their position, then fight for resources. There's nothing sick, or even racist, about it. Why not celebrate that? Why call it 'nothing but trouble?'"

Duster's closing statement from the final diversity report called for moderation in judging the current campus climate.

"A more appropriate title might have been *The Beginning Report*," he wrote. "It is our view that we are now only beginning to see the contours of the nature of social life on the globe for the next century. We need to have more humility about what works and what can work across ethnic, cultural, and racial divides. Perhaps Berkeley's students are once again at the vanguard of an important social development with far-reaching implications."

AMERICAN CULTURES

There is very little an institution such as the University of California can do to force harmony between different groups, but understanding can be encouraged. Troy Duster believes Berkeley took the correct approach with its "American cultures" courses, a graduation requirement that looks at multiculturalism by incorporating three of the five major cultures in 119 approved classes. Among them were an economics course in race and ethnicity in the labor market, one on journalism and the underdog in American society, and another in history on the conflict of cultures on the American frontier.[2]

In putting together the program, Ronald K. H. Choy, assistant director of the American cultures program, said he and his colleagues learned from Stanford's experience. When Stanford replaced courses on Western culture with ones dealing only with other cultures, there was an outcry that the university was abandoning the teaching of culture in a Western context. Berkeley decided to take a different path, introducing students to how various cultures interact. But the fact that the United States was founded on principles of Western culture cannot be ignored.

"We learned from their mistakes," said Choy of U.C.'s rival, Stanford. "It's not [that] Western Civ is the best. It's how we function as a society." Pretending, for instance, that African culture exists on its own in the United States without Western influence is just as wrong as saying only Eurocentric views should dominate.

Alex Wierbinski took a course that traced social movements between 1945 and 1975. He was disappointed. "It was current political focus rather than history," he said. "A lot of information, but little synthesis." He was also bothered by the delight some took in attacking him—the only white male in his study group of six feminists, four blacks, three Latinos, and two Asians. One feminist constantly assailed Alex. He said she accused him of not understanding her because "you have a penis!" He then referred to her "as the unit without a penis." At least for Alex, the class did not foster much harmony.

The following term, I decided to look at one of these courses. I chose "Inter-Ethnic Group Relations: The Case of African Americans and Korean Americans." It was taught by two doctoral students, Montye Fuse, black, and Joon Kim, Korean.

A year earlier, a black woman who resided in the African American Theme House accused the Korean-born owner of Johnston's Market, a store on Durant Avenue near the campus, of spraying mace on her in a dispute over a bottle of orange juice.[3] A meeting was held at the African American Theme House. Asian students were invited "and it resulted in a two-hour yelling match," Montye said. "There was this ideological divide as well as a physical divide." The black students began a boycott. The Korean students promised to break it.

"I didn't want the community to evolve into separate camps," Montye said. At the next meeting, organized by the Asian students, some three dozen Korean students showed up.

"I was one of two African Americans in the room," said Montye. "I got upset. I said you don't understand the rage in this community, the history of oppression. The African American has been oppressed by capitalism all through history, and now by these Korean merchants. I was hedging my bet, because I know many African Americans on this campus are from well-off backgrounds. But I was generally upset with these young Korean American men. They decided they didn't want to empathize with that suffering. I went home and said why not initiate a class ourselves?"

He said he felt it was important not to dwell on negatives, given the demographic direction of California. "The communities are already in Balkanization. We're bound to have more ruptures like L.A. My vision is California can have communities that build coalitions." Building them meant focusing on areas of common interest—in this case, between blacks and Koreans. Montye said the Korean market owners might be barely eking a living after putting in 14-hour days. The black patrons might not have jobs.

"The lack of economic opportunity between these two groups—coalitions can be built around that. They have to realize they are not enemies of each other, but that they have a common enemy." That common enemy was business, both international and domestic, making decisions without regard to workers. "I'm susceptible to the charge that this is idealistic. It's a plan that comes from an upper-class person at an elite university."

In class a few days later, Montye and Joon sat at a long table inside Dwinnelle Hall in the heart of the campus, as the room filled with 19 students. There were some four whites, a broad mix of Asians, a few Latinos, and a few blacks.

The students were barely settled when Joon asked a woman to read a report she had prepared on the book *Separate Societies: Poverty and Inequality in U.S. Cities,* by William W. Goldsmith and Edward J. Blakely.[4] Economic and political forces, the authors argue, are not putting an end to poverty, but instead are causing it. The international economy is shifting jobs overseas, or to outer suburbs, helping to increase the "sharp geographic isolation" of the inner city. The authors say intense racial and class clustering is "the melting pot in reverse" and that "American society is like water just above the freezing point, dangerously close to dissociating into separate parts." Their argument brings the conservative one almost full circle, but the authors see class differences, not "tribalism" as a cause. The separation is profound. Goldsmith and Blakely note that in Los Angeles 79 percent of the blacks would have to move to a white census tract to even out the racial distribution.

After the student read the report, the group joined in a discussion. An Asian woman said that sometimes people choose to be ghettoized.

"Give us an example," Montye asked.

"Chinatown."

"Asians congregate in Asian communities for support systems," a male student added. "And in that sense, that type of ghettoization actually benefits them."

Joon listed three types of urban communities on the blackboard: ethnic enclaves, class-based communities exclusively for the rich, and ghettos. He said the impetus creating ethnic enclaves has changed. In the nineteenth century, for instance, Jews were forced to live in them, because they were not allowed to live in certain parts of town.

One student asked why some groups are able to break out of the enclaves, as the Irish did in the 1850s. Today, Asians are able to make it, but why do many Latinos and blacks languish?

"I think it has to do with historical oppression," an Asian woman said of blacks. She added Asians are more inclined to be entrepreneurial, whereas others live in poverty.

The discussion suddenly turned to capitalism.

A white student asked why companies do not exploit the ghetto, which seems a likely source of cheap labor. Both Montye and Joon said it is even more economical to go overseas, where companies do not have to deal with American labor law.

These companies are taking jobs away, said a woman, "so people are forced to fight for such a small piece of the pie. They start feeling tensions with each other."

Montye said that tension can be a basis for developing connections between communities.

"It's difficult to believe coalition building is going to grow across class lines," responded one student. "Even the working class has trouble building coalitions in time of recession."

A black student shook his head. "Equal division of wealth, justice in the courts, and equal everything else, then it will be a just society."

"That," said Joon, "is the Utopian dream."

"You got to dream it," the student replied to laughter.

Another day in the class, Joon and Montye showed a film about the Los Angeles riots. The discussion went down the same hall of mirrors: the students, through their readings, tried to make sense of a separate society. The assignment was to come up with solutions.

An Asian student said enterprise zones should be tried—to create opportunity where none now exists.

"Little jobs for little people," someone responded.

"Another factor is the fear of crime, in terms of businesses closing," said one Asian student, who lived in the southeast part of San Francisco. "There's not a single Safeway or Lucky or anything. We have to drive a ways for food. If you don't have a car, you basically live on corner stores. The last Safeway that closed, they had a public forum and they said with the shoplifting rate they lost more money per month than they actually sold. The theft, breaking in, armed robberies, things like that were so high they couldn't afford to run the business."

Montye asked if it was realistic to make every community equal. "Under the economic system in which we live, is it ever possible for East Oakland to look like Concord?" Montye said of the ghetto versus the white suburbs across the Berkeley hills to the east. "I mean in terms of people having jobs, having nice homes, and so forth?"

"Not with capitalism the way it is," said a woman.

"Exactly," Montye said. "Even if East Oakland could someday come to look like Concord, then East Oakland would simply move somewhere else."

During a five-minute break I stood in the hall talking with an ethnic studies major who was morose. He said he was idealistic when he came into the school, but especially after this course, which asked dozens of questions with no easy answers, he felt there was no hope. He was 21 and burned out. He talked about giving up trying to change things.

When the class resumed, Montye said he was not happy with the discussion. He insisted: *What is the solution?* The ideas flowed —the neocon, neolib, the superliberal, the idealistic, but in the end, no one presented an idea that clicked. Montye's and Joon's classroom was filled with all the frustration facing policy makers and others.

REAL WORLD

In the summer months of 1994 leading up to the vote on Proposition 187, voters did not want to consider complex solutions. Anger and the attitude "get those people" were popular. Polls showed widespread support for Proposition 187, and even greater approval for Proposition 184, another measure on the ballot, commonly known as Three Strikes and You're Out.

This initiative was authored by Mike Reynolds, a Fresno wedding photographer, after his 18-year-old daughter was slain by a repeat felon in 1992 during a robbery outside a local restaurant. Reynolds's measure mandated a 25-year-to-life sentence for a third conviction, no matter how small the crime: it could even be misdemeanor shoplifting. Second offenders would have their sentences doubled, and even first offenders would spend more time in jail.

Appearing soft on crime was deadly for a politician. Motivated by a Field Poll that found 84 percent of the voters in favor of Three Strikes, the state's lawmakers were eager to get ahead of popular sentiment before November rolled around. In March

1994 the California legislature passed five bills, the harshest (a clone of the upcoming ballot measure) was approved 59-10 in the assembly and signed by the governor. Republican Assemblyman Bill Jones described it as the "toughest anticrime measure enacted in California in generations."[5] Even though Three Strikes was law, Reynolds pushed ahead with his initiative for the November ballot. He wanted to ensure the legislature would not soften Three Strikes—even though there was about as much chance of a politician turning back such a measure as there was of legalizing child prostitution.

Three Strikes would cost a *lot*: $9 billion alone to build additional prison space. The annual prison budget to run those new facilities for Three Strikes would be $3.5 billion per year by 2003. The Rand Corporation believed annual costs could soar to as much as $5.5 billion.

By comparison, the annual cost of Berkeley, the eight other UC campuses, and the California State University system was some $7 billion. Ten years before Three Strikes, the California Education Policy Center said state prisons took just over 2 percent of the entire state budget, the university system almost 9 percent. At the time of Three Strikes, prisons were taking just under 8 percent and the university just over 8 percent. With Three Strikes, the state would be guaranteed to spend much more on prisons than on higher education. The new prison money would have to come from somewhere, and the state was not exactly booming economically.[6]

As with the anti-immigrant bashing, getting tough on crime was an easy but simplistic course of action. In early 1994 the racial rhetoric was focused on Latinos. Though affirmative action was a perennial issue, the full-force attack on it would not begin for another year. Yet Proposition 184, like its Save Our State cousin a few spots away on the ballot, was part of the ongoing white electoral rebellion. Proposition 184 might as well have been called the Male Negro Control Act because it was aimed largely at black men, and because so many black men were already in prison. Liberals pointed out that the money would do nothing to stop crime before it happened and that conservatives ignored the reality that many black men take *pride* in going to prison, which has become a de facto poor house. Many steal their prison clothes to wear on the outside as a badge of honor. Prison is anything but a deterrent. But liberal ideals offered no solution. If there was one, it was reviled and ignored.

With the upswell of "get tough" rhetoric through 1994, what Donald Northcross was trying to do seemed out of place. For society to get at the real roots of the problem was not in vogue in an era of sound bites that cried for punishment. Empowerment and education is a long, slow process, the opposite of an expedient political message.

Just how slow was evident one Saturday morning in early 1994. The OK Program had entered its third year, and Don was the sole adult in a room of 23 youths. Sweat beaded down his brow as he coached students with homework and tried to keep some semblance of order as the decibel level doubled with the approach of lunch.

Don turned his back. A blue rubber ball bounced on the floor and sailed across the room. The eyes in the room inadvertently revealed the source of the missile. Don asked the young man if he had read the book he was supposed to report on. The kid said he had read 150 pages of a 170-page Harlequin romance.

"It's about a man and a woman and another man," the youth said. Don never accused him of not reading it, but leafed through the book and found a main character's name on the third page. The kid did not know anything about the character. Don asked him to read five pages. Another kid acting up had no homework. Don produced a newspaper and asked him to read two stories. The kid read through them quickly, then Don quizzed him and went through the stories with him for 10 minutes.

The day could have been a snapshot of any other, Don and Deputy Charles Turner—who was out getting lunch for the group—pursuing the dream of creating a new black community. Sometimes they had one or two other men helping—but usually they were alone. Slowly, over the months, the deputies working with Don had drifted away, as did many of the civilian adults he had trained to replace them.

"We had good numbers at the beginning of year," Turner said when he returned with bags of roast beef sandwiches. "They just fell by the wayside. A lot of them ask what this program is going to give to them. It's not them who need help. They all have a job, they all have homes, they all are living good."

Don was less willing to bad-mouth the lack of adult helpers. "I wish I could work with 20 guys who were really committed," Don admitted. He said he was going to work the churches to find additional black men.

The newspaper that Don had given the youth to study was lying on a table. A front-page story, "Blacks Urged to Stop the Violence," described a conference in Washington. There was a quote by Reverend Jesse Jackson. "What once was a crisis, a problem, has turned into a condition," he said. "Nearly half of murder victims are black. More blacks will kill each other each year than were killed in the entire history of lynchings."[7]

Turner said, "It's about time" that the trouble facing black men was finally being discussed.

"It's about two years too late," Don added.

It is lonely these days on the frontier beyond the civil rights movement. Marching in the South against American apartheid was easy compared with the social problems scarring the disenfranchised black community today—economic deprivation, drug use, broken families.

Little of the moral energy of the 1960s translates to the present, little in the way of community is found. The low number of OK Program volunteers is just one example. Black Americans are not any different from whites—have-nots on one side, successful people on the other, caught up with their own lives. Are blacks any more responsible for "their" people than whites are for the impoverished in Appalachia and elsewhere?

THREE STRIKES AND D-HOP

The message of Proposition 184 said if you sink, society will whack you by sending you to prison almost forever. This threat was supposed to impart terror, and it seemed almost personally directed at one of the OK Program youths, a young man whose street name is D-Hop. But he was not listening to the conservatives' message of impending punishment—although he was listening to Don.

D-Hop is the type of kid a white conservative might love to see locked up. At age six, his mother was murdered by her boyfriend. His gang leader was gunned down in a drive-by. His best friend died the same way. He was shunted between relatives and foster parents in Memphis and the city of Compton near Los Angeles. He had just arrived in Rancho Cordova from Oklahoma City a few months earlier. D-Hop said he had lived with his grandmother until she fell ill. He was now living with an aunt. Now 13, he was—in some ways still is—a Crip. He sold drugs, "did this, did that." Selling drugs was a way to be accepted. The money was secondary to making instant friends.

"I lost a lot of friends," D-Hop said during a Saturday study hall a few weeks before the state legislature overwhelmingly approved the Three Strikes law. "I was there when one of them got shot. Drive-by. That was in Memphis. It was a rival gang, Bloods. I was banging. I was a Crip, like, I still wear the colors sometime. But I'm not really into it."

D-Hop said he cannot get out. Back in Oklahoma, the leader who swore him into the Crips was killed. "You have to get his okay if you can get out, or you have to get killed to get out. The leader's dead, so I can't get the okay. I have to be dead in order to get out. So I'll be true to it and I still wear colors. But I ain't really banging. I try to keep it to myself."

D-Hop preferred Rancho Cordova over Compton. "I can walk around without worrying about getting shot. All I need to do is get my grades up and get an education. You see a lot of brothers and sisters that don't make it because they think you don't need this."

"It takes discipline," Don said. "It takes putting up with some garbage, stuff you don't like."

"It ain't easy," D-Hop said. "I sit down and I think about things, like what I can do. Plan it out so I know what to do and try to get along with people, trying to see how they act, so I can be cool with everybody. The teachers, I didn't really understand them when I first came here. Now I get to see how they are and they can be nice."

"Some of the things he'll be telling me, it's heavy, you know, for a 13-year-old," Don said, looking across at D-Hop. "I can understand why he's not doing as well as he could be doing, but at the same time, I won't let him use that as an excuse. After I listen to everything he's got to say, then my job is to help him see a way out of it. Where do we go from here? Do we say, 'I can't do anything now, because of the problems I had in the past?' Or do you just get angry and stay mad at everybody? Or do you say 'I want to go forward from here.' I think that any man in his right mind would say 'I want to go forward from here.'"

Don said that if D-Hop follows the components of the OK Program—good attendance, bringing his homework and school materials to class, following the rules—he'll do well.

"His grades are horrendous," Don said of his 1.67 grade point average. "I think this quarter he should do a lot better, because he's had a whole quarter to get adjusted. I don't ask for miracles. He doesn't need straight A's."

"If you keep working, you can get them," D-Hop said.

Don pointed out that the United States is the most diverse first world country on earth. "This is the first time this has ever happened. I really don't know if it can work, to tell you the truth. I'm wondering if this country is going to make it. Has this been an experiment? There's no history saying it will work. If it doesn't work, look at the alternative. The alternative is crazy. We may end up in a big race war. We're going to kill each other off? Or are we going to separate all the black people who want to go to Africa and all the white people going to go—"

"—What's that called, apartheid?" D-Hop asked.

"Apartheid, economic and political discrimination against non-Europeans in the Republic of South Africa. That's basically what apartheid means—you know, we've had our forms of apartheid already in this country—"

"—In the South and stuff like that," D-Hop said.

"Absolutely."

"No blacks allowed in restaurants," D-Hop said, "separate bathrooms—"

"—Couldn't vote."

"I read about that."

"I tell you what," Don said of his youth in Arkansas, "when we desegregated, we went to the white school. You couldn't sit in a desk that didn't have 'Nigger equal ape,' 'Nigger stink [written on it].' When you go to the rest room and you're sitting down to take a dump—you look on the wall, there it is: 'Niggers go home.' You couldn't go anyplace without seeing it."

"See," D-Hop said, "I don't like the word. You hear a lot of people say like 'What's up, nigger.' I'm like 'Man, don't call me that, that's not my name.' I've read some books in the library when I was back in Oklahoma, I went to the library in my spare time, 'cause I had good grades then, and I was looking into why people say that."

D-Hop's eyes brightened as he recalled discoveries he had made in that library, including Buddhism and Confucianism. "I didn't know Buddha was a real person. I thought he was just like a statue." D-Hop articulated the first noble truth of Buddhism. "He said everything in life, everything living in life suffers. I said that's neat. I go to church, I be praying. I be hoping I can make it in life. I believe in God. I believe I can make it. I pray for myself. I pray for my Grandma. I pray for my friends. Sometimes I get real happy and I'll be like I'm going to do this and I'm going to do that, but then something will happen and I'll sit down and think for a long time, an hour—two hours sometimes. I just don't want to be bothered and I'll think. I'll sit there and wonder what life is like, wonder what it's really like, wonder what could happen. I really want to make it in life. I don't want to be like some big movie star, making a lot of money on TV. I just want to make it—just make it, like get a good job, marry somebody, have some kids. You can be rich, [have] fame and fortune, and it could be bad. I hear you won't really be all happy when you rich like that."

A few weeks later, D-Hop moved away in yet another disruption in his life. Don does not know what happened to him.

THE COST-BENEFIT RATIO

One only needs to spend a few minutes with a calculator to figure out the cost-benefit ratio of helping a kid like D-Hop versus supporting Three Strikes.

If a young black man winds up with a third strike by the time he is 30—spending, let's say, the minimum of 25 years behind bars—he'll cost taxpayers over $500,000. Stanford University psychology professor Philip Zimbardo thinks it is actually far more because inmates over the age of 50 cost three times as much per year to incarcerate owing to health problems and special needs. The title of Zimbardo's 1994 study says it all: "Transforming

California's Prisons into Expensive Old Age Homes for Felons: Enormous Hidden Costs and Consequences for California's Taxpayers."[8] By 2020, he estimates, California will have over 126,000 elderly inmates, almost the population of state prisons in 1994; he points out that felons over the age of 50 are less likely to commit crimes, because after that age, repeat offensives rapidly drop off.

If a young man at risk such as D-Hop is enrolled in the OK Program and makes it, turning into a modest success, earning some $30,000 each year, he will *contribute* more than $300,000 in state and federal taxes in the same period he would have cost the state $500,000 in prison.

Don, who had been running the program on $10,000 per year, was awarded a $50,000 foundation grant and expanded from Mill's junior high to the nearby high school. That $50,000 is almost what it costs to keep two men in a California prison for one year.

What if the $9 billion that will be used to construct new prisons for Three Strikes was given to programs such as Don's? Even with just 1 percent of that money—a piddling $9 million—and role models to work with the kids, Don and others like him might transform thousands of young black men's lives, saving many hundreds of millions of dollars.

Such facts were pointed out by the usual suspects, such as superliberal Assemblyman John Burton, a San Francisco Democrat with an obvious safe seat. He became so frustrated with the prison binge and other punitive measures that at the end of 1994 he introduced a bill that would "make it a felony to intentionally and maliciously have a yearly income below the federally established poverty level." A second bill would require the state to provide gruel to orphan asylums. Gruel, Burton said, is the best food because it was popular in the time of Charles Dickens's *Oliver Twist.*[9]

One leading Republican did not see the dark humor in Burton's bills. He "applauded" Burton's bills if they removed people from state services who did not deserve them.

12

Can We All Get Along?

There were a number of attempts, large and small, to foster inter-racial harmony in Los Angeles after the 1992 riots. The biggest plan to get off the ground was Hope in Youth, an organization sponsored by the Industrial Areas Foundation and nine major reli-gious denominations. Its goal was to organize young people in dif-ferent communities across racial lines, to interact peacefully, and to solve some of the urban problems facing their neighborhoods—in effect, to answer the question posed by Rodney King, who in an appeal for calm during the riots asked, "Can we all get along?"

The question echoed over the next four years as California dealt with the backlash against cultural change, and it will reverber-ate over the next half century as the nation grows to resemble Cal-ifornia's racial mix. The rest of the country can draw lessons from the way the state deals with relations between Asians, blacks, Lati-nos, and whites. Thus far, the many attempts to improve cross-racial understanding have not fared well.

In southern California, the Los Angeles County Human Rela-tions Commission is one of the oldest organizations working to bridge cultural gaps, but critics say it prefers creating reports rather than actually doing anything. One commission plan that actually tried to get groups together, the Black-Korean Alliance, was started five years before the riots to ease tensions between Korean store owners and the black community following several deadly incidents.[1] Eight months after the riots, the group dissolved. There was a lack of communication and little support from citizens in both communities.

In this environment, the leaders of Hope in Youth saw a chance to try a proactive grass roots approach that could hold at least one answer as to how Californians might get along. One summer night in 1994, 6,200 young people from 200 Hope in Youth groups in 44 Los Angeles area neighborhoods gathered at the Olympic Grand Auditorium south of downtown. They had assembled, according to a brochure handed out for the event, "to meet for the first time . . . across geographical, racial, ethnic, and cultural boundaries, rejecting the noise of a thousand deaths for the sounds of public discourse, [to] unite in a shared vision of hope."[2] They were also united that summer night to convince elected officials—many of whom were present in the audience—that public funds were not being wasted.

Cardinal Roger M. Mahony of the Roman Catholic Diocese of Los Angeles is the political force behind Hope in Youth, and he had just lobbied another $2.5 million from the city for this untested project, on top of multimillions that had been already allocated from various government agencies. Other groups trying to work in different communities had been left with scraps, and they had cried foul. One of the community organizations supporting Hope in Youth then accused one major foe, black Councilman Mark Ridley-Thomas, of being antiwhite and anti-Latino. They were set to picket his house until Ridley-Thomas amassed twice as many counterdemonstrators.[3]

One would not know what a high-stakes game was being played out by looking at the beaming face of Mahony at a reception before the meeting out in the main hall. He worked the back room under the glare of television lights. It was a gathering of the luminaries among Los Angeles's social workers, activists, and religious leaders. The air was filled with praise for Hope in Youth as Mahony and other church leaders spoke to the VIP crowd. Bishop E. Lynn Brown, of the 9th District of the Christian Methodist Episcopal Church, said, "This is the best thing since Jesus Christ."

Months earlier, the goals of Hope in Youth were outlined with less hype by Reverend Rody Gorman, of St. Mathias Church in Huntington Park. Gorman, head the South East United Neighborhoods Organization (UNO), had long been active in community organizing, and he was glad to sign on with Hope in Youth when it was formed. The reason, he said, is that "riots have left a feeling [that] nothing has been done, nothing has been changed. In fact things are probably getting worse." Hope in Youth was the solution, Gorman said, because it emphasized the "in": young people would decide themselves what agenda they wanted to follow to improve their communities.

Gorman, who had a bit of a brogue and a flash of white hair, said, "We follow what's known as the 'iron rule,'" paraphrasing Saul Alinsky's credo when he created the Industrial Areas Foundation in 1940. "We don't believe in coming in and saying we have a solution. That doesn't train people to solve their own problems. Organized people can do something. Hopelessness comes out of people who are not organized." The key was to break big problems down to local issues—and even personal issues—that can be addressed. "They're not going to wipe out all evil. They're not going to get rid of gangs. None of that. But maybe we can see that these kids don't drop out of school. Maybe we can get them job training. Maybe we can even get them to get organized as business people who provide jobs."

When the show began out in the auditorium, a group of Mexican folk dancers in sombreros thunder-stomped on stage. They were followed by four black women 1970s-vintage soul singers— but no rap stars.

In the VIP back room, Mahony had talked about the rainbow found in Hope in Youth, but the crowd was very black and Latino. It was difficult to find even an occasional Asian face, and even fewer whites ones. Cheers were bilingual. "We are people of Hope!" *"¡Somos gente de esperanza!"* "We are diverse yet united!" *"¡En nuestra diversidad somos unidos!"* "We have power!" *"¡Tenemos poder!"* There were a few near-fistfights, but the stage show focused on unity and the human cost of violence. During a song about Soshi, a paralyzed 10-year-old girl, she was wheeled on stage to dramatize the result of a drive-by shooting.

The next day, Hope in Youth spokesman Larry Fondation explained over lunch that no other group at the grass roots level is trying to bring anyone together. He argued that the riots resulted in a plethora of "different bullshit academic" solutions. Some conferences purport to be bringing communities together, but "it's one person who earns $70,000 talking to another" and "they all go home to Westwood at the end," he said, referring to the tony area near UCLA. Hope in Youth, he said, is trying to build a true rainbow coalition.

Yet Hope in Youth was failing months after the public display. After having promised never to again ask for money as it did at the time of the rally, Hope in Youth again returned hat in hand to Los Angeles County to keep 60 of its 120 social workers from being laid off. The *Los Angeles Times* ran a story quoting a spokesman for Supervisor Gloria Molina saying the group was simply not visible. She could not support throwing more money at it. Even though people like Father Gorman had the best intentions—and were doing good things locally—the larger effort of engineered racial and ethnic interaction did not seem to be the answer.[4]

Even if Hope in Youth were more effective, it was not working across class lines. As an inner-city Los Angeles–centric plan, there is nothing in it that solves the real problem. Whites in places such as south Orange County need to talk with and learn from other races, such as the very Latinos who work in the service industry that fuels the tax base that supports their lifestyle.

GETTING ALONG

If harmony cannot be created under the umbrella of one group such as Hope in Youth, it does not mean that there are no answers to be encouraged, both by the government, the private sector, the media. The key is to search for the common ground where people of different races and ethnicities interact in society: the popular press, work, school.

THE MEDIA
Television news has difficulty dealing with the nuances of race. It has trouble exploring the racial animosities that grow from economic dislocation. This is a difficult story to show, and few if any

stations try. Stories about race and culture also give newspapers trouble. But a newspaper can explore such complicated issues, and if it is doing its job, it can educate its readers about their neighbors.

As California grows more multicultural, most of its newspapers are fearful of touching issues regarding race. The reasons are many. One big problem is that most top editors are whites who err on the side of so-called political correctness.

In the mid-1980s the editor of a major California newspaper insisted that voices of black anger be toned down in a series on the condition of blacks. He did not want to incite a riot. Such a Kiplingesque view of protecting blacks from themselves ignored the fact that many blacks *were* angry. In print they would be only mildly upset. After the Los Angeles riots, the same editor broke his newspaper's budget doing stories that showed why blacks were angry.

In other cases, racially insensitive comments are routinely edited out of stories for fear of offending readers of other races—especially when it is whites talking. Rather than explore the feelings that cause these comments, editors ignore them and play it safe. Even when editors are women or nonwhites, it does not help. A big reason is that newspapers have become more corporate. The buzzword of the day is "customer service," which translates into offending the fewest people possible. Many newspapers, in California and elsewhere, have become much blander and more fearful of alienating readers.

Instead of dealing with the substance of racial issues, California's biggest papers have been hung up on the "name" game. At the end of 1993 the *Los Angeles Times* issued a race and ethnicity stylebook.[5] The *Times* position is that a person from China, for example, should not be called Chinese, but "a U.S. resident of Chinese descent." African American is the suggested term for blacks—though studies show a majority of blacks prefer "black." The "American" appendage is preferred for almost all groups: Mexican American, Asian American, Native American, Arab American, and so forth. But whites are not European Americans. They are whites. They too should be hyphenated Americans, but this dilutes the use of the national origin appendage, and it also focuses on what keeps people separate.

The stylebook goes further. "Barrio" is forbidden as being "offensive." Same for "ghetto" and "inner city." There is nothing new about softening language. In 1961 the *New York Times* ran a column criticizing a report that told teachers to avoid "'speech patterns' that create feelings of inferiority." Slum should not be used, but "an older, more overcrowded area." Underprivileged children became "children with untapped potential." The column said "weasel" words permitted "society's conscience to live more easily with camouflaged ills." The same reason obfuscation was wrong in 1961 applies today. Watts and Compton are ghettos. HP is a barrio. The *Los Angeles Times*'s smoothing over of unpleasant realities will not make them vanish.

The stylebook was not warmly greeted by many reporters. It raises the specter of "numbing sameness," said a memo of protest from the newspaper's Washington bureau. One reporter who signed this internal memo said editor Shelby Coffey used the stylebook to deflect criticism from some reporters upset with the paper's internal and external treatment of minorities. In the 1990s the *Times* had become much "lighter" to counter increasing competition from the *Orange County Register.* "They're really chasing the whites to Orange County, only they don't say that," said one reporter of the paper's interest in attracting readers with money while at the same time trying to offend as few people as possible.

A few months after the *Times* stylebook was issued, the *Sacramento Bee* (which quickly adapted the book for its pages) ran an editorial cartoon depicting two Ku Klux Klansmen reading the words of Louis Farrakhan, in which the black bigot said, "You can't be a racist by talking—only by acting." In the caption, one Klansman says, "That nigger makes a lot of sense."[6]

Some black staff members were reduced to tears. Groups urged a boycott of the *Bee*, which has a long history of covering injustice. Dennis Renault, the cartoonist, said in his defense that "if you're going to depict a Klansman, you say what a Klansmen says."

One could argue that blacks often use this word themselves in rap songs and elsewhere, and there is no protest. This is called "hypocritically correct" by *Washington Post* columnist Warren Brown, a black journalist who captured the spirit of the issue when he wrote, "The ethos of hypocritical correctness encourages black people to expend energy on relatively trivial matters, such as something someone *said*."⁷ He went on to say: "Hypocritical correctness permits many of them to cover their eyes to the true sellouts . . . the absent biological fathers who don't want to be called 'nigger' but who don't want to be called 'Daddy' either."

The *Bee* cartoon actually got the community talking about race. But instead of using it as a tool for discussion, the paper cowered in apology, essentially promising that such intellectual freedom would never again be allowed. One *Bee* editor lamented that while it was one of the few institutions that could be attempting to bridge understanding and explore real feelings, the paper was so afraid of alienating readers that it wrung its hands over semantics. Meanwhile, this hand-wringing creates amusing problems. How does a newspaper refer to blacks who are not Americans? The *Bee* once ran a story about an athlete from Africa and referred to him as an African American, when in fact he was a black from Africa. Other newspapers, in using the computer search-and-replace function to replace "black" with the politically correct term have created an "African American cup of coffee."

Ethnic identification is fraught with confusion and makes many whites angry. Is the cost of the backlash worth the identification with one's heritage? "African American" to many whites suggests separateness, but Donald Northcross defends the term. He related that he was driving home from work one night, listening to KFBK-AM, the Sacramento talk radio station that gave commentator Rush Limbaugh his start. Don said he was surprised when the talk show host, a rare liberal voice in the medium, took a stand against people calling themselves "African American." The host was Christine Craft, the newswoman famous for her lawsuit against a Kansas City television station that fired her allegedly because she was "too old, too ugly, and not deferential enough to men."

"She's usually very liberal, but she thought that [term] had no use in this society," Don said. "I believe what makes America is the different ethnic groups. I went home and called the show. I never called a talk show before." He did not get through. He tried again the next night and got on the air.

"She was saying the hyphenation was destroying America. I disagreed. She's saying that in the past that we've always been together. We've never been together. We came here as Africans. But no one called us Africans. They called us negroes, later niggers. On my birth certificate it says 'colored.' We've never been called Americans. It's what we choose to call ourselves. I'm African American and proud to be American. It's the first time we've called ourselves what we want to be called. Instead of waiting for someone to do right by you, you do right by yourself."

The question remains: Who decides what a group is called? When Ivan Muñoz, who worked on Martha's campaign, applied for college, he found many universities do not have a box marked "Latino" or even "Hispanic," but "Chicano," a multiculturally correct term that means an American of Mexican descent. Many whites assume "Chicano" to mean anyone with a heritage from south of the border. Like many Central Americans, Ivan adamantly did not consider himself a Chicano. Polls show most blacks preferring black.

Rather than focus on ethnic identification, newspapers in California and other states can take a lesson from the few editors and reporters who are taking risks when writing about black and white relations. When Sig Gissler was editor of the *Milwaukee Journal*, he wanted to run a white columnist's frank letter about race to a black friend. But he backed down when some fellow white editors said it would ignite "black protest." Three years later, regretting that he had not run the letter, Gissler, who is white, launched the *Journal* on a year-long study of race, a project that was wrenching and honest and included racist comments from a white woman that ran over the objections of some subeditors. Gissler felt that by hiding her views, the paper would have censored reality. When Gissler later studied race and the media as a Freedom Forum fellow at Columbia University, he called for "greater courage and candor" among newspapers. The media, he said, have not helped readers sort through the change between the "clarity of the civil rights movement" and the "ambiguity of today."

One case of honest coverage found by Gissler was a seven-month project by the *New Orleans Times Picayune*. Editors told Gissler that before 18 staff members began reporting, they spent weeks in emotional meetings, engaging in "virtual group therapy." The ensuing series caused reporters to lose friends; 1,000 readers canceled the paper and the newsroom was divided. But reprints were used to spark racial discussion in schools. The frank coverage generated letters from 6,000 readers, and the newspaper ran 58 pages of these letters, which Gissler said "had the vitality of talk radio without its worst vices."[8]

In California, newspapers rarely look at whites' views of race. After O. J. Simpson's acquittal in 1995, most newspapers focused their coverage on black reaction. Katherine Corcoran of the *San Jose Mercury News* was one of the few reporters who wrote on white attitudes. The headline over her story said it all, "Race: The One Topic Whites Avoid."[9] Blacks talked freely to her, but few whites went on record. One woman summed up the reason when she told Corcoran: "You become a member of the Ku Klux Klan" by saying anything negative.

Katherine explored race with a white perspective in other stories, motivated by her own experience as a white liberal. She realized she and blacks did not really associate very much: no one in her circle had black friends who came to dinner and socialized in other ways outside of work. This led her to report stories such as one on the fallout of busing in one Bay area town in which she tracked down the students who were bused a quarter century earlier. The whites approached busing with 1960s idealism; the blacks with pride. But two and a half decades after the experiment, both blacks and whites had few cross-racial friends, and many had become disillusioned and tired. Little understanding had come from the busing. While this story is in some ways depressing, it looked honestly at differences.[10]

Like most of her stories on race, Katherine said it drew many letters and calls from readers. It is clear that people are hungry for information to guide them, but in their quest to appeal to everyone, many newspapers have become relevant to no one. When a racial incident occurs, instead of editing the participants into political correctness, editors should allow their reporters to explore deeper issues. When ethnic groups say they are angry, that anger should be talked about openly. By the time the situation has degenerated into riots or the electoral lynching of the California ballot initiative process, it is far too late to start doing stories about the sources of the trouble. There is risk in being open when talking about race and ethnicity, but the sooner we as a society do so, the better. It is important that the media encourage honest discussion. With candor, there is a chance for misunderstanding. But with silence, it is guaranteed.

WORK

Ivan Muñoz surprised both Martha Escutia and his family when he turned down a full college scholarship. Instead, he joined the U.S. Army. Stationed at Fort Campbell, Kentucky, he came home to Huntington Park on a four-day pass. He sported a regulation buzz cut and had lost his nose ring. It was the first time Ivan had been exposed to U.S. culture outside of Huntington Park, and he was surprised that by day, the men around him were a unit, but at night, they segregated. He did not know what to expect, having come from a community that was almost all Latino. "We don't have a problem working together, but at the end of the day there's no intermingling. They don't come over to us and we don't go to them."

The separation was primarily black and white. In the company of 165 men, there were just five Latinos. Ivan ended up socializing with them. He also had two white friends, one from California, and Ivan said it seemed that man was more accepting because he was from California.

"That was quite a wake-up, living and dealing with white people," Ivan said. "I have no problem. But there is—how should I say—a political correctness gap. When Jay Leno has [actor] Edward James Olmos on as a guest, that's [the whites'] experience with Latinos. I try to educate them. One of the first questions I was asked is what did you get during the riots? There's a white guy from L.A. and nobody asks him that.

"The NCOs lean toward the people of their own ethnic group. We have a black platoon sergeant. He talks to blacks casually but he expects more respect from everybody else." Ivan said there is also a white sergeant "who is very redneck." The sergeant had a problem dealing with blacks and Latinos, but he was reprimanded.

Such open hostility is relatively rare in California. Bill Shepherd said in his consulting work he could think of no cases of companies failing or doing badly because of racial tensions. And at UCLA, Dr. Lawrence Bobo and his colleagues who conducted focus groups on the multiethnic workplace found "few reports of interethnic conflict."[11] In a 1994 study, the UCLA researchers decided to look at the changing labor dynamics in the face of demographic change. Bobo said that much of the harmony is due to repeated close contact. It is difficult to have a bias against a racial group when you face individuals each day, united in a work environment where the goals are the same.

On the other hand, Bobo said that in many cases, the lack of conflict is due to de facto job segregation—for example, because Latino janitors work in areas separate from the managers of a company. They never interact and so there is little chance for tension. And there is plenty of misunderstanding. A Korean man told the UCLA researchers that people pretend they do not understand him because his English is not good. A Spanish-speaking man said the salespeople, owners, and production people at his company never sit at the same lunchroom tables, though this sounds more class- than race-based. Chinese Asian workers told the researchers they held broad stereotypes against blacks and felt that whites believed they were superior to the Asians. But others see Asians practicing the most separation.

Haleh Nazeri, who emigrated from Iran as a child, said when she worked at a San Jose computer firm owned by Taiwanese nationals, the blacks, whites, and Latinos got along just fine. But there was deep separation between everyone and the Chinese. She tried to bridge the gap by sitting at their lunch tables. But they continued speaking Chinese, and so Haleh felt excluded. There was nothing vindictive about this behavior—in fact, the Chinese owners treated her extremely well when it came to pay and benefits—but the separation troubled her all the same. Now, she finds herself saying "them." She said, "I don't like saying 'them.' I've never said that."

Language is also a barrier in some workplaces. Two women employed by Spun Steak, a South San Francisco meat packing plant, filed a lawsuit because the company mandated English only on the job. The women said the rule was discriminatory, but the company imposed the rule because a few workers were making "racially and sexually derogative comments in Spanish" to those who did not speak the language. The U.S. Court of Appeals in San Francisco upheld the company's right to regulate language, and the U.S. Supreme Court turned down an appeal.[12]

Such open conflict is not commonly seen. Despite the affirmative action debate, most companies are quite aware that the bulk of the future workforce will be nonwhite. If one reads between the lines in brochures lauding the polyethnic hiring practices coming from large companies, one finds the reasons are more than altruistic. Having a multicultural workforce is just plain smart business. Large companies know what the future holds.

In California, minorities account for 57 percent of the state's population of those under the age of 18, and in not too many years they will be two-thirds of the workers and consumers in the state.[13]

Even if all government-mandated affirmative action programs were ended, large corporations would not be bound by the laws, and few companies seem eager to change their policies. A company cannot, of course, mandate that workers love each other. As Ivan found in the U.S. Army, when there are just five Latinos in a group of 165 men, most of them white, the Latinos are social outcasts. What he experienced in his unit was the old American model of a white-dominated workplace. He plans on returning to California, and when he does, he will likely work in an environment of many cultures. While the different racial groups may separate at day's end, with such a mix, the close association of Asians, blacks, Latinos, and whites is likely to lead to some interaction.

UCLA's Lawrence Bobo said he already sees signs of this. He had a revelation one day while walking through a park. He came upon a multiracial group of men playing baseball. He wondered how they came together: they were not at work or school, which in his studies he had found to be the likely gathering places. It made him realize impromptu acts of multicultural harmony occur each day in California.

SCHOOLS
Despite the rise in popularity of private schools, 90.2 percent, or 5.2 million of California's children attend public elementary and secondary schools, which remain the great cultural meeting ground.[14]

However, the California Department of Education rarely coordinates efforts to bridge cultural gaps, aside from a seldom-used program to educate teachers about cultural inclusion. But many local districts, independent of the state or each other, are instituting programs that work to link children of different races.

Not long after the 1992 riots, black and Latino students violently clashed at Fairfax and Hamilton high schools in West Los

Angeles. A few years later, school officials began a program to offer a retreat for students to openly discuss race. There were "speak-outs" in which students could tell what bothered them most about different races, in the hope that the dialogue would lead to understanding.[15]

Other programs reach students when they are still too young to have ingrained racial opinions. The Slauson Western Youth Enrichment Program, run by volunteers, tried working with community leaders, but abandoned that top-end approach to sponsor field trips in which kids taste ethnic foods or visit communities such as East Los Angeles or Koreatown. During these trips, each child is paired with one of a different race.[16]

The cultural interaction takes on a distinctly modern tone between Latino elementary school students in the Los Angeles suburb of Norwalk and white students from La Mirada city schools. Computers and live video hookups connect 1,000 third-, fourth-, and fifth-graders who otherwise might never meet. The students have frequent video contact and sometimes get together in person, and the teachers bolster the program by instructing about different cultures.[17]

There are even more innovative programs. Martha Escutia supported a Los Angeles magnet school that was teaching kindergarten students in three languages—Japanese, Spanish and English—in a program that would continue into the higher grades. "It's unfortunate there are a lot of people who are going to view that as separatist. People still have not viewed bilingualism as an economic asset."

White California voters do not see the value in multilingualism. Besides the 1986 English-only ballot initiative, a strong undercurrent of support for Proposition 187 was a dislike of bilingual education. A popular lament is that the new immigrants, especially the children, are not learning English. One study that fueled this debate was done by the Little Hoover Commission, a California better-government agency, which said one million students were not fluent in English.[18] But in visits to many schools, the report's dire warnings that bilingual education was handicapping kids do not seem to hold up. The children of immigrants speak English everywhere.

Demographer Hans Johnson of the California Research Bureau

said immigrants are acting as they always have—learning the language and becoming part of the culture. "They are assimilating," Johnson said. "It's false to create this idea that there's a huge culture war now in terms of language and education."

There is plenty of evidence to support this. One day inside the waiting room of a medical clinic for pregnant women in the center of Huntington Park, there was a small sign in two languages: *"Descubre Tu Mundo—Biblioteca"* ("Discover Your World—Library"). Fifteen women in various stages of pregnancy listened to Lucía Muñoz, who stood next to the sign on the table at the head of the room. Lucía read off their names: "Rodriguez, Peña, Rocha, Gonzales, Perés, Camacho."

Lucía's job with Los Angeles County was to talk to the women in Spanish about *la biblioteca*. Lucía traveled to the waiting rooms of clinics around South East and South Central, telling women about the library in the hope that their children would get hooked on reading at an early age.

The women were wide-eyed as Lucía told them the library was free. Several women shook their heads in disbelief. "And you can even get videos?" one asked. Lucía nodded. She passed out applications for a library card. One woman asked if there were children's books in English, and Lucía handed her several to study.

"In Compton, no Latinos were in the library before the program; now there are a lot," Lucía said after the women filtered out of the room to meet with doctors. Lucía said the bulk of books checked out by the children of Spanish-speaking parents are in English.

At Huntington Park High School, Principal Antonio Garcia said that out of his 3,900 students—almost all Latino—less than half have "limited English proficiency," with a very small number "pre-literate." This latter group comes from rural Mexico, and their parents are illiterate in Spanish. The school's policy is to quickly mainstream the students rather than emphasize bilingual education.

Donald Northcross feels that blacks and other cultures need to be included in school curricula before anything else, including language, can be talked about.

"When you look at the textbooks that they're teaching from today, they're not a whole lot different than the ones I learned from years ago," he said of his segregated Arkansas school. "Everything I knew about Africa as a kid growing up was negative. My education about Africa was Tarzan. They were all half naked, they were all illiterate, they were all afraid of white people, they didn't have shoes. To call someone an African was the ultimate insult."

Yet Don does not believe in African-centric classes. "That's garbage. That does more harm than good because it seems to say that you are different than what America is about. What makes America is the diversity. There's nothing else—that's it!"

Textbooks that center on white people give the impression that whites are superior. "You just don't learn stuff through osmosis. You are what you eat. You are intellectually what you read. Minority kids often don't see themselves in the curriculum. A lot of European Americans feel like they have the right to the control in this country. Everything they've read, everything they've heard from their parents—their grandparents—is that they have basically done it all. White kids are at a disadvantage too. If they learned the stuff in the history books, they would be more sensitive and more willing to work with everybody and truly make this country what it should be. But changing the educational system, in a lot of people's eyes, is giving up power. It's kind of like giving up the store."

CIRCLES: A NEW SOCIETY

In the midst of California's ethnic transition, many are asking what it means to be American, but 200-plus years of U.S. history is not enough time for a permanent identity to emerge. In Europe, history is discussed in terms of many centuries; as is seen in California, the coming minority-majority is proving that the nation has not yet evolved culturally.

Assimilation has long meant that nonwhites conform to the white society that developed as a result of European immigration. But it can work both ways. A lot of whites accept black culture, for instance. Elvis Presley liberally borrowed from the style of black musicians, and several decades later, many rap stars have more white listeners than black ones. In California's four-way culture, the acceptance extends to all cultures celebrating the Chinese New Year or partaking in Cinco de Mayo. In the mid-1990s, for instance, Spanish-language music became a growing fad among non-Latino listeners.

Leo Briones is baffled that some whites are so resentful of people whose cultures they seem eager to experience. "Let's look at food," he said. "How many of these white people in the suburbs 20 years ago ate sushi, Thai, Mexican—real Mexican as opposed to Taco Bell? Now you have these restaurants everywhere. If you can appreciate the way we cook, you can appreciate the way we act. At what point do you have your culture polyethnic to the exclusion of your past? That's our argument as Latinos. Our past and our culture is an intimate part of who we are. We don't feel like losing that. Becoming part of an amorphous being is progressing?"

But for Bill Shepherd, enjoying food and assimilation into basic American beliefs are two separate issues. He cannot understand why different groups want to isolate themselves by using hyphenated names. "I don't walk around thinking of those distinctions," Bill said. "In many ways the minority groups are forcing a categorization with their own group, which I think is to their disservice."

Bill feels minorities should belong to the whole, the so-called melting pot. To Bill, ethnocentric identity violates the very notion of being American. This idea of the melting pot, as embraced by many whites, is not much different from what was found in the "Americanization movement" after the turn of the century, when Americanization classes were held and anything "foreign" was reviled. Citizens wanted Eastern and southern Europeans to learn English and conform to the dominant British-inspired culture. Today, whites cannot understand why blacks, Latinos, and Asians simply just do not conform to "normal" society.

In the United States today, however, an Americanization movement would be seen by many nonwhites as western and arrogant. The very ethnic centrism reviled at the turn of the century is now being celebrated. This is the critical difference Bill sees in the Latinos in his Lantern Village neighborhood, as they aggressively cling to their culture. He feels they should assimilate, as did his grandparents. But were not his grandparents, when they first arrived, looked upon the same way as he looks on the Latinos? Many Europeans lived in enclaves, the Little Italys, Polish towns, and so forth. But by the third generation many families were integrated into mainstream American culture.

It is not so easy to re-create or cling to one's culture, as even the most ardent ethnic activists have found. Mexico City elites look down on their former countrymen north of the border as being *pochos*, a derogatory term meaning those who are no longer Mexican. For many women from Asia and the Middle East, the first thing discarded is the subservient role of women in those cultures. And the controversy over bilingual education notwithstanding, just about all children of immigrants learn to speak English.

Like immigrants of days past, many are "assimilating," or at least are becoming more like each other than different. Yet the extremist positions on multiculturalism present a future with two stark choices: the United States sticks with a white-centered melting pot, or degenerates into separate conflicting societies. But other voices do offer a differing view.

Kirk Knutsen, a policy analyst for the state of California who has studied the changing demographics, sees a three-way breakdown of what could happen in California, which he diagrammed on a napkin.

In the first, the traditional "melting pot," he drew a series of smaller circles within a large circle—the large circle being European culture and the smaller ones absorbed inside.

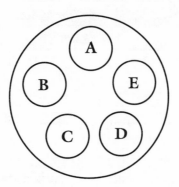

This is what many whites want to see happen with the ethnic transformation in California—Asians, blacks, and Latinos who become just like whites. Knutsen then drew circles that represent the dark vision: California and the rest of the United States become a series of separatist cultures, as in separate circles, disconnected and hostile.

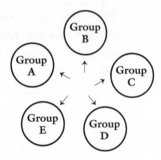

If a polyethnic society is to be successful and not riven by strife, Knutsen believes something new must be built, like interconnected circles that have a common center.

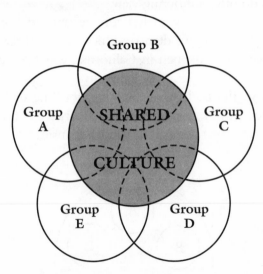

In this manner, each group can maintain identity, but still be part of the collective culture—the United States. The question that remains is what constitutes the overlapping center. Is it merely geography and language? A shared interest in a safe community, jobs, schools? How much European influence? Is there room for an amalgamation of European and Asian and Latin values?

Whatever the center turns out to be, Knutsen said it is critical that the country strives for this third set of circles.

"There is no middle ground as to how this opera turns out," Knutsen said. "We have the opportunity to build a pluralistic multicultural society or we're looking at the Blade Runner syndrome. It's a fork in the road . . . as we go toward the year 2010."

Knutsen fears the second set of circles will emerge unless things change. "I believe deeply we're not on the right road. Necessity is supposed to be the mother of invention. In this case it's the wellspring of paralysis. You see people becoming more insular, wanting to protect their piece of the pie."

Walled-in whites accelerate the process. They increasingly fear other cultures "because they see it on TV. When they used to live in Los Angeles, they would see black people on the street and it did not scare them. Now that they live in Orange County and never see a black person, they are more afraid of them."

At Berkeley, sociologist Troy Duster was much less pessimistic. Without prompting, Duster drew Knutsen's third set of circles in the air with his finger. He believes society will reach this third level, where there is room for commonality as well as the separate areas of unassimilated culture. As he sees it, California society is already working its way into this third phase, but this model, a lot less alarming than the multiculturalism rhetoric coming from the left and the right, is not part of the present discussion about race in America. It is so centrist that it has no radical constituency.

Duster says this third way of looking at cultural mixing has ill-defined borders between the center of the circle, or the common culture, and the edges that represent separate ethnic and racial scenes. He explained that the center of the circle can be seen all over California in the broad public arena where one finds a mix of ethnic groups—at work, in school, and other public places. The edges outside the overlapping center are other scenes, composed of different races and ethnicities in their homes, neighborhoods, and clubs.

"What happens is they go back and forth all the time; they're flipping between this public sphere in the center, and what might be called the fragmented experience of being in an ethnic-racial-cultural scene," Duster said. "Nobody's in the scene all the time."

The scene becomes controversial when there is something like a black engineering club on campus. Such a club might only meet for six or eight hours a year, but it is viewed as Balkanization by white students.

"When you capture it in one snapshot, either as an image for the radio, TV, film, book, you caught them in their Balkanized moment. But on closer inspection, it's a continuous back and forth. Sometimes without even knowing it they're learning . . . how to relate to each other in an osmotic way. In everyday actions, ordinary people are making multiculturalism work. They work together, they play together, and most of the time they get along. Pragmatism is the American way. The people who understand multiculturalism are not George Will . . . [or others] from the pulpit of some chair at Hopkins or Harvard."

If each culture retains its difference, Duster said it will help contribute to the betterment of society. "Only if you retain difference can you contribute to the public sphere. The obvious examples are with sensual pleasures. It's clear with ethnic cuisine. But how about the world of ideas? How about ways of problem solving?"

Duster's comments echo those made in 1924, at the peak of another xenophobic wave, when former university president Charles W. Eliot told a group of Harvard students that assimilation was a myth. Eliot said

> The fact is . . . that there has been no assimilation in the United States, and more than that, it isn't deserving that there should be any assimilation . . . that isn't for our best advantage in this country. What we want is numerous races with various history, with various gifts, with various abilities, living side by side in concord, not in discord, and each contributing its own peculiar quality to the mixed population.[19]

The "races" described by Eliot, of course, were then all white. But there's no reason that the same process can't happen today with Asians, Latinos, blacks, whites.

Duster is optimistic, but he is not Pollyannaish.

"I think that there are dangers. I don't think one needs to take the Schlesinger view of the inevitability of people fighting each other like in the hills of Bosnia or the flats of Rwanda. One would be foolish to say there's a lot of evidence that humans are just going to love each other. The evidence is on the other side. There are not very many models around the world of [different] people living together under a single political system."

The United States is now in a position to invent that model.

"There are two very different versions of assimilation. One was the melting pot thesis, which was that you must be melted down—indistinguishable. The other version was what is called Anglo-conformity, in which one group sets the standard, and every other group has to assimilate to that standard. There's a third version, which says it's not a meltdown, but it's a continuous cauldron of activity, rebirth, reformulation, and [we] emerge out of that with something new and different and better."

PART THREE

13

White Riot

On election day November 8, 1994, occasional rain clouds rolled over the Los Angeles basin. News radio was alive with speculation about how Proposition 187 would affect the nearly 3 out of 10 Californians who are Latino. Polls had shown SOS support at 53 percent, a far narrower gap than the preceding weeks, and support slipped with each passing day.[1] Though the press had mostly ignored SOS until about eight weeks prior to the vote, the surge in stories highlighted its flaws, and some progressives were confident the initiative would be defeated.

Something had to be done, but SOS was not it, or so went the logical argument that had seemed to be gaining ground. Those who wanted to believe reason would prevail did not factor in the significant number of people who lie to pollsters about race issues.

Another problem was the skewed images that filled newspapers and the evening news days before the election. In Los Angeles and San Francisco, viewers and readers saw screaming dark-skinned people marching in the streets, carrying Mexican flags and Spanish signs. Martha marched in the biggest of the early protests, and her group carried an American flag—but photographs of Latinos hoisting Old Glory did not make the news. The public saw an invading hoard brandishing a foreign flag and a foreign language—exactly the nightmare some Californians feared most. The initiative's supporters could not have paid for a better promotion.

Proposition 187 had cut deeply. There was a series of Latino student walkouts at Los Angeles high schools, and opinions surfaced even in the normally apolitical Asian community. In the window of a Chinese restaurant in Mountain View, a suburb south of San Francisco, was a flyer entirely in Chinese characters, save for one symbol: the number "187" with a slash through it.

SALAZAR

What were Latinos saying about the initiative on the day its fate would be decided largely by the white voting overclass? Chicano activists on talk radio were uttering predictable things—if it passed, there would be a Latino uprising. If these reports by the activists were to believed, there was already a great anger seething, ready to erupt. But on Whittier Boulevard in East Los Angeles, near the Silver Dollar Bar where Rubén Salazar was killed 24 years earlier, things were quiet.

Three Latinos leaning against a car watched as I sought out the bar. One of them, Francisco, left the trio and asked if I needed help. I said I was looking for the spot where a journalist was shot a long time before. He knew nothing about the killing of the man named Salazar. But he knew of others. "There was a shooting right over there, last week," Francisco offered, referring to a gang-related drive-by.

As he told about his life in East Los Angeles since he came from Mexico City five years earlier, a passing car backfired three times in quick succession. Francisco froze. A sideways glance confirmed there was no danger. He continued.

I asked about Proposition 187. He smiled and said something evasive. I suddenly felt very much the *gabacho*. Francisco was friendly but he was not going to trust any strange white man with his opinion. It did not seem he would give unless I made it clear where I was coming from. His reaction was similar to that of others that morning in East Los Angeles. This kind of fear was not evident three or four years earlier. It seemed every Latino I talked with viewed every white person as an INS agent, a spy. The Chicano spokesmen had it wrong. Among average Latinos, there was not anger, but distrust and fear.

"I think it's very bad," I finally said to Francisco.

"It's very bad," he said with brightening eyes and a shaking head. He worried about what would happen if he fell ill and needed to go to a hospital. Disregarding the less-than-stellar reputation of Mexican medical care, he said, "If you get sick in Mexico, they will treat you, it does not matter if you are American, French."

Francisco pointed to his little hole-in-the-wall storefront, where he made his living repairing refrigerators. "I fix it, you tell people. I'm right here. You tell them to come." It always seemed to come down to work for average Latinos, not politics, not revolution.

I found the bar, now called the New Silver Dollar. When I strode in, my presence startled the barmaid, who walked backward, never taking her eyes off me, to fetch the owner or manager seated in a dark nook. The man, a robust Latino with grey hair, rose to greet whatever trouble I was bringing.

He relaxed—only a little—when he learned I was a journalist. He had not been there that day in 1970—but he pointed to the stool covered in red vinyl at the center of the bar that curved in a "C." "That's where Rubén was sitting," he said. He described how the canister came through the door with the detail of a lecturing professor. "He fell backwards, landing under that pool table."

I asked about SOS. He was against it, but he was not eager to talk about anything other than Salazar. He was even more distrusting of discussing Proposition 187 than had been the men on the street. As I turned to leave, he said nothing had changed about the bar, save for the barmaids and the wall paint, though I did not believe him about the latter: it seemed to date to the Korean War.

He did not point out the most glaring alteration: a foyer. You now had to make a hard left when coming through the front door. A sturdy wall had been added as if to prevent another police tear-gas canister sailing into the bar to blast someone else in the head.

DEFEAT

Midafternoon at Martha Escutia's campaign headquarters, the office was crowded with young volunteers, on the phones urging voters to the polls, or coming and going from walking precincts. With one of the few safe Democrat seats, Martha was concentrating her energies on getting the vote out to defeat Proposition 187.

It was impossible to tell how Martha felt as she strode between the front and back rooms. Her strategy was not to push regulars, but to pull out infrequent voters. The office was targeting 5,735 occasional voters. With six hours until the polls closed, the office had already gotten 2,277 of them to cast a ballot.

Leo Briones grabbed a stack of 71 cards that identified the target voters in precinct 1430033 and rushed out the door. While driving, he launched into spin control. Puffing on a cigarette, he said that no matter the outcome, Latinos were voting in larger numbers, and this was a positive sign. Inside a voting station, a precinct captain gave Leo a list of those who had voted, and he checked them against his cards. A dozen had cast ballots. He would visit the remaining 59.

Leo hit the streets, moving quickly between houses. Many houses sported campaign posters. At one of the targeted homes, two signs were taped to the porch. One said, "These hands pick your food," and the other said, "These hands sew your clothes."

Once he visited all 59 homes, he drove home where Martha was taking a break from headquarters. "I'm nervous," she said. "I spoke to some people who were voting for the first time in 20 years. They said they were voting straight Democrat and no on 187."

On the couch with a sleeping bag drawn over her waist, she waited for the television news. She said nothing for half an hour, loudly biting her fingernails. In Mexico City at a McDonald's, the top story told of an attack by a group that smashed windows and chucked cash resisters to the floor, spray-painting "No a la 187" on the walls. No solid returns were in yet. Martha threw off the sleeping bag and headed back to headquarters.

Leo was possessed. He had printed out the last of some flyers he had produced on his computer to leave at the doors of the next batch of homes. Gunning the car up the 710 Freeway, to another polling station, he checked off the names of more voters. A young Latino couple walked in. They were nervous, both maybe 20, and they had a little girl in tow. They had come to vote for the first time in their lives. The line of Latinos snaked out the door.

This was a good sign. Two surveys estimated that 8 to 10 percent of the total vote that day came from Latinos—about the same as the record percentage that came out in 1992 for Clinton—but it was not enough. Deep down, Leo knew this, but he hoped the miserable voter registration figures of Latinos would someday improve. He was counting on the future, the children he saw with parents who came to vote.

It was almost dark. Suddenly, I found myself being directed to sit behind the wheel of Leo's car.

"Drive," he demanded.

I thought about raising the issue of journalistic ethics, but Leo was already in the passenger seat.

"Where is 5617!" he said as he struggled to find a house number. "There it is!"

Leo was out the door, darting across lawns. Doors opened, Leo gave a pitch, 7 o'clock came, 7:15, then 7:30, more doors, more faces: 15 minutes remained before he could reasonably get anyone to the polls.

"This is important," Leo breathily said as he ran to another house. Leo brought up a close election involving former U.S. Senator Alan Cranston several years earlier. "With Cranston, he won by one vote per precinct. GOTV [Get Out the Vote] meant he won."

Leo came to a house where a young man named Patrick was registered. Patrick's mother answered and said he was next door. We found him leaning against a car in the dark, talking with a neighbor.

"Have you voted?" Leo asked.

"No," Patrick replied, as if declining to take the last helping of crusted macaroni and cheese from the bottom of a pot.

"Brother, this is *important*. We need everyone."

"How long will it take?"

"Fifteen minutes."

"Oh, that's too much."

Leo begged, but Patrick just did not seem to care. Leo visited a few more homes. It was 7:45. No time left. We headed to the polling place a few blocks away to get a final precinct count. As we neared, Leo spotted a man walking at the side of the road.

"Is that Patrick? It's him! That's all it takes."

The poll captain said there was over 60 percent turnout, extremely high for the neighborhood.

Leo returned to the house to dress for the Democratic reception at the Biltmore Hotel. The early returns were just being released—with 1 percent in, the numbers were not looking good—SOS was way out front. At Martha's headquarters, the numbers remained grim. No one was much in the mood for talking. Martha stared silently at a television.

Leo asked if she wanted to come to the Biltmore.

"I'm going home to bed," she said.

Leo headed off for the hotel. In a room rented by Latino State Senator Art Torres, who was going down in defeat for his bid for state insurance commissioner, the mood was funereal.

Leo went straight for the bar and ordered a vodka and tonic. "And make it strong," he said.

With 16 percent of the vote in, SOS was being approved 66 to 34 percent. Proposition 184, the Three Strikes and You're Out initiative, was being approved by 75 percent of the voters.

The room next door to Torres's, where the anti-SOS people were gathered, was packed with high school kids who had been bused in. There was a television platform at the rear of the ballroom. In front of the cameras, for some unknown reason, the promoters whipped up the kids to dance to a song's lyrics that implored them to celebrate and have a good time.

They offered spin control for the cameras, though it is hard to imagine why they wanted to be seen celebrating the success of something they so despised. When the dancing stopped, the crowd was led in cheers of *"Sí se puede!"* yes we can, César Chávez's motto, but there was not much gusto in the cries.

Leo was bitter. "It's fucking evil," he said.

He lamented the failure of the anti-SOS campaign. "It's no time to be nice," Leo said. "You have to hit hard. You call it racist. You call it Nazi. You call it what it is and you shame people into doing the right thing."

THE MORNING AFTER

The morning of November 9, 1994, the mood at several high schools that had been hotbeds of Latino student protest leading up to the vote was sullen. Police helicopters hovered as cops swarmed the school grounds, but students said they were told not to walk out—or else. The helicopters, the somber dark-skinned faces, the palm trees—all imparted a strange sense of some tropical place of third world unrest. But the kids acted sucker-punched. They were as sad and confused as they were angry. Proposition 187 passed with 59 percent of the vote. Even if most eligible Latinos had turned out and voted as a block, the outcome would have been closer, but it would not have made a difference.

It was the morning after a riot, but the ruins were not of smoldering buildings. The destruction was seen in the faces of the kids at the high school. The whites had won a psychological victory, had "taken back" their state. Ron Prince was on the radio in a morning-after gloat. He outlined plans for taking the initiative on the road to Texas.

In Dana Point, Bill Shepherd was happy that Proposition 187 passed. But he had not felt strongly about it until election day, when about a dozen Latinos, apparently high school students, marched with a Mexican flag down the Street of the Golden Lantern near his home.

"That flipped me," Bill said. "I thought, 'That's it.' I probably would have still voted for it, but it hooked me emotionally. I spent four years in the military, took a year of my life, and went to a foreign country and lived in horrible conditions, and they have the nerve to come here illegally and walk down the street waving a Mexican flag? That pissed me off. They blew it."

The election showed Bill that people no longer fear being politically incorrect, and that some Latinos saw through the issue: he knew of a number of Latino citizens, including a long-time friend, who voted for Proposition 187 because they did not believe in an open border.

"The paper today said they're thinking about a day of non-work," Bill said of a post-election tactic to protest the measure.

There was also talk of a day when Latinos would not patronize stores to show their economic clout.

"If they want to be fair and complete, they should also have a day when they don't use government services."

Bill did not see how Proposition 187 and other California referendums shared a dark history. Bill credited the small band of students who had carried the Mexican flag through the streets with too much power. The vast majority of Latinos laboring in the city's hotel industry live in fear of the police and power and express no revolutionary zeal. But in the end, they saw a society that hated them.

Even though Latinos were just between 8 and 10 percent of the turnout on election day, among all of the four major ethnicities, they were the strongest in opposition. Exit polls showed Latinos were against the initiative by a 5-to-1 margin.[2] Even Raul Escutia, Martha's conservative father, opposed it. After 40 years in the United States, Raul cast his first vote for Ronald Reagan. When Pete Wilson ran for governor in 1990, Raul supported him enthusiastically. But Proposition 187 changed everything. Raul did not vote for Wilson, and he voted against the initiative. "It's very scary," Raul said. "It's heading into 'us' versus 'them.' We are going into a minefield."

Wilson had emphasized repeatedly that race was not the issue. But it was. The enforcement of numerous existing laws would have been enough to control illegal immigration. There was no need for an initiative that would punish the undocumented while at the same time doing nothing to stop business from employing them.

Raul said he knew of only one Latino who voted for SOS, his sister-in-law.

"She said there were a lot of illegal immigrants. Naturally we were up in arms. My wife, she is apolitical, she never votes, but even she went to the polls against 187."

Despite her workload, Maria Ha was quite aware of Proposition 187 and Pete Wilson's immigrant-bashing. Maria had turned 18 and had registered to vote.

"He's referring to everybody," she said, not just illegal immigrants. She feared it would lead to an ingrained hatred of legal immigrants like her. The San Francisco Chinatown community was talking about it. Her grandmother was especially worried—she hadn't yet been made a citizen.

"She's going, 'Oh my God.' That's really outrageous to do that. How can you cut down funding for senior citizens? I really don't like it. I know a lot of people who are immigrants and they aren't doing anything wrong. They're paying taxes. They're not on welfare."

A broad block of people besides white males from south Orange County made up the 59 percent who voted in favor of 187, and a lot of "other" voters had to join with traditional conservatives. A *Los Angeles Times* exit poll found almost half of Asian and black voters supported the proposition, as did almost two out of three whites.[3] The poll did not ask about political labels, but a lot of moderates and even some liberals must have crossed over. Even more liberals and moderates and minorities must have voted for Three Strikes, for the measure was approved by 71 percent of the electorate.

The lack of rainbow unity was extremely troubling to Joaquín Ochoa, the UCLA hunger striker. Joaquín told how he worked with Latino high school students against Proposition 187. As the kids walked out of school and marched in the streets, some told him, "We'll revolt!"

"It's scary," he said. "The kids feel so powerful." He said he told them they had better be careful. "They've got a big militia that [is] willing to pull the trigger. You know, I don't think you're going to be able to go up against F-14s."

He was not sure where the anger would lead. But Joaquín was bitter that the Latino community had not organized. "I think a lot of people tried to say the sleeping giant has awakened, something like that. It already had been slaughtered by the time it woke up."

Joaquín had not known until after the vote how much his hunger strike energized Ron Prince and Barbara Coe. When he found out, did he feel any differently about his actions? He smiled broadly but did not directly answer the question. He took great satisfaction, it seemed, in having riled Ron Prince and the hunger strike that helped energize the Latino community: the kids who were walking out of high schools to protest SOS had been motivated by the strike.

"You're going to have to deal with us, whether you want to or not. This is our land, you know, the mythical Aztlán."

The day after the election, a federal judge ordered an injunction against most aspects of Proposition 187. Within a few days, eight lawsuits were pending in state and federal courts, brought by the Los Angeles Unified School District and school districts in Sacramento and San Francisco, along with other government agencies. This quick legal action drew the wrath of some voters, who flooded phone lines at the school boards in Los Angeles and Sacramento, as well as Los Angeles City Hall, with vows that they would recall officials for wasting taxpayer money.[4]

As in times past, when California flexed its anti-immigrant muscle, the reaction quickly reached the national level. President Clinton made the first remarks on immigration in the State of the Union address of any president in recent memory. He later proposed radically increasing funds to combat illegal immigration, and for the first time, the INS in early 1996 took out advertisements inside Mexico warning its citizens that they would be dealt with harshly if they came north; at the same time more walls were built on the border. Clinton also suggested employer sanctions like those proposed long before by Willie Brown. A Wilson spokesman responded that business was innocent in the whole affair—this approach relies on "employer vilification" and the spokesman repeated that the immigrants were merely coming for services such as welfare and public schools.[5]

Other Democrats such as U.S. Senator Diane Feinstein joined Republicans in attacking illegal immigration. The Federation for Immigration Reform, a group that has long lobbied to freeze legal immigration, resurrected its cause. By 1996 many punitive measures were in the works, including a Republican proposal in the House Judiciary Subcommittee on Immigration, supported by many California Democrats, to repeal the 14th Amendment, which guaranteed citizenship to anyone born in the United States.

In Orange County, the trials began in the cases against the six youths accused of killing Steve Woods. Superior Court Judge Everett W. Dickey sentenced Hector Penuelas and Julio Perez Bonilla, both 18, to the California Youth Authority, in a nonjury trial. They would be released by age 25. Barbara Coe launched a recall drive against Dickey to send a message to other judges that they should not protect illegal immigrants. Apparently her message was heard. The next defendant, Juan Alcocer, 19, came before Judge Robert R. Fitzgerald two weeks later. Alcocer, who prosecutors admitted had not thrown the paint roller, was given 26 years to life. In the *Los Angeles Times* Shellie Woods, Steve Woods's sister, said, "I'm so glad this animal will be put away behind bars . . . I wish they all were behind bars."[6]

A recall drive was also started against Mark Slavkin, president of the Los Angeles School Board, for the board's filing a lawsuit challenging the initiative. Both recall drives sputtered.[7] The real test will come when Proposition 187 likely reaches the U.S. Supreme Court, which is exactly what its supporters want. Ron Prince said he would like to see the court reverse itself on the 1982 *Plyler* v. *Doe* case, in which it ruled 5-4 that illegal immigrant children have a right to a public education.[8] It is a far different court today, and SOS backers believe it will reconsider, if not on all aspects of the case, at least some of them. Plyler affirmed for the first time the 14th Amendment's equal protection guarantee to anyone within U.S. borders; children should not be penalized for their parent's actions. SOS backers do not think the court will extend that reasoning, for example, to adults seeking nonemergency medical services.

With Proposition 187, the voters had unleashed an ancient genie, and California's history shows that only bad will come from it, at least for a while. Once again, California led the United States in the bashing of nonwhite immigrants. A spinoff group inspired by Ron Prince, the Orlando-based Save Our State Committee, was seeking a Proposition 187-type initiative to place on the Florida ballot in 1996, and a host of federal actions were considered. What happened on November 8, 1994, was an orderly white riot against cultural change, and the xenophobia of voters will echo harshly in the coming years, until whites in California and the rest of the nation learn that there is little basis for fear.

THE SLEEPING GIANT

Democrats should pay attention to the emerging voting power of Latinos, a group that alone could shift politics first in California and then nationally. European immigrants quickly joined the main-stream when courted by the political machines in East Coast cities. As corrupt as machine politics were, the system was quick to incor-porate newcomers with the promise of jobs and other perks in ex-change for votes. The machine is dead, but the power of the vote is still there to be tapped.

A look at some numbers reveals the potential of the Latino vote. Each year in California, 150,000 Latinos turn 18 and more Latinos are seeking citizenship. In Los Angeles County at the time of the Proposition 187 vote, an average of 735 applications for cit-izenship were filed each day with the Immigration and Naturaliza-tion Service, many from Latinos. It reached an 877 daily average one month after the vote; by February 1995 it jumped to 1,440, and by April there were 2,200.[9] Martha Escutia's grandparents were among those who said they were going to seek citizenship. Latino leaders credit Proposition 187 for this surge. Once Latinos become citizens, they are "supervoters." Eighty-one percent regis-ter to vote compared with 70 percent for the general population.

The prophecy made by former Republican cabinet members Jack Kemp and William Bennett that Proposition 187 could drive the Latino vote into the Democrats' hands seems to have been borne out by the 5-1 ratio by which Latinos voted against the ini-tiative. Antonio Gonzalez, president of the Southwest Voter Re-search Institute, which has long worked to enfranchise Latinos, said that Republicans have virtually ceded Latinos in California and the Southwest to the Democratic Party.

How Democrats capitalize on this huge block of voters is a challenge to the party. Gonzalez says the national Democratic lead-ership is becoming more aware of the Latino vote. In the summer of 1995 Vice President Al Gore came to a meeting of Gonzalez's group as it started a drive to register 100,000 new Latinos for the 1996 election. Gore said the Democrats must create a future in which the "demagoguery of this day and time" can be passed off with an "amused shake of the head."[10]

The California Democratic Party, which for so long was domi-nated by black Assemblyman Willie Brown (later mayor of San Francisco), is "driven by the old guard coalition of labor, blacks, and liberals," said Gonzalez. "It's a Sacramento–San Francisco

Cadillac liberal philosophy. They're still living in the past in determining what the Latino vote is about."

Latinos respond to door-to-door vote-getting drives, said Gonzalez, not slick mailers and television campaigns. Martha Escutia later admitted that she knew Proposition 187 was going to win, but in her campaign office on election night it was important to engage the community by the get-out-the-vote drive. She was thinking of the future, not the lost present.

To energize the Latino vote, Martha believes old-fashioned grass roots organizing is key. She echoes the sentiments of many liberals who think the Democratic Party has moved away from its base and are only marginally different from Republicans in how they raise money and run campaigns. "People are forgetting there is a great value in getting regular people involved in campaigns," Martha said.

The personal approach works with Latinos, according to a test by the Colorado Latino Voter Registration and Education Project.[11] It picked 11 precincts in a Commerce City election in 1995, according to the *Rocky Mountain News,* and members knocked on the doors of Latino-surname voters and urged them to vote. In these precincts, there was a 15 to 20 percent increase in voter turnout.

The Catholic church could also play a role in organizing the Latino community. The traditional reluctance of the church to enter politics was broken during the Proposition 187 campaign, when Cardinal Roger Mahony of Los Angeles pushed his priests to urge people to vote from the pulpit. The *National Catholic Reporter* says there may be a major "church–state battle" and that California "could see massive campaigns of civil disobedience led by Latino faith communities. The mobilization . . . may hold the key to how the future Latino majority can finally relegate to the historical sidelines the white minority trying to dictate the conditions of their lives."[12]

Gonzalez said that with some work, Latinos could soon be 14 percent of the voters in California, roughly a 50 percent increase over present numbers. But with some real effort, this could be raised to 19 percent, a huge block vote that when combined with traditional white liberals, blacks, and some Asians, could turn California away from the politics of division typified by Pete Wilson—but only if the party acts.

The end of de facto apartheid does not have to come at the expense of white voters. Gonzalez thinks the white community shares many things in common with Latinos, most of whom are culturally conservative.

"The ultimate values are the same. It's not about immigration, it's about old America rejecting the new America. They cannot win that fight. They should not win that fight. The country has been East-West oriented, but the new reality is a North-South reality"—the "have" societies versus the "have-nots." "Pete Wilson is California's last East-West governor. I see the next political period as [one] of real conflict. But I'm not pessimistic. Demographic forces are on our side, but it will be a long fight. This is a marathon."

14

The New Frontline

Just weeks after the Proposition 187 vote, Thomas Wood, executive director of the California Association of Scholars, and Glynn Custred, an anthropology professor at California State University in Hayward, proposed the California Civil Rights Initiative. It would bar the state (but not private business) from using race, sex, color, ethnicity, or national origin as a criterion for either discriminating against, or granting preferential treatment to, any individual or group in employment, contracts, and education.[1]

Governor Wilson did not wait to endorse the measure, as he had with Proposition 187; his support was almost immediate. He had not yet formally announced his candidacy for president, but he made affirmative action the centerpiece of his campaign. His support was in language that made the issue seem reasonable to many whites. In 1995, before the University of California's Board of Regents' vote to end affirmative action, Wilson rescinded all executive state-mandated affirmative action programs in an eight-page letter "to the people of California." He quoted letters sent to him by an Asian and a Latina who were against affirmative action.

Forging a new approach to equal opportunity here is a necessity if we are to succeed and prosper. . . . We are divided by a system that offers preferences and privileges to some, but not to others. We are divided by a system that flies in the face of the American notion of fairness. Americans today are rightly concerned that we have lost our sense of community. We must not allow "E pluribus unum" to be debased and undermined by misfired good intentions that artificially tribalize Americans and drive us apart.[2]

The public gave the initiative overwhelming support. The first Field Poll in March 1995 showed 60 percent of voters in favor of repealing affirmative action, 35 percent against. A large majority of whites were in favor, but each nonwhite group was opposed. Pollster Mervin Field told reporters he had never seen an issue gather such high awareness so quickly.[3]

The initiative was already the topic of discussion one sunny Saturday during the OK Program study hall in Rancho Cordova. Don Northcross had just shown the high school students a film about an interracial group discussing cultural issues, including whites' fear of affirmative action. He described a black man in the film who said his fear was not of white supremacists.

His fear comes from decent hard working, church-going, law abiding white citizens who are not educated about the facts of affirmative action, what it was intended to do, how it was implemented, and how it's fallen short of the goals that it was made to reach. They're going to come out for this thing in record numbers, I guarantee you. Whether or not they're going to the polls because they dislike you or not, the results are going to be the same.

The OK Program was entering its fifth year. From its nadir a year and a half earlier, the program had a surge in volunteer adults. Don now had some 30 men working with him and there were over 100 kids enrolled from both the junior high and high schools. The young men in the room had been with the program from its first days. They were now juniors and seniors, a few over 6 feet tall. Gone were the bouncing balls and other acts of cutting up. In 1996 these youths would be entering college and the working world. They listened seriously as Don talked about the CCRI.

"I grew up when there was no affirmative action and I've seen what it was like after," Don told the young men. "You don't have to ask me which I prefer. This is the most serious issue I've ever seen. You have to understand the Civil Rights Act was passed 30 years ago. South Africa just started voting last year. We got just 30 years ahead of South Africa in a lot of ways. I couldn't drink out of certain water fountains as a kid. I had to go in the back door. People think that's hundreds of years ago. I tell you that so you can understand you ain't out of the woods. You can't relax."

A student named David interjected. "A lot of black folks who are Republican feel in a way that I made it, why can't you?"

Don nodded and mentioned Shelby Steele's book, *The Content of Our Character.* Among the points Steele makes is that white guilt and black dependency have conspired to make things worse for blacks. "I agree with a lot of things Shelby says," Don said. "But I think Shelby [and] most black conservatives go too far with their philosophy about self-help when they take all responsibility away from the government. But I certainly don't think we can sit around and not take our responsibility simply because the government is not living up to [its]. We have to work hard."

At the same time, Don emphasized that hard work and ability are worthless if there isn't equal opportunity.

"Just look at people like my father," Don said. "My father was the hardest working man I ever knew. My father drove 80 miles a day round-trip to work for 30-some years, raised seven kids. He supplemented his income by plowing the fields with mules. But because he came along in a time where the laws hadn't been changed that would judge him more fairly, that would present him more opportunities, he didn't make it as far. So it's an insult to people like my dad when people say, 'I worked hard and made it.' Years ago it didn't matter how hard you worked. You got enough to carry you and your family to the next crop season, no more. There have always been hard-working black folk, believe me. Slave labor is the hardest work you can do."

Don said black conservatives ignore those who gave their lives for civil rights, without which they would not be allowed in their present positions in universities and the courts and politics. "People went to jail, gave their lives, literally, so that the system would change," Don told David and the others.

No matter how far you go, you got to realize you're standing on the backs of somebody else. Because some of those people whose backs you're standing on were just as smart as you are, and they worked just as hard as you, but they didn't have the opportunities you have. We've got to the point where we feel like everything is just hunky dory. We're in for a rude awakening. When we relax, you'll see what happens. They'll take it back from you.

My mom used to tell us the story about a hog under the apple tree. She said there was a big apple tree [with] huge branches that spanned across the hog pen. And every year when the apples would get ripe, [they] would fall into the hog pen. He had a keen ear, and every time he'd hear one fall, [the pig would] find it and eat it up. She said from watching that hog for three seasons, she noticed that he never looked up to see where the apples were coming from. She said many of us are just like that hog. All of these opportunities are symbolic of the apples. They're everywhere, compared to the way they used to be. And many of us are just racing from opportunity to opportunity. And even worse than that, not only do we not stop and look up and say thank you for these opportunities, we're not planting any apple seeds to make sure the next generation has apples, too. We're busy eating up the apples. I guess we think we deserve these apples. I urge you, don't get so carried away eating up the apples and, number one, forget where they came from, and number two, forget to plant some more seeds.

Some of this stuff is hard to hear, makes you angry. It's not to make you angry. It's meant to motivate you, to let you know where you come from, to let you know that those old people that went through this, they deserve much more than what we are giving them. You are their future, you are their hope. That old slave, my great-great-granddaddy, probably [laid] awake nights after a hard day in the fields and just dreamed of the day that his offspring could go back to Africa, could be in a place where they had their own land.

It was late and the students had places to go—a production of a play, sports practice, jobs. The eight remaining students climbed into Don's van. One by one the kids piled out, until the last stop at two big apartment buildings. Clusters of Russian immigrant men were talking and smoking in the parking lot, amid playing children. Several *stara babas,* babushka-headed old women, lugged grocery bags up stairs. Every available railing and pole had a line anchored to it, and freshly laundered clothes caught the last rays of sun. The Russians turned to stare at the van. During an early OK Program study hall, a student asked Don why the Russians from the former Soviet Union who had moved into Rancho Cordova already seemed to be doing better than black people. Don presented the question to the group for discussion.

"Because they're white," said one youth, who then cringed, fearing he had said something wrong. Don then lectured about the different kinds of immigrants—refugees and those who came seeking a better life. Blacks, he said, differ from every other group, not only because they were brought against their will, but because their skin color always sets them apart. While this sounds elementary to an adult, it was a revelation for the kids, who had not considered history. "The first thing people did was change their name to sound more American," Don said of European immigrants. "Within a generation, they had intermarried, they had moved into certain other neighborhoods, there was no obvious attempt to exclude them anymore. They don't have to ask you where you're from. They know you're of African descent. You stick out like a sore thumb. You can move from one neighborhood to the other, but you still stand out."

While it is unclear how the Russians will adapt to the United States, Don speculated during that earlier study hall that in a few generations, their offspring will more or less blend in with other whites, as has been the pattern for two centuries of white immigration. This left him feeling frustrated about where blacks are headed. The uncharted territory of life without affirmative action is a grim prospect. As Don drove out of Rancho Cordova, he spoke about the sponsors of the affirmative action measure, Glynn Custred, Thomas Wood, Pete Wilson, and others.

"They hide behind this thing, take government out of our lives, make it fair for everybody. Now we're going to get back to 30 years ago when things were fair! Who do they think they are kidding? These guys are saying this with a straight face. They're interested in maintaining total power and control. They hate somebody telling them that they have to share with other people. We're supposed to relax and feel like they have our best interest at heart— when history has proven over and over again that they can't be fair? If it happens, it will be like things were basically 30 years ago, where white males were in a position to decide on who got jobs and didn't have to answer to anybody."

AFFIRMATIVE ACTION:
THE PAST AND ITS FUTURE

Fairness in hiring had its beginnings on June 25, 1941, when Franklin Roosevelt issued Executive Order 8802, which forbade discriminatory hiring practices in defense industries under government contract. Dwight Eisenhower issued a presidential order in the 1950s mandating employment opportunities for disadvantaged groups. John F. Kennedy issued an executive order similar to Roosevelt's. But affirmative action did not really take shape until after the 1964 Civil Rights Act, when it meant a temporary program in which blacks could catch up. Lyndon Johnson rejected it, calling it "compensatory preferential hiring," and Senator Hubert Humphrey warned that "it should not lead to an excess in its application for all Americans."[4]

In 1969 President Richard Nixon required companies doing business with the government to set up "goals and timetables" for the promotion of blacks and then went a step further by including other categories: Asians, Pacific Islanders, Latinos, Native Americans, and Alaskan natives. Nixon changed his position when he decided to shore up his conservative base, all part of his growing political emphasis on the racial wedge issue. By 1972 he was attacking affirmative action.

By the 1990s the supposed aggrieved white male was the reason for the backlash. But the belief that blacks were dominating jobs was a myth, at least at the top. A 1995 federal study showed that while white males made up 43 percent of the workforce, they held 95 percent of senior management jobs.[5]

Conservatives have long howled about affirmative action. But if one scratches the psyches of many liberals, they resent it too. The same liberals who supported civil rights in the South are uncomfortable when they have to compete with blacks for jobs. Later, blacks themselves became uncomfortable when affirmative action meant making room for Latinos. And as was seen at Lowell High

School, Asians were not happy when things came full circle and they had to make way for white students.

One wonders where liberals really stand. *Nation* writer Katha Pollit lambasted left-liberal opinion magazines for preaching but not practicing. Pollit said in her 13 years at the magazine, only briefly was there a nonwhite person on the editorial staff. She found the same track record elsewhere. There were no nonwhites on the staff of *Atlantic, Harpers, The New York Review of Books,* and *The Utne Reader.* There was one nonwhite each at the *Progressive, Mother Jones,* and *In These Times.* Pollit asked, "If we don't live our politics, why should anyone else?"[6]

Just how does one define a group in need of affirmative action? At UC Berkeley, before the regents' 1995 vote, there were two separate admissions categories for Latinos and Chicanos, the latter a classification targeted for help. Two people with Mexican heritage could conceivably fall into either group. "It's difficult to differentiate between them," admitted Bob Laird, the undergraduate admissions director. The school had a special category for Filipinos, but after detailed study, officials phased out affirmative action for them and folded the group into "Asians." At the same time, Berkeley was broader in its use of affirmative action than other schools because it had special status for the economically disadvantaged, including whites.

Not all whites would be happy with a system based purely on grades. Whites who want to do away with affirmative action should consider the admissions policies at Lowell High School. Through the 1980s and early 1990s, the school admitted whites with *lower* test scores than Chinese Asians; it admitted Latinos and blacks with even lower test scores than whites and Asians. This system was scrapped in early 1996 for one that is race-neutral and accommodated disadvantaged students—20 to 30 percent of the 600 or so spots in the 1996–97 class will have to come from families on welfare or in public housing.[7] It is almost certain more Chinese Asians will gain entry, because applicants competing for the roughly 400 remaining spots broke down as follows: 667 Chinese Asians, 385 whites, 234 Latinos, and 102 blacks.

How would most whites react if they were nudged out in favor of more Chinese Asians not because of preference, but performance? Would a school of all Chinese Asians—or whites—be desirable when one considers that learning includes socialization and acculturation to the society in which one lives? Test scores and grades are just one measure of someone's ability. They are an indicator, but so are other equally important factors, like community participation and special skills learned outside the classroom. "Merit" is a broad term that goes beyond a score. And there is a big difference between mandatory quotas and a policy that simply seeks diversity.

THE WEDGE ISSUE ROLLS ON

Supporters of the California Civil Rights Initiative expected a romp when it came to gathering signatures to place the measure on the ballot, but they needed 312,000 additional names than had been required for Proposition 187. Because the measure was a constitutional amendment instead of a statutory one like 187, it required 693,230 registered voters signatures—but it needed at least 1 million to withstand those disqualified by the secretary of state's office.

CCRI backers fumbled. They did not factor in the possibility that large businesses, often champions of conservative causes, would not give them money—these firms did not want to be associated with the divisive measure, knowing it is not good business to support something that flies in the face of common sense in such a polyethnic state.

By November 1995, the group was choking, plagued by inexperience. It had spent $500,000 and had only some 200,000 signatures. A few weeks later, UC Regent Ward Connerly stepped in. With the help of Pete Wilson, he was able to raise $900,000, a substantial portion of it from the state and national Republican Party, which hoped to use affirmative action against President Bill Clinton in 1996.[8] Republicans planned to "beat Clinton over the head with it" in California, said one state Republican official, who felt the strategy would work for the Republican presidential nominee as well as Proposition 187 had worked for Wilson.[9]

One million mailers were sent out, and the bounty paid to signature-gatherers was raised to $1 each in the final weeks before the February 1996 deadline. In the end, 800,000 of the nearly 1.1

million names were harvested by the paid gatherers, the balance from volunteers.[10]

Connerly was praised by the party. At a state Republican gathering in early 1996, he was one of only six blacks among 800 attendees. He received a standing ovation for his CCRI campaign.[11]

As 1996 progressed, opponents girded for a fight. Some looked hopefully to what had happened in Washington state, where backers of an initiative failed to collect enough signatures to place a measure on the ballot in late 1995.

But just as with Proposition 187, the extreme outer Right had taken control and polls continued to show it winning. In a state on the brink of being "minority-majority" but in which 8 out of 10 voters are white, it would take a miracle to defeat the CCRI. Polls showed most Californians are against special preferences but support affirmative action if the question is phrased differently, so long as there are no rigid quotas.[12] But the message of the Right was heard most loudly. Rather than brokering reasoned adjustment— such as studying ways in which affirmative action could be refined—the solution was presented in all-or-nothing terms.

Every aspect of the initiative was carefully orchestrated. The words "affirmative action" do not appear in the ballot language, which in part says, "neither the State of California nor any of its political subdivisions or agents shall use race, sex, color, ethnicity, or national origin as a criterion for either discriminating against, or granting preferential treatment to, any individual or group in the operation of the State's system of public employment, public education or public contracting."[13] It is no coincidence that this sounds suspiciously like the wording of 1960s-era laws against discrimination.

Another part of the text reads, "Nothing in this section shall be interpreted as prohibiting classifications based on sex which are reasonably necessary to the normal operation of the State's system of public employment or public education." This seemingly innocuous wording, some argue, could mean a pregnant woman could be demoted or laid off if the pregnancy was seen as interfering with her job.

Opponents counted on fighting the initiative as a gender issue, not just a minority issue, reminding voters that affirmative action and equal rights have been responsible for advances made by women in jobs and pay. Also, opponents planned a "Freedom Summer 1996," reminiscent of the Freedom Summer of 1964, when students descended on Mississippi to register black voters. In California, organizers planned to use several thousand students from at least 130 college campuses to register voters and educate the public.

With the 1996 vote approaching, the task grew daunting. Liberal support was clearly lacking: there had been a low turnout for the 1995 march with Jesse Jackson after the University of California Regents' vote to end affirmative action. There was big talk inside the meeting, however. UC Berkeley ethnic studies professor Carlos Muñoz, for example, flatly decreed in testimony, "You vote for the proposal, you vote for making America an apartheid nation. . . . War is what we don't want. If that's what it comes down to, it will be war."

But what war? Muñoz was assuming that minorities were united in their desire to fight whites and that liberals would leap into the fight. The split on his own campus was obvious two months after the regents' vote, when the student newspaper at Berkeley ran an editorial endorsing the regents' decision. "Race-based affirmative action needed to end because it is racist," said an unsigned editorial in the *Daily Cal*, the voice of the radical Left in the 1960s.[14] The mixed-race editorial board voted 6–4 to endorse the regents. The split at Berkeley is mostly between a conservative Asian-white axis versus Latinos and blacks and liberal whites. But a large group of students were not sure what to think.

At a protest against the regents' decision, 5,000 people crowded Berkeley's Sproul Plaza—a relatively small turnout, many of them high school students. Most of the 30,000 UC students were studying for midterms. At the edge of the plaza, three UC students debated affirmative action, trying to figure out what it meant. One of them, Theo Hummer, acknowledged, "There are a lot of people who are confused about all the information."

"There's a big split," added Tonia Hsieh. "Last night in my dorm a big discussion went on for one hour." The women were debating what "qualified" meant. Hsieh leaned toward disregarding race as a factor, letting in those with the best scores—which would benefit Asians. They are most affected, because many are turned away in favor of other groups, including whites. Hsieh is Asian.

Theo, who is white and went to high school in Mississippi, differed. She said that four of her classmates applied to Berkeley. "Two of them were white and two were Asian. Both whites got in. We were all qualified." Hummer said she liked affirmative action because it improved her education. She came to Berkeley to get away from Mississippi. She said she did not meet her first Asian until she was 14 years old. "Affirmative action adds to the quality of my education when I'm surrounded by people of different backgrounds."

Given the diversity of opinion among these women, it is not surprising that Democrats, women, and nonwhites disagreed greatly about how to fight the proposed ballot measure. Some progressives vowed not to repeat the same strategy mistakes made with Proposition 187. Education was to be the key.

Polls show whites believe more has been done to advance relations between blacks and whites, while blacks feel there is still a lot of racism. This oldest racial dynamic—that is, in black and white relations—which dates back to slavery through the civil rights years to the present, shows that the nation has a long way to go in a society that is white and black as well as Latino and Asian. Perhaps the best that can be hoped for, as the old saying goes, is that the law can't make a man love me, but it can prevent him from lynching me. This is the best argument for some form of affirmative action that brings inclusion for nonwhites. If nothing replaces the loss of affirmative action to nudge nonwhites into the mainstream, it will spell huge trouble in a society with a white minority. It is one more guarantee that the future will hold unrest.

15

End of the Rainbow
or a New Society?

When the first interviews for this book were conducted in 1991, Californians had not yet seen the Los Angeles riots, Proposition 187, the Three Strikes prison law, or the anti–affirmative action initiative. These events moved at a stunning pace, comparable in some ways to the anti-Chinese tumult in the 1870s and the anti-Japanese eruptions early in the century, when the state's racial outbursts affected the nation.

In those periods, whites successfully barred "those people." But no longer can nonwhites be kept out. The tide of history that has caused the browning of America cannot be stemmed. The most extreme whites should realize the change is inevitable, destined to occur because of their forebears' actions: the Mexican-American War, Vietnam, Korea; slavery; the past and continued importation of low-cost labor.

Although there are ethnocentric nonwhites who are just as racist as some whites, California's electoral discord has emanated from whites. There is ample evidence that white tension could escalate. What will California be like in 2010, when nonwhites make up 60 percent of the population, especially if whites are still the voting majority? And how will California's actions influence the rest of the nation as non-Hispanic whites fall from 76 percent of the U.S. populace in 1990 to just over half in 2050?

There is no solid block of white opinion in California, despite the voting patterns dominated by a frightened electorate. By just looking at the outcome of elections, it is easy to forget that many whites are simply confused and afraid to discuss racial issues. I listened to many guarded opinions, but it was not until a Berkeley protest over the end of affirmative action that I witnessed a moment of rare candor within the monolithic group called "whites."

Some 5,000 people crowded in front of Sproul Hall, roaring as a woman shouted into a microphone. Many carried signs, one proclaiming "Pete Wilson is the Mother of All Fuckers." At the edge of this wrathful scene, either bravely or stupidly, stood a lone student wearing a placard over his chest that said "California Civil Rights Initiative." Christopher Gray, in a suit coat and tie, was gathering signatures to place the measure on the 1996 ballot.

One signer, a balding white man in his late thirties, attracted a small crowd, including a tall white South African. Gray told the South African, who lived in California, that the initiative would end bias, not create it—the logic being that affirmative action was state-sponsored racial discrimination. "We're not for racism," Gray insisted.

"It's really sweet how you people make it sound so innocent," said the South African. "It's racist. I wish you guys would be honest. I would have more respect for you."

The balding man tensed. "Racism should not exist. But it does exist, and where it comes up it should be dealt with. But I am not for giving preferences to groups."

The South African countered that it is vital to make up for centuries of inequity. "There were set-asides for white men in the eighteenth and nineteenth and twentieth centuries," he said.

"So it's okay to make another wrong?"

"I'm from South Africa, and let me tell you, you are not very far ahead of us. There are still problems. If anyone was to argue with me that we [South Africa] should return to apartheid, I would call them a racist. It's wrong."

"Are you calling me a racist by implication?" asked the balding man.

"Yes."

"Then you are a jerk. That's the problem. You reduce it to an argument that you are a racist or you are not. What you don't understand is that this is why you are fucking losing this battle. You don't know who I am. I believe in the premise of innocent until proven guilty. I am a white man talking here, and I am against institutional powers that are racist. But I am not in favor of giving preferences to groups. You can't pass a law saying, 'Be nice to everybody.'"

He told the white South African that past injustice was wrong, but that people should "just get over it."

"Yes, it's easy for you to say," argued the South African. "You got over it. People at the bottom are under it. This discussion is not going to solve anything. We don't have any common ground. But I think we are going to end up farther apart than we are now. I think that you and I will end up on opposite ends of an incredible explosion in this country."

The South African walked off in disgust.

The balding man turned to Gray. "Sorry for starting a debate in front of you. I just see this country growing farther and farther apart, and it scares me. You can't have an honest disagreement with people. They call you a racist."

This exchange struck at the root of the conflict among California whites. It is not a matter of Klan-like cross burners versus those opposing intolerance and hate. The South African and balding man epitomize the complex differences as whites try to chart a course in a new racial landscape.

QUESTION FOR WHITES

Whites will dominate the evolution of the new society because they now hold electoral and economic power. This "white question" is an inverse of Kipling's "white man's burden." In California the burden is not the paternalistic attitude of whites toward dark-skinned people, but their attitude toward their own role in a society in which they are not the majority. The future of California and the nation lies in whites recognizing that interdependence based on common interests—jobs, schooling, safety—is necessary.

At the same time, nonwhites must also be inclusive. Some Latinos, blacks, and Asians do not believe they need whites in a political coalition because whites will be "just" 40 percent of the population. This attitude is as dangerous as white isolation. Given present circumstances, the "majority" of nonwhites will be incredibly divided and many will not vote. There is much talk about the rainbow coalition, but it clearly has not come to exist in California. The white 40 percent will be a significant and powerful minority. The Left will have to understand the difference between activism and organization. Ernest Hill, Donald Northcross's friend at UCLA, says a big part of the failure of the Left-progressive alliance lies in the lack of willingness to organize; instead of registering voters as in the South, Ernest says college students "want to be at the microphone, enjoying the spotlight. But no one wants to be out doing the work to change the community."

All the same, the pressure is on whites. They can choose to be inclusive or ever more isolated. Whites ignore dealing with this question at their own peril, for power can and will be chiseled away from them. If they continue to resist cultural change, the result likely will be a long period of unrest, which could include a series of riots.

Many whites are choosing isolation and are starting to resemble third world elites. The census data that show "white islands" in California south of Sacramento and San Francisco may be the future residential patterns for other regions as the percentage of nonwhites increase throughout America. The walling seen first in suburban California is becoming more common in states as dissimilar as Texas and New Jersey.

California's white islands seem to be getting even more starkly separated from the larger society. Census data present only a snapshot of the ethnic makeup of a neighborhood, as is pointed out by William W. Goldsmith and Edward J. Blakely in *Separate Societies*.[1] A neighborhood that now has a white majority with a Latino presence could merely be in transition. It could, by the next census, "tip" like Azusa near Los Angeles and become minority white. Rather than a snapshot, the authors say a movie would more accurately reflect what is happening. Thus the maps at the beginning of this book based on the 1990 census are deceiving: areas outside the white-dominant islands that seem integrated could merely be in transition as more whites flee to wealthy zones such as the non-barrio areas of Dana Point.

The siege mentality could grow more fierce, even in the liberal white islands found around San Francisco. Whether or not an area is liberal or conservative does not seem to matter when it comes to fear and how to react to it. Dana Point Mayor Judy Curreri said that when she campaigned for office, she spent a lot of time behind the walls. Residents told her they worried about crime in Bill Shepherd's neighborhood.

"It wasn't, 'We want a better life for the people in Lantern Village,' which is how I think," she said. "It was 'I don't want crime, and crime might come from there to me, therefore I'll put money there.'" Judy said even though there is a selfish interest in what is going on outside the walls, she worries about the future. "I wonder if we will see that in another decade or five years."

Judy believes a time may come when the wall dwellers become even more sequestered. Judy and others throughout California worry about white detachment, which could lead to more funding cuts for public services and education, which would further starve the nonwhite majority of opportunities. This third world model bodes ill for the nation.

Judy's worry is based on an open secret in Dana Point: the wall dwellers pay a large chunk of the city's budget, second only to the hotel bed taxes, but they get little in return. "We don't go in and maintain their parks, we don't maintain their streets," she said. They also use fewer police services, almost none of the code enforcement effort, and they often send their children to private schools. Former city councilman Mike Eggers put it bluntly: "Monarch Bay is an effective donor community."

BEHIND THE WALLS

The gate-guarded and walled neighborhood of Dana Point's Monarch Bay is situated on a bluff overlooking the Pacific just north of the Ritz-Carlton Hotel. I approached the guard booth, from which a man emerged and checked a sheet attached to a clipboard. "Go ahead, sir," he said, as he found my name and handed over a red pass.

I felt out of place, having just left Martha Escutia's assembly district, with its sad but earnest *campesino* faces and bare earth yards. It was as if an hour or so before I had been "in country" and had reentered the first world by passing through the "Orange Curtain."

My entry visa was resident Eileen Krause, a Dana Point councilwoman who had left office the previous summer. After I had sat through a number of meetings, she invited me to dinner. Eileen's neighbors included the inventor of a popular computer game and the owner of a foodstore chain. Monarch Bay did not look all that different from any suburb—sidewalks devoid of people, houses with dominating garage doors, perfectly landscaped yards—but it was different because I was *In* and everyone else speeding down the Pacific Coast Highway was *Out*.

The Krauses' live-in Japanese housekeeper answered the door, then rushed back into the kitchen to finish cooking dinner. In the hall leading to the living room was a picture of Ronald Reagan, arm raising a wineglass, inscribed to the Krauses, whose daughter had worked at the White House. A letter signed by Reagan commemorating their twenty-fifth wedding anniversary was also on display.

Eileen arrived home, followed shortly by her husband Bob, and we sat at one end of a long table beneath a heavy cut-glass chandelier. The housekeeper served a dinner of chicken under cream sauce, asparagus, stuffed mushrooms, mixed domestic and wild rice, a dessert of fresh blueberries, strawberries, raspberries, and kiwi beneath a mild sweet glaze.

The Krauses bought this house of their dreams after starting in a tract further inland. In 1977 they opened their business, Air Cleaning Technology, which installs and services pollution control equipment. High tech has been good to the couple. The Krauses are futurists: they see today's problems leading to a better tomorrow. Eileen was bullish on all aspects of California because the future is in new technologies, in which the state continues to excel.

"You got a lot of entrepreneurs, a lot of bright people who are willing to do things," Eileen said of the development of new products like zero emission vehicles. "I think the state of California has so much going, because of its climate, its people, and its proximity to everywhere." A big asset, she said, is the mix of cultures. She does not see the state fragmenting into separate camps. "You don't have the segregation, with the blacks over here, the Catholics go here, whatevers live there."

At their company, Eileen said they have a mix of different ethnicities among their 18 workers: black, Chinese, Filipino, Iranian, Latino, Vietnamese, white. Eileen said there is no ethnic tension. "Where else in the whole world can you go where you have so many different kinds of people?" Eileen asked of California.

"The demographics are changing," she explained. "I don't see that as a negative. I like it. I grew up in a culturally diverse area. I mean it's normal for me to learn a lot about different kinds of people. I'm real comfortable with that." Eileen described herself as "optimistic about a lot of things," so she was surprised by what she learned at an Orange County gang summit that had been held the previous year.

"There were a thousand people there," Eileen said. "The one common thing that came from all the cities—was fear. I am naive and don't pay attention to where I'd be afraid to go somewhere, but there was a young lady at our table; she knew she could go to a place and be there until a certain time, but then she had to leave. There were men who wouldn't let their wives go to the mall at night."

She took safety for granted. "We moved here because it was closer to the beach," Eileen said. "It wasn't a factor in my mind at all. It really is nice, because it's quiet. There is no car noise, there's no solicitors—it's just very calm. There's a real plus to that."

Bob disagreed. "I look at it from a safety standpoint. I think there's much less risk." He added, however, that there was still some minor crime. "We've had things stolen out of the car. Usually that kind of crime is internal. Probably kids."

The conversation moved to other topics. After dinner, we took a walk with Max, the dog. We tramped down the center of the empty street, toward the ocean's roar. Far below, a group stood around a beach fire. We cut through the fence into the greens of the Ritz-Carlton golf course; the sea and a cricket army drowned out our conversation.

"This is why you live in California," Bob said, pointing to the dramatic view of shadowy hills and foaming breakers.

Fear and trouble were the last thing on my mind, but Eileen returned to the subject. She vowed the gang panel to which she belonged was going to do more than just create a report.

"One common thing about gang leaders, they're all bright," Eileen said. She is hopeful because she thinks this makes it possible to change them.

"You have to be proactive," she said. "The thing that to me is incredible, you look at how much money we spend on jails, prisons, cops, and then you look at how much money we invest in our kids, it's incredibly lopsided."

I pointed out that such talk sounded as if it was coming from a liberal Democrat—not a Republican.

"No," she said, "that's pure business. You invest and you end up with some good results. You spend $20,000 a year for prison, or $4,000 a year on schooling for a kid."

Perhaps Eileen is not typical of the wall dwellers. The others I met at council meetings seemed much less aware of societal problems. But as Judy says, they at least seem to have enough contact with the outside world to want to deal with crime in Lantern Village, which is why Bill Shepherd received most of Monarch Bay's votes for city council. In fact, a majority of the residents spent most of their lives living outside walls. Walled suburbs, after all, are a relatively new phenomenon. But one wonders what will happen to the children of the children who grow up behind walls and know no other reality.

A visitor to Dana Point learns there are three kinds of whites in town: those inside the walls, those outside, and a third subset, extremely small in number, far below the economic station of their walled and unwalled brethren, who live in a small trailer park secreted in a corner of town. (Whites on both sides of the walls have been scheming for years to eradicate the trailer court dating to the prewealthy days but have so far been unsuccessful.) Those outside the walls, including Bill Shepherd, speak not with contempt of the one-third or so of the town who live behind the walls, but with a certain sense of "otherness," as if they are a caste apart.

Bill lives less than 2 miles away and has a different view on how to deal with the problems Eileen is talking about. It is easy to intellectualize what whites should do and think, but when faced with crime right on their street, theory is quickly jettisoned. Bill had a revelation after he suffered a serious fall while helping a neighbor cut down a tree that threatened to topple in a storm. He said he gained a new understanding of the wall dwellers. In the early stages of recovery, he had to use a walker and learned what it is like to be 80 years old. When he went down his street, he felt vulnerable. He thinks if he does not move to a rural area, a walled development is in his future. "It's definitely safer," he said. "I feel I could walk around Monarch Bay at any hour, day or night."

FOUR CALIFORNIANS AND
FOUR YEARS OF CULTURAL TENSION

The walls in California come in many forms, and the four years following the Los Angeles riots saw all kinds of barriers rising between ethnic and racial groups.

Just after the riots, Martha Escutia lamented that Los Angeles was filled with ethnic and racial groups acting like piranhas, snapping at each other, rather than working for a common goal to rebuild the city. But several years later, she in some ways had joined the piranhas. She was angry that blacks and Jews and others did not come out in numbers to fight Proposition 187. Of the new battle against affirmative action, Martha said, "Of course, this is [blacks'] Proposition 187. I want to see them try to get other parties to help them out. I'm going to sit back and watch." Martha was even angrier at Latino citizens who sided with Governor Wilson's immigrant-bashing, and those who do not become citizens and vote.

"If they don't want to become active players in a system of government, I have no use for them. I don't like people who complain. Yet they're the ones that don't go out and vote. All they are is a bunch of whiners."

Leo Briones was more upbeat. He sees sanity triumphing—he believes that different races will eventually get along in the first polyracial society of the developed world. "That's where America has the greatest advantage. Because we are truly a village. We're the first experiment. It's outrageous to assume that you live in California and you can't get along with your neighbor."

This made Martha think about her pessimism. She agreed that there was hope in the long term. "It's just sheer demographics. Our time as Latinos is not ready yet. Our time will come in about 5 or 10 years."

But when will the time come for blacks? For Don, the long history of turbulent race relations does not hold promise. As he watches affirmative action being attacked, he readies young black men for a racially fragmented world. At a time when Californians were about to make a decisive vote on affirmative action, Don saw that a little attention could have a big payback. The first OK Program youths were entering college, and one was in training to become a law officer. Some of these men were now going to help other black youths make it in a multicultural world. Don was expanding the program. Locally, it entered two more Sacramento area schools, and Don opened a training center that will teach law officers from other states how to replicate the OK Program.

As for the future, Don said he hoped politics would change. "We can't get past the party issue to find out what we can do together for the country. To me, that's dangerous. That's probably doing as much to destroy the country as the drugs and the gangs and everything else. It has to change if this country is going to move forward." A collective mentality is a noble goal, but in the meantime, he feels blacks have to help themselves. But many whites will see this as "tribalism," even if whites have been doing the same thing for years through fraternal orders or church groups.

Asians, meanwhile, present the most mixed message: the greatest success as well as hidden troubles. But of three major ethnic and racial groups, they fared the best during California's white backlash, in spite of rumblings about Asian immigration and the number of Asians at universities. One wonders if Proposition 187 and other actions have been a warmup for a time yet to come, when sentiment again turns against Asians.

Events thus far have made some of California's Asians uneasy—and more politically aware. Maria Ha, for one, "was mad at the election results." She was frustrated more Asians weren't voting—and that so many are conservative. "I think the country as a whole right now is really conservative Republican. If things continue, it's going to be really hard, especially on minorities. It is already." Triple-digit tuition increases at Berkeley have compounded her concerns. She wanted to be a practicing optometrist so she could help her sister go through college. "By the time I graduate, I hope I can afford her tuition," Maria said.

There was much talk about the awakening Asian community in 1996, but there was little evidence of this. It seems many Asians will continue to become just like the white overclass. No one can fault success, but Asians seemed destined to mirror the division and fear found in whites, with many Asians continuing to vote conservatively. Many study for high-skill, high-paying professions such as medicine, perpetuating the "model minority" stereotype. More Asians will probably be admitted at Berkeley if the University of California Regents uphold the end of affirmative action; Asians could climb from 41 percent to as much as half or more of the freshman class.

Bill Shepherd does not view more Asians in college as a bad thing. Regardless of color, Bill did not want to see qualified people who "have the ability to be successful and to create jobs for those who have less abilities" denied access to college, while those less qualified take their place. "Asians have been successful in this country," Bill said. "And my feeling is if they can do it, why can't blacks [and] Hispanics?" Ultimately, Bill thinks a thriving business climate will end racial tension. "We'll get along if we can sit here as a black man and a Hispanic and do business together." He said it is hard to bomb a country you have business interests in or hate the man you work or do business with.

Yet Bill has grown pessimistic, in a different way from Martha, Don, and Maria. He came to a harsh realization months after the Proposition 187 vote. One clear afternoon, while he stood on his back porch looking through binoculars at the distant islands off the Mexican coast, he recalled a recent city council meeting in which Lieutenant Paul Dennis Ratchford publicly presented crime statistics for the first time in the town's history.

The reason for the sudden openness was to report good news: crime was going down. The council was pleased, Bill said, but he pointed out what Ratchford did not—the figures for Lantern Village were off the charts in comparison with the rest of the city. He said the city manager did not like negative publicity because it was bad for tourist business. The city manager, a position more power-ful than mayor in most West Coast cities, asked Bill not to be so vocal. Bill said he agreed not to complain publicly so long as the city was doing something to help Lantern Village. But Ratchford's sunny crime figures, he felt, were a facade to hide the effects of the killing of Steve Woods and other problems. "I never have believed in conspiracy theories," Bill said. "But I'm changing my mind."[2]

This masking of reality in Dana Point is emblematic of the situ-ation throughout the state. Money interests are always protected. In Dana Point, the tightly regulated sector of Lantern Village, with its overcrowded and overpriced apartments and garages, will con-tinue to be the home of many. This is not to say the village will end up like the center of Huntington Park, a transplanted Mexican city—it won't—because that would negatively affect the Dana Point tourist industry. Instead, city officials will vacillate between pressure and tolerance. The cops will stop people like Antonio for balding tires and let him know his place, the code enforcement of-ficers will make sure the exterior of the apartments do not become eyesores. Neither the Latinos nor Bill will end up very happy. Lantern Village will be a nether world.

Proposition 187 had little impact on Dana Point. There was a slight rise in fear among Latinos, but none worried about losing services because few took services. Even if the measure is upheld by the courts, illegal immigrants will not suddenly pack and leave, though they may suffer more and look over their shoulders. There is work to be done and money to be earned, and business will go on in Dana Point.

CALIFORNIA'S ERUPTIONS AND THE NATION'S FUTURE

The federalization of California's immigration and affirmative ac-tion backlash continued to gain momentum through 1996. U.S. Representative Lamar Smith of Texas, the Republican chairman of the House Judiciary Committee's immigration panel, said Proposi-tion 187 "was the tidal wave that washed up on the shores of the Capitol."[3] In March, the House passed by a vote of 387–333 a bill that would double the size of the U.S. border patrol, would bar illegals from schools, and would forbid them to apply for some welfare benefits in behalf of their citizen children, among other provisions.

In mid-April, when the Senate version of this bill was being debated, the CCRI was qualified for the November ballot by the California secretary of state. Bolstered by California, similar measures moved forward in other states. The legislatures in Arizona and Pennsylvania were considering bills to end affirmative action; in Louisiana, the Republican governor signed an executive order halting it; South Carolina conservatives were planning a ballot measure.

There were also increasing numbers of California-like situations in decidedly un-California-like places. In Worthington, Minnesota, which was almost 100 percent white, a pork-processing plant was expanded in 1989 and added 400 jobs. As in other places in the Midwest, the company had trouble finding locals to fill the jobs. (One Kansas meat-packing plant that processes 32,000 head of cattle per week sends recruiters to the Mexican border.) In Worthington, the $7.50-per-hour jobs drew Mexicans, Vietnamese, Laotians, Ethiopians, and some Sudanese. "It's not Lake Woebegone anymore," complained one school official. Another citizen called it "Worthington's descent into purgatory." Police have been harassing the newcomers, and locals will not advertise apartments for fear of having to rent to nonwhites. The reaction is even harsher in Wausau, Wisconsin, where the largest number of Hmong in America live, many first invited by local churches. A school official who voted to bus Hmong students to white grade schools received a 3 a.m. telephone message, "You're going to get a bullet in your head." He and four other school officials were later recalled from office.[4]

California acted as a catalyst in the period between the Los Angeles riots and the 1996 presidential election, which triggered reactionary sentiments nationwide. A major player in all of this was Governor Wilson, first with Proposition 187 and then with the CCRI. Pete Wilson and other conservative torch-bearers of wedge issue politics are bitter and divisive. To make matters worse, they offer nothing positive about where society should be heading. Unlike the late Governor Pat Brown who articulated a strong message about how California should lead the nation, Wilson and his kind wallow in negative messages. Instead of saying what can be done, they focus on what cannot be done.

No Democrat or independent has emerged to definitively conquer wedge issue politics, to capture the spirit of progressive populism, as Franklin Roosevelt did in the 1930s when he talked about the real villain, the "forces of organized greed," that threatened the country.

But equally ominous and no less cataclysmic is a society separated by class differences, racial strife, and fear, much of it due to these same forces. Racism has always been with us and probably always will be, but it runs rampant when opportunity is scarce. The changing demographics of California and the nation in the midst of economic uncertainty is a crisis that requires the same fundamental shift that was created by Roosevelt.

In late 1995 I drove across the country and talked with people from Ohio to California. I heard a great deal of anger. Workers were bitter at industrial downsizing and the lack of reward for their labor. There was a lot of scapegoating. Conversations were filled with anger toward immigrants and nonwhites. The natural inclination was to blame "others," just as people had blamed Jews and Gypsies for the economic problems in prewar Europe. This is the kind of mood that lent support for Pat Buchanan in the 1996 Republican presidential primaries.

In several cases, I shifted the discussion to corporate irresponsibility and found the anger especially pronounced. Many American workers have been "downsized," and if they have not, they know friends who have been laid off or demoted. There are few people who do not feel threatened. While the anger first focused on immigrants and minorities, a larger hostility crosses race boundaries. Rather than pander to base fear, a leader could educate and inform Americans not only about the real cause of their troubles but about solutions. It is defeatist simply to say that hate cannot be changed, that the inevitable result of a multicultural society in a time of shrinking economic opportunity is so-called Balkanization. There was plenty of hate and anger in the 1930s, but leadership overcame it.

The Democrats thus far have done nothing. As *Roger and Me* filmmaker Michael Moore has said, "The Democrats are all whiny, wishy-washy politicians who shift with the wind. The Republicans are creating the wind. It's an evil wind, but Americans like it when you stand for something. . . . [T]o the disenfranchised, angry, alienated, unemployed worker in Michigan, what are the Democrats, the liberals, offering?"[5]

As Roosevelt proved, anger can be channeled into a positive force. Progressives would be wise to focus on common issues that affect working people and the middle class—regardless of race. It does not have to be a "class war," as George Bush termed it any time the Democrats brought up issues of economic disparity. What is needed is an ethos of responsibility and real values, as was shown with stark clarity by Aaron Feuerstein, when his Massachusetts textile factory burned down in 1995. Feuerstein not only promised to rebuild, but he paid the salaries of his 3,000 workers for two months. Words like "stunned" and "surprise" were used to describe his actions because everyone expected him take the insurance money and close, or ship jobs overseas.[6] While a golden era never existed when all American corporations were community-minded, not all that long ago rebuilding and taking care of workers were too common to make Feuerstein's actions a story.

Profits are meaningless and will be threatened if lowland ghettos teem with disenfranchised masses, engulfed in periodic riots, while the small elite live in upland walled fortresses designed to keep "those people" out. But these walled neighborhoods essentially become prisons that the wealthy are afraid to venture beyond. This is not America. Law enforcement is powerless to stop crime and strife based on disenfranchisement. The FBI's Dr. William Tafoya, who predicts race riots that will eclipse any that the nation has yet seen, was a self-proclaimed "typical conservative" before his research. Now, he says policing and the criminal justice system will have to change to include issues such as education and community development.

"The jails are like the interstates," Tafoya said of the prison-building frenzy in California. "Once you've cut the ribbon, you've already got gridlock. It doesn't solve the crime problem. Business as usual is absolutely the wrong thing to do after the Los Angeles riots. We can do something about it. But we don't have the national will." The answer, he said, is jobs and education. "Some view that as very simplistic, or too overwhelming to tackle." He said if we can alleviate poverty, the problem of a multicultural society will be solved.

Americans can be led into working for a collective good. The political center must recognize common interests among racial and ethnic groups that cross color lines. As liberal commentator Jim Hightower says, "The majority of us . . . as the old saying goes, might not have come over on the same boat but are in the same boat now."[7]

In an era of distrust of government and limited resources, the answer simply is not programs. Yet there are many things the government can do to promote economic security and social harmony. As Martha Escutia notes, the United States should encourage bi- and trilingualism through schools that in the primary grades prepare children to compete in a global economy. A kid who speaks Spanish, Japanese, and English fluently and knows a skill will never lack for a job. And the government could promote, through tax incentives and other means, the development of technologies such as zero or ultra-low-emission vehicles. Tax incentives can also be used to encourage companies to keep plants in the United States, and if that does not work, severe penalties could be levied for shipping jobs overseas.

By its sheer size and unique nature, California can be the testing ground for many of these things. The state will lead America into the society of the future, and it can also lead the world as white societies everywhere become increasingly polyethnic. California's destiny need not be to resemble the Balkans or be the northern version of a banana republic. It could show how a multicultural society can work.

It is important to keep in mind that as grim as race relations sometimes appear, much works in California. All one has to do is compare the situation with Europe, where minorities account for no more than 6 percent of most countries. It does not take much to imagine what race relations would be like if Germany was even 20 percent nonwhite. In everyday life, people get along in California. As the Krauses' firm shows, multiethnic companies are profitable as well as congenial.

Over the course of American history, many writers, historians, and others have pointed out that the United States has never really established its identity. The ultimate test of whether or not this identity can be forged will take place in the multicultural society of California, said Grantland Johnson, a regional administrator for the U.S. Department of Health and Human Services in San Francisco. Johnson, who supported Donald Northcross's OK Program when he was a Sacramento politician, added: "If California is successful, the country can be successful. If you can't succeed in California, you will not succeed in the country."

Even in the best-case scenario of increased economic opportunity and politicians who lead instead of wallowing in divisiveness, the success of this new society will in the end come down to individual citizens, who in their own hearts will have to deal with what it means to be part of a polyethnic nation. To paraphrase what Donald Northcross said to the young former gang member he was trying to help, we can choose to whine and say nothing can be done to improve race relations; we can elect mean-spirited politicians; we can retreat behind walls like cowards; we can blame others for our own problems; we can choose hate instead of engaging in positive action; or we can ask ourselves, do we go forward from here? Any smart man or woman will say, "I want to go forward."

Notes

Unattributed demographic statistics throughout the book are from the U.S. Bureau of the Census. Unless otherwise noted, conversations, facts, and descriptions of events are from field observations or from the hundreds of interviews conducted by the author between 1991 and 1996.

CHAPTER 1: THE BRINK

1. California Department of Finance, Demographic Research Unit, *Population Projections by Race/Ethnicity for California and Its Counties, 1990–2040* (Sacramento: 1993).

2. U.S. Bureau of the Census, *Population Projections for States, by Age, Sex, Race and Hispanic Origin: 1995 to 2020* (Washington, D.C.: Government Printing Office, 1996).

3. *Los Angeles Times* exit polls, 1992 and 1994; The Field Poll.

4. On the rapid spread of California affirmative action backlash, see Bureau of National Affairs, Inc., *Daily Report for Executives,* August 2, 1995.

5. California Higher Education Policy Center, "Affirmative Action Debated at UC," *Crosstalk,* vol. 3, no. 2 (April 1995).

6. Interview with demographer Hans Johnson; Deborah Sontag, "New Immigrants Test Nation's Heartland," *New York Times,* October 18, 1993.

7. Louis Uchitelle, "1995 Was Good for Companies, And Better for a Lot of C.E.O.'s," *New York Times,* March 29, 1996.

8. Edmund G. (Pat) Brown, *Reagan and Reality: The Two Californias* (New York: Praeger, 1970).

9. Carey McWilliams, *California: The Great Exception* (Westport, Conn.: Current Books, 1949).

10. Reynolds Farley, Howard Schuman, Suzanne Bianchi, Diane Colasanto, and Shirley Hatchett, "Chocolate City, Vanilla Suburbs: Will the Trend Toward Racially Separate Communities Continue?" *Social Science Research,* no. 7 (1978).

11. U.S. Bureau of the Census, *1990 Census of Population and Housing, Summary Population and Housing Characteristics—California,* (Washington, D.C.: GPO, 1991). This information, which was used to draw the maps at the front of the book, was extracted from "census designated places," which are clusters of several or even dozens of census tracts, based on neighborhoods, small cities, or areas of counties. I found that using data by the many thousands of individual census tracts was meaningless: they were too narrow to show broad residential patterns. Likewise, using data on cities or counties presented too large a picture. In drawing on the data, I ignore regions of rock and ice and mountain wilderness where no one lives, or desert areas with few people scattered across hundreds of otherwise empty square miles.

12. John Wildermuth, "The Dream Dies Hard in L.A," *San Francisco Chronicle,* October 12, 1995.

13. Much of the general history of California's treatment of nonwhites here and in several other places in the book is from the Works Progress Administration, *The WPA Guide to California* (New York: Hastings House, 1939).

14. National Advisory Commission on Civil Disorders, Otto Kerner, chairman, *Report of the National Advisory Commission on Civil Disorders* (Washington, D.C.: 1968).

15. Peter Brimelow, *Alien Nation: Common Sense about America's Immigration Debate* (New York: Random House, 1995).

16. Arthur M. Schlesinger Jr., *The Disuniting of America* (New York: Norton, 1992).

17. William L. Tafoya, "Rioting in the Streets: Dejá Vu?" *C.J. The Americas,* vol. 2, no. 6 (December–January 1990). I first interviewed Tafoya by phone in 1990 for a newspaper article. When he moved to the FBI's San Francisco office, I was surprised to hear him say the agency was not keen that his report, conducted as doctoral research at the University of Maryland, appeared to have been generated by the FBI; thus his com-

ments about how crime can be prevented are presented as his own, not the bureau's.

18. Timothy Egan, "Los Angeles Riots Spurring Big Rise in Sales of Guns," *New York Times,* May 14, 1992.

19. Daniel M. Weintraub, "Crime, Immigration Issues Helped Wilson, Poll Finds," *Los Angeles Times,* November 10, 1994.

20. *LA 2000: A City for the Future* (City of Los Angeles, 1988).

21. Jane G. Pisano, president of LA 2000, "The Potential for Greatness Remains," *Los Angeles Times,* January 5, 1994.

CHAPTER 2: CALIFORNIANS AND CALIFORNIA

1. On the history of the Mexican-American War and the actions of Juan Escutia, see Jack K. Bauer, *The Mexican War* (New York: Macmillan, 1973); Bradford E. Burns, *Latin America: A Concise Interpretive History* (New York: Prentice-Hall, 1986); Edward D. Mansfield, *Life and Services of General Winfield Scott* (New York: A. S. Barnes, 1852); Alfonso Teja Zabre, *Breve History De Mexico* (Mexico City: Andres Botas, 1947); Salvador Gutiérrez Contreras, *La Acción Heroica de Juan Escutia En la Defensa de Chapultepec y la Intervención Norteamericana de 1847* (Mexico City: Gobierno de Nayarit Comisión Editorial, 1990); Departamento Del Distrito Federal, *El Asalto Al Castillo de Chapultepec y Los Niños Heroes* (Mexico City, 1983).

2. I learned what Martha whispered when I later asked what she told Vasconcellos.

3. On population doubling, see Carey McWilliams, *The California Revolution* (New York: Grossman, 1968); on driver's license transfers, see California Department of Finance, Demographic Research Unit, "California Drivers' License Address Changes" (Sacramento, 1994).

4. Jerry Hagstrom and Neil R. Peirce, *The Book of America: Inside Fifty States Today* (New York: Warner Books, 1983).

5. California Department of Finance, Demographic Research Unit, *California Drivers' License Address Changes.*

6. Louis Sahagun, "Perils of Small Town Dreams," *Los Angeles Times,* December 16, 1993.

7. Author's UC source and James Richardson, "UC Kills Affirmative Action," *Sacramento Bee,* July 21, 1995.

8. Carey McWilliams, *California: The Great Exception* (Westport, Conn.: Current Books, 1949).

9. Edmund G. (Pat) Brown, *Reagan and Reality: The Two Californias* (New York: Praeger, 1970).

10. On the rise of the politics of division see Thomas Byrne Edsall and Mary D. Edsall, *Chain Reaction: The Impact of Race, Rights and Taxes on American Politics* (New York: Norton, 1991).

11. Pete Wilson, "An Open Letter from Governor Pete Wilson to the People of California," Governor's Press Office, Sacramento, May 31, 1995.

12. Dan Morain, "Petitions Turned in for Affirmative Action Ban," *Los Angeles Times,* February 22, 1996.

13. Ramon G. McLeod, "White Male Workers a Shrinking Minority," San Francisco *Chronicle,* August 10, 1993.

CHAPTER 3: WHITE

1. On Dana Point history see Doris Walker, *Dana Point Harbor/Capistrano Bay: Home Port for Romance* (Dana Point, Calif.: To-the-Point Press, 1981); Dana Point Historical Society, "History of the City of Dana Point," information sheet, Dana Point City Hall.

2. "The Ritz-Carlton," brochure in hotel lobby.

3. City of Dana Point Planning Department, interview with Assistant Planner Gregory Pfost, March 22, 1994. I had difficulty determining the number of walled communities in south Orange County—no agency documents this trend—but the situation in Dana Point seems fairly representative. Pfost drew in the walled communities he knew on a map, and then I field-checked them.

4. Interviews with Edward J. Blakely, dean of urban planning at the University of Southern California, whose research led him to the 4 million estimate.

5. *Market Profiles/Residential Trends,* interview with Fred Schlosser, June 14, 1994. Schlosser's figure of 500 walled neighborhoods is a rough estimate.

6. Interview with Jenny Kopfstein, El Pollo Loco employee, Summer, 1992.

7. Interview with City of Dana Point, finance office, March 22, 1994.

8. Interview with Ken Peacock, Dana Point code enforcement officer, July 28, 1994.

9. Interviews with Orange County Sheriff's deputies; also City of Dana Point Police Services, "City Council Workshop. Police Services—Services, Goals and Objectives," March 21, 1995.

10. Orange County Sheriff's Department, "South County Gangs," intradepartment memo, November 3, 1993.

11. Jim Carlton, "Sky for a Roof: Capistrano Beach Seeks Solution to

Workers Who Have No Place to Live," *Los Angeles Times,* September 23, 1988.

12. Lantern Village Neighborhood Steering Committee, "Phase 2: Draft Action Plan" (1993).

13. City of Dana Point, *Good Home Good Neighbor: A Fotonovela from the City of Dana Point Community Development* (1994).

14. Robinson Jeffers, "The Eye," *Selected Poems* (New York: Vintage Books, 1963).

15. On this and the following history of Orange County and Spanish exploration see Works Progress Administration, *The WPA Guide to California;* Leo J. Friis, *Orange County through Four Centuries* (Santa Ana, Calif.: Pioneer Press, 1965); John A. Garraty and Peter Gay, *The Columbia History of the World* (New York: Harper & Row, 1972); Thomas More, *Utopia* (New York: Norton, 1975); Richard Henry Dana Jr., *Two Years before the Mast: A Personal Narrative of Life at Sea* (New York: Random house, 1936).

16. On James W. Towner and the "Bible Communists" and conservative history of Orange County see Robert Scheer, "A Frontier Dream Has Come of Age/ Orange County at 100," *Los Angeles Times,* June 4, 1989; Spencer C. Olin, "Bible Communism and the Origins of Orange County," *California History* (Fall 1979); Robert V. Hine, *California's Utopian Colonies* (San Marino, Calif.: Huntington Library, 1953).

17. Rob Kling, Spencer Olin, and Mark Poster, eds., *Postsuburban California: The Transformation of Orange County since World War II* (Berkeley: University of California Press, 1991).

18. William Glaberson, "At the Orange County Register, Journalism for the Age of the Mall," *New York Times,* January 10, 1994.

19. Orange County Sheriff's Department.

20. On Europe's turning against immigrants, see Tyler Marshall, "No Melting Pot: Europe Busy Closing Doors to Foreigners," *Los Angeles Times,* May 7, 1989; William Drozdiak, "Rolling Up a Worn-out Welcome Mat: French Fear Loss of Identity, While Immigrants Seek a New One," *Washington Post,* July 13, 1993; Jonathan Kaufman, "New Face of the Old World: Influx of Immigrants Is Forcing Europeans to Deal with Diversity," *Boston Globe,* October 15, 1991.

21. On population expansion and the demographic transition model see Ralph Thomlinson, *Population Dynamics: Causes and Consequences of World Demographic Change* (New York: Random House, 1965); Glenn T. Trewartha, *A Geography of Population: World Patterns* (New York: John Wiley & Sons, 1969).

22. United Nations, "Trends and Characteristics of International Migration since 1950" (New York: 1979).

23. United Nations, "World Population Prospects—The 1992 Revision" (New York: 1992).

24. Ibid.

25. U.S. Bureau of the Census, "Population Projections for States, by Age, Sex, Race and Hispanic Origin: 1992 to 2050" (Washington, D.C.: GPO, 1992).

26. Stephen Castles and Mark Miller, *The Age of Migration* (New York: Guilford Press, 1993).

27. On Europe's nonwhite population see Charles Dawson, "Making Sense of Today's Euro-Population Trends," *Campaign,* January 11, 1991; William D. Montalbano, "Italian Baby Boom Goes Bust," *Los Angeles Times,* June 24, 1994.

CHAPTER 4: LATINO

1. Facts and figures about District 50 are from the Speaker's Office of Majority Services, "AD 50 District Profile: Demographics, Registration and Issues of Concern," California State Assembly (Sacramento: 1993); California Department of Finance, Demographic Research Unit (Sacramento).

2. Joel Brinkley, "80's Policies on Illegal Aliens Are Now Haunting California: Politicians Wincing after Getting Their Wish," *New York Times,* October 15, 1994.

3. Ann Wiener, "5-1/2-Hour Bus Tour Rekindles Jewish Past," *Los Angeles Times,* February 23, 1988.

4. Carlos Muñoz, *Youth, Identity, Power: The Chicano Movement* (New York: Verso, 1989).

5. *La Raza* Magazine, vols. 1 and 2 (1970).

6. Hunter Thompson, "Strange Rumblings in Aztlán," *Rolling Stone Reader* (New York: Warner Paper Back Library, 1973).

7. On the history of the creation of District 50 see Tina Griego. "Group Seeks to Convert Seven Small Cities into a Unified Political Force," *Los Angeles Times,* August 4, 1991; Jill Gottesman, "2 Assembly Seats Ripe for Latino Candidates: The Newly Created 50th District Is the Most Heavily Latino in the State," *Los Angeles Times,* May 21, 1992; "Elections Legislature," *Los Angeles Times,* June 4, 1992. Also, interviews with Martha Escutia and local activists.

8. Alameda Corridor Transportation Authority, "Alameda Corridor Update," July 1993.

9. Ron Russell, "Bakewell Vows to Continue Shutdowns of Non-Black Work Sites; Recovery: Activist Condemns Recent Violence But Re-

fuses to Apologize for Tactics That Have Raised Tensions between Latinos and African-Americans," *Los Angeles Times,* July 24, 1992.

10. Johnathan L. Fried, Marvin E. Gettleman, Deborah T. Levenson, and Nancy Peckenham, *Guatemala in Rebellion: Unfinished History* (New York: Grove Press, 1983).

11. Paul Lieberman and Richard O'Reilly, "Most Looters Endured Lives of Crime, Poverty; Riots: Thieves Ranged from Addicts to Students. Majority Were Repeat Offenders, Times Analysis Shows," *Los Angeles Times,* May 2, 1993.

12. Charlotte J. Erickson, "Emigration from the British Isles to the U.S.A. in 1841," *Population Studies* (London: March 1990).

13. Robert Reinhold, "In California, New Talk of Limits on Immigrants," *New York Times,* December 3, 1991.

14. California Department of Social Services, "Assistance Units with Citizen Children of . . . Undocumented Alien Parent(s)" (Sacramento, October 1991).

15. S. J. Holmes, "Perils of the Mexican Invasion," *North American Review,* May 1929.

16. Emma Reh Stevenson, "The Emigrant Comes Home," *Survey Graphic,* May 1, 1931.

17. John Steinbeck, *The Harvest Gypsies: On The Road to the Grapes of Wrath,* introduction by Charles Wollenberg (Berkeley, Calif.: Heyday Books, 1988).

18. John Dillin, "Clinton Promise to Curb Illegal Immigration Recalls Eisenhower's Border Crackdown," *Christian Science Monitor,* August 25, 1993.

CHAPTER 5: BLACK

1. Pete Wilson, "Eulogy for Former President Richard M. Nixon," *Vital Speeches,* vol. 60, June 1, 1994.

2. Homer Clance, "Guidelines for Minority Hiring Okd: City Will Bring Staff to Parity with Population," *San Diego Union,* February 9, 1972.

3. Carey McWilliams, "Pete Wilson of San Diego," *Nation,* March 12, 1977.

4. For the history of blacks that follows see James Adolphus Fisher, *A History of the Political and Social Development of the Black Community in California, 1850–1950* (Ph.D. diss., State University of New York at Stony Brook, 1971); Rudolph M. Lapp, "The Negro in Gold Rush California," *Journal of Negro History* (April 1964).

5. Tammerlin Drummond, "A Lost Horizon: Allensworth Was the

Dream of an Ex-Slave Who Envisioned a Place Where Blacks Could Live Freely," *Los Angeles Times,* November 17, 1991.

6. On covenants and job loss see Fisher, *History of the Political and Social Development of the Black Community in California.*

7. Laura Mecoy, "Compton Teen's Beating Mobilizes Latino Forces," *Sacramento Bee,* August 12, 1994; Jonathan Tilove, "Latinos Claim Black Prejudice at Hospital," *Newhouse News Service,* December 19, 1993.

8. Tina Griego. "Group Seeks to Convert Seven Small Cities into a Unified Political Force," *Los Angeles Times,* August 4, 1991.

9. Ernest Hill, *Satisfied with Nothin'* (Los Angeles, Calif.: Pickaninny Productions, 1992; Simon & Schuster, 1996).

10. Ibid.

11. Edward N. Luttwak, "With a Rare Opportunity, Ford Blew It," *New York Times,* October 24, 1993.

12. Lawrence Bobo, Camille L. Zubrinsky, James H. Johnson Jr., and Melvin L. Oliver, *Work Orientation, Job Discrimination, and Ethnicity: A Focus Group Perspective,* Occasional Working Paper, vol. 4, no. 1, UCLA Center for the Study of Urban Poverty, Los Angeles, 1993–94.

CHAPTER 6: ASIAN

1. On the history of Asians in California see Ronald Takaki, *Strangers from a Different Shore* (New York: Little, Brown, 1989); Federal Writer's Project, *WPA Guide to California* (New York: Hastings House, 1939); Thomas W. Chinn, ed., and Mark H. Lai, Philip P. Choy, assoc. eds., *The History of the Chinese in California* (San Francisco, Calif.: Chinese Historical Society of America, 1969); Elmer Clarence Sandmeyer, *The Anti-Chinese Movement in California* (Urbana and Chicago: University of Illinois Press, 1991); Charles F. Holder, "America's Treatment of the Chinese," *North American Review,* August 1900.

2. Ho Yow, "The Attitude of the United States towards the Chinese," *Forum,* June 1900.

3. William A. Piper, "Immigration of Chinese into the United States," speech to House of Representatives, Thursday, May 18, 1876.

4. Immigration and Naturalization Service, *INS Fact Book* (Washington, D.C.: GPO, 1993).

5. Carey McWilliams, *California: The Great Exception* (Westport, Conn.: Current Books, 1949).

6. "Japanese Will Lodge Protest to Land Law," *San Francisco Chronicle,* November 6, 1920.

7. Annals of the American Academy of Political and Social Science,

"Present-Day Immigration—With Special Reference to the Japanese" (Philadelphia: 1921).

8. Lowell High School, "Ninth Grade Admissions Worksheet," October 1991; Katherine Seligman, "Furor over Lowell High Admissions," *San Francisco Examiner,* March 29, 1993; Nanette Asimov, "Math Is Off at S.F.'s Lowell High," *San Francisco Chronicle,* September 9, 1993. Also author's interviews with school officials.

9. Institute for the Study of Social Change, University of California, Berkeley, *Diversity Project* (November 1991).

10. Maya Suryaraman, "White High School Kids Form Own Ethnic Clubs," *San Jose Mercury News,* May 29, 1994.

11. Interview with Bob Laird, director, office of undergraduate admissions and relations, University of California at Berkeley, July 13, 1994.

12. Asian Pacific American Public Policy Institute and the Asian American Studies Center at UCLA, "The State of Asian Pacific America: Economic Diversity, Issues & Policies" (1994).

13. Annals of the American Academy of Political and Social Science, "Present-Day Immigration."

14. Leon Bouvier and David Simcox, "Foreign-Born Professionals in the United States," Center for Immigration Studies (Washington, D.C.: April 1994).

15. Material on the cutbacks at the University of California here and elsewhere in the book is from numerous interviews and some key documents from the university, including "University Relations: What's Going On; Information about State Budget Support for UC Berkeley," May 13, 1993. State studies were also important, including "Update on Long-Range Planning Activities," California Postsecondary Education Commission, Report of the Executive Director (Sacramento, September 16, 1991); and Kirk Knutsen, "Beyond Business as Usual: A Framework for Options for Improving Quality and Containing Costs in California Higher Education," California Postsecondary Education Commission (Sacramento, 1993). In addition, several newspaper articles were particularly helpful: Erin Allday, "UC Officials Foresee Dire Financial Future"; Julie Agullar, "Depts Struggle to Stay Afloat; Programs Are Shrinking, Professors Are Leaving"; and Henry K. Lee. "University Buckles Down for Lean Times"—all three in the *Daily Californian,* April 30, 1993. Also Larry Gordon, "Berkeley Battles the Blues," *Los Angeles Times Magazine,* June 13, 1993.

16. Douglas S. Massey and Nancy A. Denton, *American Apartheid* (Cambridge, Mass.: Harvard University Press, 1993).

17. Lawrence Bobo and Camille L. Zubrinsky, "Attitudes on Residential Integration: Perceived Status Differences, Mere In-Group Prefer-

ence, or Racial Prejudice?" Department of Sociology, University of California, Los Angeles, November 8, 1994.

18. Background on Asian voting patterns came from George Skelton, "Voters of Asian Heritage Slow to Claim Voice," *Los Angeles Times,* August 19, 1993; Clarence Johnson and Dan Levy, "Minorities Find Power Is Elusive: S.F. Has Never Elected Person of Color as Mayor," *San Francisco Chronicle,* October 31, 1994.

19. Mark Gladstone, "Senate Rejects Wilson's Choice for UC Regent," *Los Angeles Times,* March 4, 1994; Renée Koury, "Wilson Takes Flak on Minority Selections for UC Regents," *San Jose Mercury News,* February 24, 1993.

20. Seth Mydans, "Asian Investors Create a Pocket of Prosperity," *New York Times,* October 17, 1994.

21. Author heard a promotion for the station's morning show, June 3, 1992.

22. L. A. Chung, "SF Included Asian Indians in Minority Law," *San Francisco Chronicle,* June 25, 1991.

23. Dan Walters, *The New California: Facing the 21st Century* (Sacramento: California Journal Press, 1986).

CHAPTER 7: THE NEW WEDGE

1. Jerry Roberts, "Governor's Poll Ratings Nose-Dive," *San Francisco Chronicle,* May 27, 1993.

2. Amy Wallace, "The Mystic behind Wilson's Mystique," *Los Angeles Times,* October 12, 1994.

3. Peter Applebome, "Orval Faubus, Segregation's Champion, Dies at 84," *New York Times,* December 15, 1994.

4. Pete Wilson, "Why Does the U.S. Government Continue to Reward Illegal Immigration . . . at Such Costs to the American People? An Open Letter to the President of the United States on Behalf of the People of California," paid full-page advertisement in the *New York Times,* August 10, 1993.

5. Jerry Gillam and John Schwada, "Wilson Defiant over Immigration Issue," *Los Angeles Times,* August 19, 1993.

6. "Over the Line? Citing Question of Mayor, Activists Say Border Patrol Targets All Latinos," *Los Angeles Times,* September 2, 1993.

7. Thomas Byrne Edsall and Mary D. Esdall, *Chain Reaction: The Impact of Race, Rights and Taxes on American Politics* (New York: Norton, 1991).

8. Richard Polanco, assistant speaker pro tempore, "Latino Caucus

Takes On Illegal Immigration," California State Assembly, press release, August 25, 1993.

9. Robert J. Lopez, " '86 Immigrant Hiring Ban Used in L.A. Case," *Los Angeles Times,* August 9, 1994.

10. Associated Press, "Disneyland Fined $395,000 for Immigration Violations," May 7, 1993.

11. Danielle Starkey, "Latinos Divided over Immigration," *California Journal Weekly,* September 6, 1993.

12. S. J. Holmes, "Perils of the Mexican Invasion," *North American Review,* May 1929.

13. When I was in Chiapas, Mexico in 1984, I was startled to learn that neighboring Guatemalans were paid about $1 per day, in contrast to the $3 daily minimum wage in Mexico.

14. Louis Freedberg, "Growers Push for 'Guest' Field Hands," *San Francisco Chronicle,* June 30, 1995.

15. Editorial, "Poll Guard Lesson Lost on County GOP; Despite Settlement, Republican Party Here Fails to Grasp Why 1988 Incident Was Wrong," *Los Angeles Times,* November 22, 1992.

16. Henry Pratt Fairchild, "Americanizing the Immigrant," *Yale Review* (July 1916).

17. Some 1,200 foreign language papers. See "Put the Bars Up Higher," *Saturday Evening Post,* September 26, 1925.

18. "Skimming the Melting Pot," *Literary Digest,* March 1, 1919.

19. John A. Garraty and Peter Gay, *The Columbia History of the World* (New York: Harper & Row, 1972).

20. Ibid.

21. Anthony DePalma, "Racism? Mexico's in Denial," *New York Times,* June 11, 1995.

CHAPTER 8: CONSERVATIVES

1. Dan Morain and Mark Gladstone, "Racist Verse Stirs Up Anger in Assembly," *Los Angeles Times,* May 19, 1993.

2. Pete Wilson, "Why Does the U.S. Government Continue to Reward Illegal Immigration . . . at Such Costs to the American People? An Open Letter to the President of the United States on Behalf of the People of California," paid full-page advertisement in the *New York Times,* August 10, 1993.

3. Editorial, "Squeezing the Crowded Out: Courts Strike Down Santa Ana's Go-It-Alone Occupancy Policy," *Los Angeles Times,* September 2, 1992.

4. Citizens for Responsible Immigration, "Credo," membership application form.

5. Elizabeth Kadetsky, "'Save Our State' Initiative: Bashing Illegals in California," *Nation,* October 17, 1994.

6. Gebe Martinez and Doreen Cavajal, "Creators of Prop. 187 Largely Escape Spotlight," *Los Angeles Times,* September 4, 1994.

7. Kadetsky, "'Save Our State' Initiative."

8. Meeting, California Coalition for Immigration Reform, Fullerton Savings and Loan, in Garden Grove, July 28, 1994.

9. Pete Wilson, "Illegal Immigration: The California Lawsuit," press release, April 29, 1994.

10. Pamela Burdman and Edward Epstein, "Wilson Goes After Kemp and Bennett: Governor Responds to Prop. 187 Attack," *San Francisco Chronicle,* October 20, 1994.

11. National Public Radio, "California Voter Panel Discusses Immigration Issue," *All Things Considered,* June 1, 1994.

12. Editorial, "Immigration Shakedown," *Orange County Register,* June 29, 1994.

CHAPTER 9: PROGRESSIVES

1. J. Yentsun Tseng, "Student Protest Closes California Hall," *Daily Californian,* April 8, 1993.

2. "UCLA's 'No' on Chicano Studies Dept. Brings Violent Protest," *Chronicle of Higher Education,* May 19, 1993.

3. "Six Fasting to Press for a Chicano Studies Department at UCLA," *New York Times,* June 2, 1993.

4. Fox Butterfield, "Political Gains by Prison Guards," *New York Times,* November 7, 1995.

5. California Coalition for Immigration Reform, material from a sheet entitled "Attn: Citizens & Legal Residents . . . Is This America's Public Enemy #1???"

6. Steven A. Holmes, "College Fund Is Threatened over Speeches," *New York Times,* May 4, 1994.

7. Tom Hayden, California state senator, release, "Why College Doors Are Closing" (1993).

8. Interview at the home of Elaine Kim, March 16, 1994.

9. Evelyn C. White, "Blacks Divided on Immigration," *San Francisco Chronicle,* October 10, 1994.

10. Gary Lee, Roberto Suro, "Latino-Black Rivalry Grows," *Washington Post,* October 13, 1993.

11. Carey McWilliams, *California: The Great Exception* (Westport, Conn.: Current Books, 1949).

CHAPTER 10: ORANGE CURTAIN

1. Anna Cekola and David Reyes, "Tragic Death Left Scar on San Clemente; Exposed a Racial Divide in Their Town," *Los Angeles Times,* March 4, 1994; Len Hall, "Parks Have Worn out the Welcome . . . Once Seen as Neighborhood Assets, They Are Now Viewed by Some in Dana Point as Havens for Crime and Violence," *Los Angeles Times,* January 25, 1994; Mike Davis, "Legal Lynching in San Clemente: Behind the Orange Curtain," *Nation,* October 31, 1994. These articles along with author interviews are the basis for the reconstruction of events that occurred December 15, 1993.

2. Jodi Wilgoren, "Tays Say They're Still Numb at Loss of Son," *Los Angeles Times,* January 14, 1993.

3. Anna Cekola and Len Hall, "Girl's Shooting Called 'Random Tragic Incident,'" *Los Angeles Times,* December 15, 1993.

4. Frank Messina, "Shots Fired at Youths Leaving Charity Dance," *Los Angeles Times,* December 14, 1993.

5. City of Dana Point Police Services, *Annual Report* (1992).

CHAPTER 11: THE CAMPUS AND THE SUBURBAN GHETTO

1. Institute for the Study of Social Change, University of California, Berkeley, *Diversity Project* (November 1991).

2. "American Cultures Fellows and Courses," Center for the Teaching and Study of American Cultures, Wheeler Hall, University of California, Berkeley (June 1993).

3. Allen Matthews, "D.A. Won't Charge Berkeley Grocer," *San Francisco Chronicle,* May 20, 1993; Yumi L. Wilson and T. Christian Miller, "UC Group to Boycott Market Where Black Was Maced," *San Francisco Chronicle,* March 2, 1993.

4. William W. Goldsmith and Edward J. Blakely, *Separate Societies: Poverty and Inequality in U.S. Cities* (Philadelphia: Temple University Press, 1992).

5. Vlae Kershner and Greg Lucas, "'Three Strikes' Signed into California Law," *San Francisco Chronicle,* March 8, 1994.

6. "'Three Strikes' Law Could Undermine College Opportunity," California Higher Education Policy Center, October 1994.

7. Headline in the *Sacramento Bee*; wire story from William J.

Eaton, "Blacks Urged to Stop the Violence," *Los Angeles Times,* January 9, 1994.

8. Philip Zimbardo, "Transforming California's Prisons Into Expensive Old Age Homes for Felons: Enormous Hidden Costs and Consequences for California's Taxpayers," Stanford University Report (1994).

9. Greg Lucas, "Burton Offers Bill That Would Make Poverty a Crime," *San Francisco Chronicle,* December 13, 1994.

CHAPTER 12: CAN WE ALL GET ALONG?

1. Jake Doherty, "Black-Korean Alliance Says Talk Not Enough, Disbands," *Los Angeles Times,* December 24, 1992.

2. Brochure, *Hope in Youth,* July 19, 1994.

3. James Rainey and Miles Corwin, "Anti-gang Agency Given $2.5 Million . . . City Council Fails to Override Riordan Veto, Guaranteeing Funding for Fledgling Hope in Youth Organization," *Los Angeles Times,* June 8, 1994.

4. Mary Anne Perez, "Molina Criticized over Halt in Funding," *Los Angeles Times,* February 5, 1995.

5. Shelby Coffey III, Inter-office memo, "Guidelines on Ethnic, Racial, Sexual and Other Identification," *Los Angeles Times,* November 10, 1993.

6. Dennis Renault, editorial cartoon, *Sacramento Bee,* February 4, 1994.

7. Warren Brown, "Political Correctness in the Driver's Seat: Racial Issues Are Getting Waylaid by Words," *Washington Post Weekly,* June 20–26, 1994.

8. Sig Gissler, "Newspapers Quest for Racial Candor," essay in *Media Studies Journal: Race—America's Rawest Nerve,* Summer 1994; and author interview.

9. Katherine Corcoran, "Race: The One Topic Whites Avoid," *San Jose Mercury News,* October 8, 1995.

10. Katherine Corcoran, "A Nation Divided: Participants in '70s Sequoia School Integration Project Mirror Today's Racial Gap," *San Jose Mercury News,* January 15, 1996.

11. Lawrence Bobo, Camille L. Zubrinsky, James H. Johnson Jr., and Melvin L. Oliver, *Work Orientation, Job Discrimination, and Ethnicity: A Focus Group Perspective,* Occasional Working Paper, vol. 4, no. 1, UCLA Center for the Study of Urban Poverty, Los Angeles, 1993–94.

12. Jim Doyle, "High Court Lets English-Only Job Rules Stand," *San Francisco Chronicle,* June 21, 1994.

13. California Department of Finance, Demographic Research Unit.

14. "Public School Enrollment as a Percent of Total Enrollment in California Schools, by County, For Selected Years," California Department of Education (1994).

15. Scott Collins, "Fairfax, Hamilton Students Meet to Discuss Race Relations," *Los Angeles Times,* April 14, 1994.

16. Karen E. Klein, "Voices: Racism Takes a Vacation; Regular Field Trips Help Asian, Black and Latino Preteens Understand One Another's Cultures," *Los Angeles Times,* February 20, 1994.

17. Howard Blume and John D. Wagner, "Virtual Integration: High-Tech Video System Connects Latino Pupils in Norwalk and White Counterparts in La Mirada, But Is It Desegregation?" *Los Angeles Times,* May 26, 1994.

18. "A Chance to Succeed: Providing English Learners with Supportive Education," *Little Hoover Commission,* Sacramento, July 1993.

19. Johan J. Smertenko, "Those Inferior Foreigners," *Outlook and Independent,* September 25, 1929.

CHAPTER 13: WHITE RIOT

1. Pamela Burdman, "Prop. 187's Lead Keeps Shrinking, Field Poll Finds," *San Francisco Chronicle,* October 27, 1994.

2. Daniel M. Weintraub, "Crime, Immigration Issues Helped Wilson, Poll Finds," *Los Angeles Times,* November 10, 1994.

3. Ibid.

4. Rich Connell, Beth Schuster, and James Rainey, "Officials Attacked for Using Tax Funds to Battle 187," *Los Angeles Times,* November 11, 1994.

5. James Bornemeier, "Clinton Moves to Curb Illegal Immigration . . . He Orders Crackdown on Employers Who Knowingly Hire Undocumented Workers," *Los Angeles Times,* February 8, 1995.

6. Rene Lynch and Ching-Ching Ni, "Long Prison Term in Woods Slaying Stirs Emotions . . . 'I'm So Glad They Put Him Away,' Victim's Sister Says," *Los Angeles Times,* January 28, 1995.

7. "Proposition 187 Watch: Forgetful Recall," *Los Angeles Times,* April 19, 1995.

8. Kenneth B. Noble, "California Immigration Measure Faces Rocky Legal Path," *New York Times,* November 11, 1994.

9. "Average Daily N-400 Receipts," U.S. Department of Justice, Immigration and Naturalization, Los Angeles District Office, 1995.

10. Jeff Leeds, "Latino Rights Activist to Get Medal of Freedom . . . Vice President Gore Tells Pasadena Audience That Presidential Honor

Will Go Posthumously to Willie Velasquez, Who Led Latino Voter Registration Drive," *Los Angeles Times,* July 15, 1995.

11. Hector Gutierrez, "Voter Drive Draws Out Hispanics, Study Indicates," *Rocky Mountain News,* January 26, 1995.

12. John Ross and Ruben Martinez, "After Prop 187, New Bonds of Solidarity," *National Catholic Reporter,* December 9, 1994.

CHAPTER 14: THE NEW FRONTLINE

1. "California Civil Rights Initiative; The Text of CCRI," *Californians against Discrimination and Preferences* (1995).

2. Pete Wilson, "An Open Letter from Governor Pete Wilson to the People of California," Governor's Press Office, May 31, 1995.

3. Gerry Braun, "Move to End Affirmative Action Gets Early Support," *San Diego Union-Tribune,* March 7, 1995.

4. Alan F. Reeves, former regional director, U.S. Department of Defense, Contract Compliance Program, "What's Behind White Male Anger," *San Francisco Chronicle,* February 21, 1995.

5. U.S. Congress, Glass Ceiling Commission (1995).

6. Katha Pollitt, "Subject to Debate: Affirmative Action," *Nation,* March 13, 1995.

7. Nanette Asimov, "Single Standard for Admissions at Lowell High," *San Francisco Chronicle,* February 28, 1996.

8. Dan Morain, "Petitions Turned In for Affirmative Action Ban," *Los Angeles Times,* February 22, 1996; David Tuller, "Preferences Ban Is Likely to Qualify for State Ballot," *San Francisco Chronicle,* February 14, 1996.

9. Dan Morain, "1996 Expected to be Boom Year for Initiatives," *Los Angeles Times,* December 9, 1995.

10. George Skelton, "Battle over UC Policy Comes at Key Time," *Los Angeles Times,* January 29, 1996.

11. Dave Lesher, "Preference Foes Say Initiative Is Back on Track," *Los Angeles Times,* February 13, 1996.

12. Susan Yoachum, "Wording Affects Polls on Affirmative Action," *San Francisco Chronicle,* September 14, 1995.

13. "California Civil Rights Initiative; The Text of CCRI."

14. Editorial, *Daily Cal,* September 21, 1995.

CHAPTER 15: END OF THE RAINBOW OR A NEW SOCIETY?

1. William W. Godsmith and Edward J. Blakely, *Separate Societies: Poverty and Inequality in U.S. Cities* (Philadelphia: Temple University Press, 1992).

2. "City Council Workshop. Police Services—Services, Goals and Objectives," Orange County Sheriff, City of Dana Point Police Services, March 21, 1995.

3. Cassandra Burrell, Associated Press, March 21, 1996.

4. Unpublished research by Associate Professor Stephen G. Bloom, School of Journalism and Mass Communication, University of Iowa, 1996.

5. Terry Morris, "Moore Follows Own Direction: Speaks to Sociology Class at UD," *Dayton Daily News,* November 8, 1995; Lawrie Mifflin, "The Rib Tickler's Approach to Social Provocation," *New York Times,* July 16, 1995.

6. Tom Curley, "Mill Owner's Heart Is Fabric of Mass. Town," *USA Today,* January 29, 1996.

7. Evan Smith, "Jim Hightower: A Hellraising Texas Radio Personality Fights to Stay on the Dial," *Mother Jones* (November/December 1995).

Index

ABOUT THE AUTHOR

Dale Maharidge teaches journalism at Stanford University. He was also an assistant professor of journalism at Columbia University and was a Nieman Fellow at Harvard University. From 1980 through 1991, he was a reporter in California at the *Sacramento Bee*. His second book, *And Their Children After Them*, with photographer Michael Williamson, won the 1990 Pulitzer Prize in nonfiction. His first book, *Journey to Nowhere: The Saga of the New Underclass*, also with Mr. Williamson, inspired two songs on Bruce Springsteen's 1995 album, *The Ghost of Tom Joad*. He lives in the San Francisco Bay area and on a small homestead on the northern California coast.